Nick Danziger

RORY MACLEAN has known three Berlins: West
Berlin, where he made movies with David Bowie and
Marlene Dietrich; East Berlin, where he researched
Stalin's Nose; and the unified capital where he lives
today. He is the author of nine books and has won awards
from the Canada Council and Arts Council of England
as well as a Winston Churchill Traveling Fellowship. He
was an International IMPAC Dublin Literary prize nominee and is a Fellow of the Royal Society of Literature.
Visit his Web site at rorymaclean.com.

ALSO BY RORY MACLEAN

Additional Praise for *Berlin*

"A wonderfully enjoyable, poetic, and instructive tour through the history of this fascinating and changing city. A book that magnificently combines real history and pure reading pleasure. Not just for those interested in Germany, but for anyone interested in the history of Western culture."   —Stephane Kirkland, author of *Paris Reborn*

"Grandly ambitious . . . Splendid . . . This book is a wonderful achievement, not justly to be summarized in the few hundred words of a review, but hauntingly representing, as in a tangled dream, six hundred years of history."   —*The Telegraph* (London)

"MacLean's wonderfully knowledgeable overview of the city's history helps explain the place's enduring fascination."
                                                       —*The Guardian* (London)

"Vivid, imaginative . . . brilliant. What makes MacLean's history of Berlin stand out is that this is an intensely human document, a rich tapestry spanning five centuries and woven together through intimate portraits of twenty-one of its former inhabitants that collectively reveal the narrative of the city. . . . Their stories are wholly engaging, written with the flair of a novelist."
                                                       —*The Observer* (London)

"Superb . . . [MacLean] has a knack of approaching his subjects obliquely, catching them unawares. . . . Original and well-researched. MacLean is a highly visual writer, and his dialogue is crisp and believable. [He] deserves to win all the prizes going."
                                                       —*The Tablet* (London)

"Inventive, exhaustive, and energetic. *Berlin* is . . . a human story. MacLean tells it with a wonder, a sadness, and a compassion."
                                                       —*Herald Scotland*

RORY MACLEAN

BERLIN

PORTRAIT OF A CITY
THROUGH THE CENTURIES

PICADOR ST. MARTIN'S PRESS NEW YORK

picadorusa.com
twitter.com/picadorusa • facebook.com/picadorusa
picadorbookroom.tumblr.com

Picador® is a U.S. registered trademark and is used by St. Martin's Press under license from Pan Books Limited.

For book club information, please visit facebook.com/picadorbookclub or e-mail marketing@picadorusa.com.

Quotations from Christopher Isherwood's *Mr Norris Changes Trains* © 1935, and *Goodbye to Berlin* © 1939, reprinted by permission of the Wylie Agency. Quotations from *The Berlin Stories* © 1935, reprinted by permission of New Directions Publishing Corp. Quotations from *Christopher and His Kind* © 1976, reprinted by permission of Farrar, Straus and Giroux, LLC, and the Wylie Agency.

The Library of Congress has cataloged the St. Martin's Press edition as follows:
MacLean, Rory, 1954–
    Berlin : portrait of a city through the centuries / Rory MacLean.—First U.S. edition.
        p. cm.
    Includes bibliographical references and index.
    ISBN 978-1-250-05186-8 (hardcover)
    ISBN 978-1-250-05240-7 (e-book)
    1. Berlin (Germany)—History.   2. Berlin (Germany)—Description and travel.
3. Berlin (Germany)—Social life and customs.   I. Title.
    DD860.M25 2014
    943'.155—dc23

2014026162

Picador Paperback ISBN 978-1-250-07490-4

Our books may be purchased in bulk for promotional, educational, or business use. Please contact your local bookseller or the Macmillan Corporate and Premium Sales Department at 1-800-221-7945, extension 5442, or by e-mail at MacmillanSpecialMarkets@macmillan.com.

First published in Great Britain by Weidenfeld & Nicolson, an imprint of Orion Publishing Group Ltd, an Hachette UK Company

First published in the United States by St. Martin's Press

First Picador Edition: October 2015

10 9 8 7 6 5 4 3 2 1

'The past is never dead, in fact it's not even past.'

Christa Wolf

CONTENTS

PROLOGUE

Imagine

Dawn casts the shadow of a vanished palace upon the mist. A king's flute solo drifts on the air. Saplings take root on the forgotten railway siding where Lenin paused before sparking his revolution. Victory flashes gold through the thick Tiergarten trees. Ashes from Sachsenhausen's ovens are caught in dusty whirlwinds above the Holocaust Memorial. Children's laughter echoes along narrow, naked parks where the Wall once stood. In a banal car park, tourists stand, transfixed, atop Hitler's hidden bunker.

Why are we drawn to certain cities? Perhaps because of a story read in childhood. Or a chance teenage meeting. Or maybe simply because the place touches us, embodying in its tribes, towers and history an aspect of our understanding of what it means to be human. Paris is about romantic love. Lourdes equates with devotion. New York means energy. London is forever trendy.

Berlin is all about volatility. Its identity is based not on stability but on change, as wrote historian Alexandra Richie. No other city has repeatedly been so powerful, and fallen so low. No other capital has been so hated, so feared, so loved. No other place has been so twisted and torn across five centuries of conflict, from religious wars to Cold War, at the hub of Europe's ideological struggle.

Berlin is a city that is forever in the process of becoming, never being, and so lives more powerfully in the imagination. Long before setting eyes on it, the stranger feels its aching absences as much as its brazen presence: the sense of lives lived, dreams realised and evils executed with an intensity so shocking that they rent the air and shook its fabric. So much of it has been lost or reinvented that the mind rushes to fill the vacuum, fleshing out the invisible, linking facts with fiction. As neither are fixed, an animated dialogue sparks between present and past, between the observed city and the place portrayed in ten thousand books, films, paintings and fanciful architectural utopias. Yesterday echoes along today's streets and the ideas conjured up by Berlin's dreamers and dictators seem as solid as its bricks and mortar. The hypnotic and volatile city comes alive in the mind.

A lifetime ago I was a teenage traveller 'doing' Europe. During a happy, footloose summer I climbed the Eiffel Tower, tripped down the Spanish Steps and felt the earth move under the stars on an Aegean beach. Then on the last week of the holiday I saw the Wall. The sight of the heinous barrier shook me to my core. At the heart of the Continent were watchtowers, barbed wire and border guards instructed to shoot fellow citizens who wanted to live under a different government.

I knew the history. I understood what had happened. But I couldn't conceive how it had happened. The individuals whose actions had divided Germany and Europe – the wartime planners, the Soviet commissars, the Stasi agents – weren't monsters. They were ordinary men and women. I longed to understand their motivation, how they came to act as they did, yet at the same time I was repulsed by their crimes and needed to feel their victims' suffering.

Throughout that week I was drawn again and again to the Wall. I stood for hours on the wooden observation platform at the end of a bizarre cul-de-sac overlooking vanished Potsdamer Platz. I stared in silence across the death strip, stunned that a clash of ideas could be set in cement at the centre of a city.

Then on the final day of the holiday I crossed into the East. At Checkpoint Charlie I stepped over a white-painted line and slipped through a gap in the Wall. Gates lifted then closed behind me. Cars and pedestrians were corralled into a concrete chicane of sharp double bends. A Soviet MiG flew low over the deserted Brandenburg Gate, touching the sound barrier, shaking the windows and my faith in the inherent goodness of man.

I surrendered my passport to an armed, buttoned-up officer, paid for a visa and stood in the drizzle under the gaze of a Volksarmee lieutenant dressed in field grey. He carried a loaded rifle. Beyond his squat lookout post, the doors of the surrounding buildings had been bricked up. The entrances to underground stations were sealed. Along Friedrichstraße – once the bustling Fleet Street of Berlin – stretched a bleak and narrow transit route of flat concrete-rendered façades, from which residents and memories had been sucked away.

On that last – and first – day I walked away from the tightly controlled border area and made for windswept Alexanderplatz. I carried with me a collection of Alfred Döblin's 1920s short stories. Before the war and Wall, Berlin's greatest biographer had wandered through the central square's cobbled courtyards and cloth shops, noting the idle youths in cheeky caps, the clockmakers and the '*very* cheap women'. Around him locals had called out in guttural Yiddish. Fishmongers had sold fat herring on ice, chalking price lists on the cellar doors of their high, angular houses. Fairground barrel organs had clamoured outside the Münzstraße cinemas. Above a workers' bookshop a painted hand had rested on an open book, beneath a sickle, ears of corn and the words, 'To produce more you need to know more.'

But in the 1970s the monstrous expanse of grey concrete offered me no hint that fifty years earlier it had been Döblin's 'quivering heart' of Berlin. Almost nothing had survived of the old town, due to the combined efforts of Albert Speer's fantasies, British Lancaster bombers and Communist city planners. Around me I heard neither voices nor birdsong. The tiled 'Fountain of Friendship among People' was bone dry. The cavernous, colourless Centrum department store seemed to sell nothing but Russian *Melodiya* LPs. Smudges of brown coal smoke hung in the air and the blackened station smelt of blast dust. A maroon and beige S-Bahn train rattled over the arches. I clutched my book so tightly that my knuckles turned white. Alexanderplatz appeared to be deserted, apart from a young couple pushing a pram. Beneath the tarnished World Clock – in which planets jerked like dying atoms around a nuclear centre – they paused to adjust the baby's blanket. I glanced into the pram. Their baby was a plastic doll.

A single building of human proportion caught my eye. On the square's western edge beyond a tram shelter, the Marienkirche was Berlin's second parish church, built on a sandy rise in an unknown year during the thirteenth century. Its canted angle alone echoed the old street plan. Yet as I darted towards it I saw that bullet holes still peppered its old brick walls. The mingy light which seeped through its dirty windows dragged the spirit down into the lurking shadows, instead of drawing it up to heaven. In its doorway a lone woman shivered in her bare stockings as a cobbler whetted his knife and shaped the new heels of her boots.

Death stood in the vestibule behind them. He seized the hands of cardinal and pope, king and knight, magistrate and fool, and led them on their last journey. I moved with them into the body of the church, along the length of the pale, twenty-metre Gothic mural. The *Totentanz* had been painted with childlike simplicity around 1469 and survived blitz, firestorm and agnosticism, hidden under whitewash for almost half a millennium. Its awkward line of dancers had been invisible when – for example – Nietzsche had walked past them and first felt Berlin's 'hidden will to death'. Goethe, Voltaire and the Brothers Grimm had followed him into the Marienkirche, sensing rather than seeing the *Totentanz*, as had visitors and residents Chekhov, Kafka, Döblin, Nabokov and Günter Grass. In this same vestibule Anita Berber – the black-lipped erotic dancer painted by Otto Dix – had been stirred to create her own naked death dance and Nick Cave had paused, hearing in his head the lyrics of 'Death is Not the End'. During his sojourn in the city Jean-Paul Sartre may even have imagined here a world where the dead lived alongside the living, unseen by them and unable to touch them.

'Come you all with me and join the Dance of Death,' called the grisly, shrouded leader in Low German verse, glancing back at his cavorting charges, and I realised that he was also staring at me, as he'd stared at everyone who had passed this way, drawing us all into the dance.

For an instant I pictured myself taking hold of the doomed dancers' hands. I stepped out of the church with them as the sun emerged from behind the clouds. Alexanderplatz was no longer deserted. In a wink it had become crowded with plague victims and Habsburg Army whores. Medieval storytellers and cackling fishwives rose into life. Vengeful Red Army soldiers taunted bent-back rubble women. In the throng I spotted gum-chewing GIs and charred British bombardiers clutching flaming parachutes. I saw Napoleon astride his white charger and SS Panzergrenadiers prance around murdered Jewish children. I watched John F. Kennedy's motorcade stop at a baker's stall to buy a dozen sugar-dusted *Pfannkuchen* with plum filling.

Not only that, but among the dead appeared the city's iconic creations: David Bowie's heroes kissed by the Wall, Wim Wenders' angels winged above a torch-lit Nazi parade, Sally Bowles went shopping with Marlene Dietrich and le Carré's George Smiley watched the packed trains leave for Auschwitz. As far as the eye could see Berlin's legends, both real and imagined, joined hands together with Death – and me.

The light changed, ending my reverie and the summer. I left the church and flew home to Canada and my ordinary world. But there's a part of me that believes we go on existing in a place after we've left it and soon I felt compelled to return to Berlin. Over the next decade I came back again and again to make movies and to start my first book, trying to see through the whitewash and patina of daily life, falling in and out of (and back in) love with the haunted, ecstatic, volatile city.

Then in 1989 the sun came out again. *Ossis* and *Wessis*, East and West, danced together on the Wall, holding hands, waving sparklers, not in a last waltz with Death but in jubilation for new beginnings. I made a trail of footprints across the smoothed sand of no man's land, linking two worlds. Around me thousands of Berliners hacked away at the barrier with pickaxes and hammers. A swarm of buzzing Trabants – the cardboard car for comrades, belching blue smoke, breaking down, being pushed – circled gangs of soldiers dismantling the concrete slabs. At Checkpoint Charlie the Russian cellist Mstislav Rostropovich – who had been harassed, intimidated and stripped of his citizenship by the Soviets – played an impromptu Bach suite. Beside him an old man dropped to his knees and cried. Road crews rejoined severed streets. 'Ghost' U-Bahn stations were freed of their phantoms. Within a year 155 kilometres of the Wall vanished, leaving in its place only a discreet line of paving stones and peculiar, twisting cycle paths. In this city my own actions became memories, and a part of Berlin's history too, not so much because I did anything of importance here, but because others did, and their deeds became enmeshed in my life.

Now, after forty years of visits, I've settled here to try to map this place, divided as it is between past and present, conformity and re-bellion, the visible and the invisible. I stand in Alexanderplatz, busy with tattooed tourists and old Berliners basking in the sunshine, holding iPhones and lapdogs, flashing neon wristbands or folding themselves into blankets outside the cafés. I start to walk away from them, at once back and forth in time, spiralling out from the square and into the city. I know that no true map can be drawn by simply trekking across town and noting interesting facts. To chart both the seen and unseen, and to navigate the potency of Berlin's vigorous mythology, one needs to know its mythmakers: the artists, thinkers and activists whose heated visions have become no less real than the city's bitter winter nights. It is Berlin that made them, as they made Berlin, transforming a mean and artless outpost into the capital of Europe.

This book portrays the city through those men and women,

alongside some of the countless others whom one has never heard of, whose lives can only be divined: Germans and foreigners, native daughters and adopted sons, politicians and painters, a broken-hearted king and a reborn pop star, a diabolical genius and at least one angel. Each of them is different, each an individual. But one characteristic unites them all, as well as their modern counterparts. In this laboratory of creativity and evil, in this *Heimat* of fantasy and Death, Berlin dared them to imagine.

CHAPTER 1

Konrad von Cölln,
and True Love

Detail from the Dance of Death (*der Totentanz*) fresco from the Marien-kirche, Berlin, c.1469. (*akg-images/ullstein bild*)

Marienkirche, 1469

He never liked to scribe the words, never liked to clip their wings, to fix them in time like the poor, glass-eyed song-birds stuffed and mounted in the Kurfürst's Room of Wonders. Words spoken were thoughts alive, unfettered, tracing ever-changing patterns in the air and mind, blown to and fro by a breath of fancy or gust of laughter. A gilding here, an embellishment there, the deed of a hero or the tender-hearted longing of a shepherdess tweaked and tailored for Cölln, Berlin, Spandau or Treptow. Each town was different, each ballad rejigged to suit the place, the time, the mood and appetite of the crowd. That was the artistry, the freedom, and that had been the swallow's flight of his calling. Without it his words lost their music, and his music its resonance, like a thrush snared on the branch and stunned into silence. Yet now, on this dull September evening in the Marienkirche, Konrad needed to write down the words, to tether the lyrics and melodies of the old *chansons*. In the lamplight the fresh paint on the mural, on his father's portrait, looked as wet as the tears on his cheeks.

He lifted the flask to his lips then stumbled back through the vestibule and out into the boneyard.

His father Gottfried von Cölln had been a *Minnesänger*, a wandering poet and a vassal of the prince. In the year of Our Lord 1448, soon after Kurfürst Frederick 'Irontooth' had ordered the building of the Schloss, Gottfried had led Berliners to defy him, opening the Spree floodgates to swamp its foundations. 'Irontooth' responded as he had when he'd disbanded the town council, with viciousness. Five hundred knights – more skinhead bully boys than nobles – took to the streets, smiting the rebels, throwing into the Spree their statue of Roland, prized symbol of citizens' rights. Gottfried's *Unwille* had been the single rebellious act of his life, after which he had to flee of course. But not before bidding his wife a farewell so fond that it led – nine months later – to the birth of Konrad.

For the first decade of the boy's life, Gottfried had wandered through German lands, tramped abroad to Prague and Paris, taking whatever God sent him: sun, rain, mist, snow, famine or feast. In far Lusatia he ate pike broth and stag's liver pasties. On the banks of the Elbe he drank hot cordial spiced with cloves and gillyflowers. He was robbed, beaten and left for dead in the Alps of Savoy. He watched the sun rise over the Mediterranean. And in every place he sang, to fill his heart as much as to earn his crust.

At the courts of margraves and princes, Gottfried told the old tales of mighty soldiers of long ago, of maidens with garlands of fresh roses in their hair, of saints wise and demons wicked. He sang in Latin, French and Occitan. He even joined with a harper and a fiddler to form a travelling band, honing his powers of enticement.

At the same time he collected other traditional songs. On the Petit Pont and in Provence, he plucked *sons d'amour* and wanderers' melodies from the air as swallows catch insects, locking them in his memory, always favouring the courtly romances of a more chivalrous age.

But, as the traveller brings settled folk a little hunger for freedom, so he came to pine for his own hearth. Ten years to the day after his departure, the wayfarer stood on his threshold, holding out a calloused hand to the boy hiding behind his mother's skirts. Gottfried then pulled young Konrad through the earthen lanes, over the wooden Langebrücke to the Schloss by the Spree, to stand before the Kurfürst. He dropped to his knees and groaned for forgiveness. He said that he had followed his heart and the poem of the road, unravelling its twists and bends, its *Wort und Weise*, until it told him to return home to Berlin. He recited:

> Revertere, revertere
> iam, ut intueamurte.

> Return, return now,
> so that we may look at you.

Kurfürst 'Irontooth' – splendid in his red tunic shot through with gold – might have drawn his sword, or called upon a ruffian knight to give him satisfaction. Yet he chose not to rush the moment, and to humble the rebel poet. Instead he led both Gottfried and his son into his *Wunderkammer*.

In this Room of Wonders were stuffed birds and the spurs of a knight who had fallen at the siege of Constantinople, books rare and precious, a lock of the emperor's hair and a splinter from the true Cross. Young Konrad gawked at the splendid riches but the sight did not humble Gottfried. Rather he was moved to speak of the soul's unappeased hunger for beauty, as well as the troubadours' joy in summer and love, in noble quests and in sweet, blessed ladies who await the return of their betrothed. 'There is no greater power, no stronger magic in the world, than music to save the tender blossoms of life,' he said.

At first the old ideals seemed to touch 'Irontooth', for he replied without apparent anger, 'Then *Minnesänger*, you will sing once for me.' There and then in the *Wunderkammer*, flanked by Ovid's *Amores* and a mirror said to reflect holy light, Gottfried sang the *Roman de Horn* as if his life depended on it:

> Lors prent la harpe a sei, qu'il la veut atemprer . . .

When he tunes the harp,
and touches its strings,
and makes them sing;
Lord, what heavenly harmony!

A *chanson de geste* was followed by a pair of lyric pieces. Gottfried slid the words into the music like a hand into a glove, jerking his head as he threw out the lines, growing so excited that he seemed about to fly. He recounted tales of lost love and Christian heroes until the shadows fell across the room and in the lane below cowled priests answered the call to Vespers.

Throughout the performance the Kurfürst said nothing. When Gottfried finished, he stated simply, 'You have a gift, and you will never use it again.'

Twenty years later, on that dull September evening, Gottfried's son Konrad stumbled out of the Marienkirche. He had no bone to pick with graveyards. Unlike some who were unsettled by their sweet, heady stench, he didn't find the air unpleasant. Cemeteries felt strangely comforting to him, in their levelling of prince and pauper, in that they were a destination to which all men travelled. In any case he didn't want to go home yet, drunk and dishevelled as he was, to sit by the cold hearth listening to his mother weep.

He picked his way around a tangle of wooden crosses. The new stone was set beyond the shallow hollow of an old plague pit against the church wall. Konrad noted that the workmanship was fine, the letters carved well and deep, the chisel cut still sharp to the touch. Murderous 'Irontooth' himself had paid for the stone, if one could believe it, as if to hide his infamy from eternity. Here lies a good man. Here ruled a just prince. Here the Word was cherished, and other such lies.

Konrad dropped against the slab and felt the soil ooze between his toes. He couldn't remember where he'd left his boots. He wanted to believe that his father was still near, that he'd catch sight of him in a crowd on the Mühlendamm bank or among the monks at red-brick Lehnin. Yet at the same time he thanked God that his father's two decades of suffering had finally ended.

Overhead the light drained from the sky and the limbs of the elms seemed to reach out to one another in the dusk, clinging together for support through the coming night.

'Shove over,' she barked, startling him awake. Konrad must have fallen asleep, judging from the stiffness in his bones. He didn't know the hour.

'Don't throw your arms and legs about so,' cautioned the woman as he made room at the slab. 'Keep your elbows in or you'll knock over a ghost.'

Konrad was irritated. His mourning solitude had been disturbed and he was cold. 'There are no ghosts here,' he replied as silhouettes of crosses danced across the broken earth, cast by torches on the Neuer Markt. 'Only flesh rotting into earth.'

'Sacrilege,' she accused, jabbing a finger at him. 'We walk among a multitude of ghosts who are visible only to the messenger of souls.'

In the half-light the woman's face was not wholly unpleasant. Her hair was uncovered and loose. But her arms were fat and he was in no mood for conversation.

'Are you a messenger of souls?' he taunted.

'I am Lola.'

He could have kicked her, driven her away or walked off himself but her proximity stirred him, as did the warm hand now placed with skill on his thigh. He knew well that certain women – whom some called swallows – were drawn to churches and cathedrals like the feathered travellers themselves. He understood from the moans and titters around them that it was not the dead who were coming to life among the graves. Like these hidden others, he too decided to reach for comfort in the cold night, so that he might forget death for an hour and a coin or two.

'So you *are* alive,' laughed Lola.

At dawn she was gone, taking her superstitions with her. Konrad rose to drag himself home, crossing the waking market with its stout horse dealers, its bakers whitened by flour, its yawning peddlers of pepper and cumin seed. Pigeon-breasted farmers' wives in dusty sandals snored over baskets of onions. Stinking beggars displayed their stumps and called for alms. A Jew in ringlets and spotless black frock coat paused at a cloth merchant's stand, unfolding rich reams of Flanders indigo and perse. A wrestler in bearskin with hair wind-wild challenged passers-by to a tug-of-war.

Medieval Berlin was a dirty patchwork of squalid hovels and mean manors stitched to a low, lazy twist of the Spree. Along its sandy banks fisherboys hawked the morning catch, their high voices lifting in a kind of babbling river music. Brawny lads stripped to the waist unloaded barrels of Rhenish wine and sacks of rice from Arborio. A matron from a noble house craned her neck to select the finest trout, the freshest loaf, the thickest wedge of cheese, tucking each prize into her willow basket. Urchins raced by the Mühlendamm mills like dogs on a scent. Blue-tunicked soldiers sauntered through the mêlée, plucking any ware that took their fancy.

Konrad crossed the river to the Cölln side, to the better half of the sister settlements, behind a lone scholar with a curl of crisp linen rising above his dark jacket. The man slipped into the Dominicans' cloister – the so-called Dom – and Konrad turned left into narrow Brüderstraße with its clustered, peak-roofed dwelling houses. Around him the *Klang* of canaries yellow and foreign and ironsmiths at their forges hung in the air, as did the smell of beeswax and roasting chestnuts.

In these shadowed courtyards he had learnt his father's craft in secret, memorising for over twenty years the formal songs which Gottfried himself had been banned from singing, coming to master the flute, the vielle and the viol. Gottfried had been a strict teacher, his standards sharpened by frustration, and Konrad never seemed able to live up to his expectations. He tried so hard for perfection that a tightness held him back, until finally he rejected his father's staid and dated *Minnesang* music, as well as its courtly Latin and French lyrics.

Konrad wanted instead to sing as a free man, in the drinking houses and at the fairs of common folk. He loved to croon on impulse and in German, composing spontaneous tunes for artisans and peasants, even though they had almost no money to pay him. He played and sang until the music moved them onto their feet, into song, to dance. He uncaged his father's chivalrous *Lieder* and let them soar, rewording them on the fly, spinning them anew for his audience and age, proud of never repeating himself in performance.

Often payment came to him in pleasure. He gorged himself on *Berlinerinnen*, becoming a skilful and energetic lover both on and off stage, a lustful carnivore who could not imagine feasting for ever on a single female. But the sport had its dangers, for the Kurfürst had imposed strict penalties for petty crimes. Loose-liver fornicators could be hung by the neck. Adulterous women were apt to be killed by the sword. Likewise, thieves who stole from the Church were buried alive and liars were boiled in an iron cauldron. Public executions took place on every second Wednesday at the Oderberg Gate, a death rattle east of the Marienkirche. The corpses were hung on the Langebrücke as a warning to others.

Konrad mourned away the September day at home until evening, when he re-crossed the long bridge to Berlin. The weather was grey and wet, a Baltic rain blowing cold and sea-scented from the north. Berlin was a place incapable of tenderness, he thought, a volatile and moody virago who only ever ran fiery hot or bitter cold or drenched herself in tears.

He had told his mother that he wished to look again at his father's painted likeness. In truth he went back to the church for the living as much as the dead. When he saw Lola, her skirts dirty from practising her trade on the damp grass, he felt another flash of irritation. Like most Berliners, she was ignorant and uncouth, preferring carousal to contemplation. As she drew him near he jumped away, unable either to stand tall or lie down. He wanted to gather up his feeble defences against loss yet at the same time he could not wait to surrender to it. In response she simply warned him about striking out at ghosts and, when night closed around them, her persistence softened the man, though only his heart.

'Lola Lola', he called aloud like a child. Lola Lola.

Afterwards a woodsmoke mist rolled across the earth and he

began to speak of his father, gesturing down at the mound on
which they lay.

'I will write down all his old songs,' he told her, the smoke bringing tears to his eyes. 'I cannot bear to lose them too.'

In the fifteenth century lyrics were rarely recorded. Songs passed
by mouth from master to apprentice, father to son with an emphasis
on accuracy and external form: numbers of syllables, orthodox
rhymes, rote learning. Gutenberg's press was but a dozen years old
and had not yet overtaken the oral tradition. The few manuscripts
in Berlin's *Wunderkammer* had come from a scriptorium, copied and
bound by Franciscan or Dominican hands. No learned scribe had
ever bothered to fix the old poems to the page. Now, in the shabby
outpost, Konrad dared to imagine doing just that, with Lola at his
side.

Theirs was not a usual courtship. He did not send her fragments
of sugar and sweet notes. She did not withhold her favours. Instead
they continued to couple like rats in straw and, after their wedding, he moved her into his house. By day he became a scribe at
his father's table, bent over sheaves of cloth parchment, recalling
and writing down songs. By night in his parents' old bed he was a
farmer glad to plough his wife's fertile field.

> Unter den Linden, an der Heide,
> da unser zweier Bette was,
> da muget ir vinden, schöne beide
> gebrochen Bluomen unde Gras.

> Under the linden trees, and on the heath,
> where we made our bed,
> we left the grass and blooms,
> so flattened by beauty.

Konrad could not spell of course, or at least words were not yet
put down with a standard arrangement of letters, yet the handicap
did not diminish his eagerness. Strangely Lola's reluctance to give

up her old trade also heightened his sense of urgency. He beat her, as was his right, locking her in the granary until she agreed to stop. She called it her own hunger, and it grew more acute with the loss of their firstborn. In the spring before the meadows were sown she held the babe in her arms. When it died, she placed a Bible at its head in the crib.

'Er tuot ein scheiden von mir hin, das mir nie scheiden leider wart . . .' wrote Konrad that sad morning, recording the old German refrain:

> He leaves me, and no leaving brings me more pain,
> I give him my heart to guide his journey.

*

Berlin and Cölln were minor towns, sharing a provost and mayor, bypassed by Europe's main trade routes, much less important than busy Magdeburg and Frankfurt-an-der-Oder. Within their compact defensive walls gossip spread as swiftly as the pox, between women warming themselves by the fire, through servants at the Rathaus pump, to courtiers in the Schloss. When the Kurfürst heard of Konrad's ink-horned undertaking, he summoned him to the court.

Kurfürst 'Irontooth' held strong views on legend and legacy, as he did on most matters. He recognised that his Brandenburg was a headstrong borderland of little learning, peopled for the most part by the dispossessed. They'd tramped in from every corner of the Holy Roman Empire and beyond. His subjects needed both to be built up, so that they might serve him, and to be cut down so as not to rebel.

The Kurfürst understood the power of chronicle and in his chambers he instructed Konrad on which lyrics were to be preserved. Konrad was to glorify the leaders of the Germani tribes, from Hermann who had destroyed three Roman legions to Albert the Bear and 'Irontooth' himself. He was to describe war as destiny. He was never to call their land Slavonia, or Slavic, but rather a place forever German.

'Do this and you shall sit at my table and sing for me. Fail me and you – and your whoring wife – will sing a different tune, when you suffer the same fate as your father.'

As he'd been born under the sign of the Scorpion, 'Irontooth' never forgave nor forgot. Over the years he had forbidden Konrad's father to perform, taking away his voice, making him as mute as one of his stuffed songbirds. Two decades after the flooding of the Schloss foundations, when he had exacted pain enough to polish his power, the Kurfürst had taken final revenge. Gottfried had been dragged from his home and lashed to a wooden platform. A dozen wooden blocks had been rammed beneath his body and he was battered with clubs. When his arms, legs and spine had been broken he was threaded onto a large wheel and hoisted onto a post at the Oderberg Gate. Then as he died, as maggots devoured his still-living flesh and crows pecked out his eyes, 'Irontooth' had instructed that Gottfried be portrayed as the singing fool – holding Death's hand, dancing with a drum at his feet and musical bells on his two-tone tunic – in the Marienkirche *Totentanz*.

Konrad was no hero. He had no wish to be broken on the wheel. He simply wanted to share the stories which moved him. He began to fear the loss of his own life as much as the loss of those whom he loved. His fear made him timid, and he trimmed the course of his endeavour. Not only did he stop his own performances, he also started to shape his father's *Lieder* to please his patron. On the page he recorded the bravery of a pure, northern race, romanticising their battles, demonising the uncourtly knights of archaic West Francia and Slavic Moscovy. He preserved only appropriate epics for posterity.

As a result he acquired a green velvet coat, a fur cap and a satchel of good leather in which to carry his pages. Noble folk who once laughed at his careless tunes now lowered their eyes in respect as he prepared to join the Mastersingers' Guild. Whenever he felt uneasy with his compromise, 'Irontooth' rewarded him with a reading at court, after which he was free to partake of any willing lady in the audience, as long as her maid kept watch at the bedroom door.

He even had silver enough to make a weekly call at the Flemish bathhouse. Indeed it was there, at the turning point of his life, in the arms of a most-favoured Brussels nymph (whose slender feet and firm breasts transported him into a particular ecstasy) that he thought he heard his father's voice.

The sounds of copulation do not vary much from lover to lover yet, through the bulging bathhouse wall, the passionate groans next door brought to his mind Gottfried's plea long ago for forgiveness. Konrad uncoupled himself from his fair partner and without dressing burst into the adjoining room. The grunting stranger – so set on his task that he wasn't distracted by the interruption – was unfamiliar to him but Konrad recognised the woman beneath as his own wife.

'You live by prostitution,' he accused her.

'We live by prostitution,' she replied.

Konrad's last Sunday dawned with him back in the Marienkirche boneyard, the imagined voice of his father and his wife's true words ringing in his ears. His chin was disjointed and pocked by pebbles. His velvet coat was ingrained with dirt. His breath stank of *Brandewin*. His arms were spread wide over the grave mound as if to embrace it.

He had not been home, not slept in his bed, not washed and refreshed himself for the day. His unruly, natural ways were inappropriate on this of all mornings, he told himself, for it was the day that he was to perform an approved poem and be admitted to the guild.

Poetry was a mechanical art to be learnt through diligent study, according to the guild. Its creation had nothing to do with inspiration. To gain membership Konrad had agreed to submit himself to rules which dictated both the manner of delivery and a song's subject, as well as permissible structure, rhymes, melodies and cacophonies. He made himself accept that words could never be altered, except upon the instruction of a superior authority.

Konrad hurried home to change, passing synagogue and stagnant city moat, keeping to the back lanes so as not to be espied in his shameful disarray. He returned to town as red and white banners were hung from the Rathaus roof. In the gathering crowd were Dominican fathers in black robes, blond soldiers dressed in mail, weavers and cobblers, gypsies carrying baskets of violets and heather, calling out promises, offering eternal health and happiness for the smallest sliver of silver. At the centre of the throng unfolded a commotion of clerks busy with self-importance, aldermen in gold chains of office and guild judges flaunting their gem rings and certainties. Konrad moved between them with outward confidence, at once familiar and aloof, even as the voices raged in his head.

As soon as 'Irontooth' had settled himself on the dais, and his knights taken their positions, the ceremony began. First, an elderly poet recited a precise *lectio* from Isaiah. Then a visiting Master delivered the St John's Day verses. Next the *Zunftmeister* – the leader of the guild – performed a well-crafted rendition of 'Geblümte Paradiesweis', the flowered paradise melody. Finally it was Konrad's turn.

Konrad stood with his back to the crowd to face the judges. To ensure that none of his verses contradicted the Gospel, a Bible lay open before the first *Merker*. The second judge was to evaluate his prosody: rhythm, stress and intonation. A third and fourth man would decree if the rhyme and tunes were correct, consulting the guild's *Tabulatur* law book if necessary. Any faults were to be chalked on a board behind their high table, though none were expected from compliant Konrad.

He bowed deeply as stipulated in the *Tabulatur*. In his breast pocket was his prepared text, pressed against his heart. His plan was to perform Heinrich von Morungen's traditional 'Ir tugent reine ist der sunnen gelich', which celebrated a noble lady's 'pure excellence like the sun that makes dark clouds bright'. But when he opened his mouth, a different song rang out across Spandauerstraße.

It wasn't a Beowulf fragment, a French *rondet* or a Moravian epic. The song was none and all of these things, a fusion of tradition and innovation, and as the words rose unbidden to his lips he turned away from the judges to address the crowd. Before them – and for them – he shook himself free of fear and envy. His heart filled with love for his shamed father, his imperfect wife and Berlin. His voice swelled larger than it had ever been before, rapt with its own timbre and volume. His song liberated his thoughts, giving them wings, nailing to the air all the Kurfürst's lies and cruelties, breaking all the rules.

The judges were struck dumb, unable even to rise from their carved thrones to chalk up errors, not because the song was particularly beautiful (it wasn't), but because it was his and – through a kind of blessed alchemy – the audience's too. As Konrad finished, a hush fell over Berlin, broken only by the rustle of sparrows mating in the ivy.

'Irontooth' did not need to speak. He lifted a single finger. Two knights moved forward to take hold of Konrad and the dumb crowd parted without a word to let them drag him away. Later that morning they cut out his tongue. His house was seized, his possessions scattered, his wife Lola burnt at the stake for witchcraft and communing with the dead. 'Irontooth' had the satchel of papers brought to him and – after destroying a number of inappropriate Slavic songs – locked the rest away in his *Wunderkammer*. On Monday morning the poor poet was beheaded, and his corpse left to rot above the Langebrücke as a stifled warning to others.

In time Gottfried's and Konrad's names were forgotten. Yet a part of them lived on in Berliners' imagination, despite the attempt to erase them from history by whitewashing away the Marienkirche Dance of Death. Over the centuries fading memories of Konrad's dissent and his father's flooding of the Schloss's foundations came to be conflated, and out of the stories grew a myth of the people's own defiance, the *Berliner Unwille*. In truth the majority of burghers were not free-thinking, independent people. They remained in the thrall of their volatile virago, bound by her moods and tears, never staging a successful revolution. But the myth strengthened their resilient spirit, enabling them to endure the many coming tragedies, all because a man had sung the story of his love and his city.

CHAPTER 2

Colin Albany,
and the Players

The Great Comet of 1618, title page of *Cometa Orientalis* by Gothard Arthusius. The Latin inscription below the artwork translates as 'Dangerous
times shall come'. (*Royal Astronomical Society/Science Photo Library*)

Berliner Schloss, 1618

L ook at him. Look at him look. A callow youth on the palace
steps, gazing up at the night sky in wonder. Look at him,
light of frame and good sense, with lifted, fine-boned face, downy
cheeks and freckled nose. His gazing eyes are sea green in colour.
His hair has the glow of beach sand at sunset, and he twists it into
a long lovelock which touches his shoulder. His clothes are smart
and tidy: white hose, belted russet coat, a muffin cap dressed
with figaro feathers. His smile is sudden, unexpected, disarming
(or so he is told by his master John Spencer), mirroring the optimism of a happy life, of good times, and a naivety of that which is
to come.

He is in his thirteenth year in that autumn of 1618, watching the
Great Comet dazzle Berlin, as it does every city from Lemberg
to London. It fills the sky and his thoughts with its meteor-bright
head, its lizard-long tail, its reddish hue.

'Blood-coloured hue,' blusters Dandy Hohler, his friend and
faithful Anthony and Duke of Venice, who stands beside him on
the Schloss steps.

'Keep your imagination until you sleep, Dandy,' young Albany tells him with a laugh.

'Instabunt tempora periculosa,' he quotes from the Epistles, as he is apt to do when at a loss for words. 'Dangerous times shall come from this angry star.'

Berlin already had a history when Colin Albany walked onto its stage, right enough, although like most players he was convinced that little of value ever existed before him. The shiny-faced lad believed in the city's legacy of pure-bred heroes, in the defiant bear of antiquity which had named it, in it as an *altes deutsches Stammgebiet*, an ancestral German home, even though the diversity of faces in the market seemed at odds with that notion.

He also believed in his fellow countrymen's noble history in the Brandenburg borderland. For centuries Scottish knights had flocked hither to offer their swords to Kurfürsts for the propagation of Christianity. Shipmasters and mercers named Lawdre, Gordon and Young had brought trade from Leith and Edinburgh. Above all in the 1300s 'Black' Douglas, the terroriser of the English, had led a train of men-at-arms to fight for the Teutonic Order in defence of Danzig (after which all Scotsmen became free men of that city, and the Douglas arms was placed over the Hohe Thor). Of course he did not yet know of the tens of thousands of Scots, some say as many as 55,000, who would soon be drawn from the great Highland recruiting depot and slaughtered in the terrible coming war.

Colin Albany began as a sort of soldier of fortune. His history, his entrance, had opened in ancient Stirling, in the shadow of the Church of the Holy Rude. His father was church steward, his mother a waiting-woman-cum-midwife, and together they eased him into life near the old stone walls where King James had been crowned. He was an only child and so filled his solitude with imaginary companions, growing up in their company as if in a summer haze, never noticing the winter rain or Lower Town hunger. As soon as he found his feet he took to dressing up as a knight errant to scale the castle cliffs with his make-believe siblings. When he found his voice he exercised it as well, proclaiming to the whole world (or at least to anyone who would listen) that he would have both adventure and poetry in his life.

He, being a silly gaby, loved the attention of an audience. When, at the age of twelve, he found that drab and *dreich* Stirling provided insufficient applause, he headed south to London like King James himself, never to return. His father had schooled him in the divine Gospel and an earthly suspicion of strangers, and packed him off with the advice to know himself, to avoid bad company and to stand steadfast, all of which he promptly ignored. Instead the boy fell into a world of ruffs, rouged cheeks and powdered faces, and with the thespians at the Curtain found companions who chased loneliness out of his heart.

He was then a person of slender form, with lean hips and arms, so he made a suitable eyas, an unfledged hawk who takes on women's roles in the theatre. On the boards in old Shoreditch he played nurse, maid and courtesan. He proved his worth as the wench Jaquenetta in *Love's Labour's Lost*. Within twelve months he had been raped as Lavinia in *Titus Andronicus* and hung as goodly Cordelia in *Lear*. He also played both Tib and Mrs Bridget in Jonson's *Every Man in His Humour*. His physique and pale complexion befitted the fashion of the age.

One Saturday afternoon Master Spencer spotted him in the wings, pinching the seams of his skirts, about to step on stage as Rosalind. He was casting about for players to join his peripatetic *Englische Comödianten*, a troupe which was to tour the Low Countries en route to Brandenburg. The prince of that place, Johann Sigismund, was enamoured with English theatre and wished to engage a company for his court. At the end of *As You Like It* Spencer invited him – despite his muffing half a dozen lines – to join his *Comödianten*. There was little money in the enterprise, he was told, but the promise of foreign adventure (and of a new suit of clothes with high-quality embroidery) sparked his interest. He willingly agreed to travel with a dozen other John-a-dreams to Berlin.

So he came to be a strange vagabond in this strange city. Its location – he would be obliged to tell you – was plain to the eye. The place had been two settlements and to his mind their joining together had preserved the worst of both parts. Its riverbank stank and its squares lacked charm. Its hulking palace was so unattractive that he wondered why citizens had tried only once to flood it. Its vaunting, tin-topped landmen were quick to quarrel, always ready to settle even the smallest disagreement with swords. Truly, its streets were rich only in mud, taverns and bearpits. No ale-washed resident was ever far from his next glass, a dubious wager or the grave. Drunks who did not trip over and drown in the mire were lost to the pox, or to their wives who beat them to death for trekking dirt over their sacred, scoured thresholds. He had never seen homes as pin-clean and *ordentlich* – or lanes as filthy – as in Berlin. Yet despite its roughness, the place enchanted him with a strange magic.

Look at him. Look at him now on that first, fateful, bright-starred night. The actors are improvising a mangled version of the Scottish play. He is Lady Macbeth with lousy wig and blood-stained hands. Dandy Hohler is his Thane of Cawdor, wrestling with the unreachable dagger which is suspended over the stage (Dutch and German audiences prefer to see the imaginary blade). In an unexpected change to the text, a palace courtier enters stage left. He whispers into Johann Sigismund's ear. Advisers gather around the prince. The hushed tones are more arresting than any of John Spencer's barked stage directions. The players' performance shudders to a stop. Master Spencer lets go of the rope, sending the dagger into the parquet floor.

'It is war, gentlemen,' says Sigismund, who has just united his Brandenburg with the tiny Duchy of Prussia. 'God save you, and goodnight,' he adds, then vanishes from sight for ever more.

Exit Johann Sigismund.

They do not know yet that the blood-letting will endure for thirty years, that Europe's unbridled religious war will all but destroy the Germans. They will not live to see it fix fear into hearts for the next 400 years. They know only that the company will go unpaid for the evening's performance.

'Eight things a Comet always brings,' grumbles Dandy, with his usual lightness of touch. 'Wind, Famine, Plague and Death to Kings; War, Earthquake, Floods and Dire Things.'

Within twelve months Sigismund is dead. Spencer deserts the players and makes for home. Three thousand English Protestant mercenaries march through Berlin en route to Prague, bellowing curses and battle songs, set on stopping the Catholic Habsburg advance. When they and others fail in the task, and retreat, the Austrians seize German lands and demand an obligation for Brandenburg-Prussia's safety. Hostages are taken to encourage swift settlement. Yet despite the payment of 60,000 guilders, the Imperial Army seizes Berlin.

Albany had stayed on at the palace for he had found himself a sister. She is his age, as pretty as a peach, and he loves her as no lad had loved before, as if she is the missing half of him, as the old heathen poets once wrote. At the instant he'd seen her, his heart had flown to her service. Actors ever need a female who is quick with a needle, and this skill had brought her into the company. She made costumes, stitched britches, breathed on his neck as she repaired the lace on his collar. Her manner was formal with the other players but with him – in his skirts and bonnets – she was at ease, as if they were the young does in a herd. They lay together in their Schloss wardrobe, talking of follies and futures, foolish with childish games, until her father arrived to take her home.

Now look as Berlin is abandoned to the wanton capers of Austrian soldiers. Its buildings are burnt, its oaks turned into gallows, the Kurfürst's *Wunderkammer* seized. Girls take to drowning themselves in the Spree rather than be raped again. His sister's mother is shamed then thrust into an oven and roasted like a pig. Her father is clubbed to death with the butt end of muskets. She herself manages to escape and hide in their wardrobe. But Albany is not the first to find her there. Upon their frocks and props his sister is mounted by a Croat trooper. He cuts her then stuffs half a petticoat into her mouth to silence her, thereby depriving her of air. Albany seizes Macbeth's dagger and stabs the jack-slave again and again until his red blood flows over their pretty rags.

His screams alert other Imperials but not before Albany slips into Rosalind's dress. As the soldiers enter the little room he pulls his sister to her feet and spins a tale of a second Croat who had attacked his comrade in terrible jealousy.

'My liege, he defamed us both then turned on his brother,' Albany hams to an Austrian officer and begs for his protection. In the kerfuffle his performance does not disappoint and he and his sister manage to steal away, running over the old Langebrücke, past the timbered, communal houses of the Jews on Jüdenstraße and out the Stralower Gate.

Young Albany has no plan, other than to avoid the Catholic camps and make for the Köpenicker woods. In his lunacy he fancies some chance for them there, in a hidden glen, living on snared birds and beech-nuts until the tide of misery washes away from Berlin. But his sister is blooded from the assault. They walk but an hour then take shelter in a burnt-out farmhouse. He makes a pine-bough bed for them but fails to cheer her with a supper of herbs. Her pain keeps them awake, as do the shrieks of tortured peasants in a nearby village.

At dawn she is still losing blood. At noon she cuts off a strand of her hair and curls it around his finger as a love band. At dusk he holds her in his arms as her breath stops, until her body turns cold.

There are no tools to bury her so he wraps her in their skirts, within her well-stitched threads, and builds a cairn. As he works, the last whimper of childhood goes out of him like the wind from the bellows of a bagpipe. He feels nothing when the weight of stones shifts and settles over her mortal coil. He lights a fire to protect her from the wolves but its light attracts soldiers and he must run deeper into the forest.

There he hides through the summer, feeding himself on wild fruit and snails, with no will to live but a perverse determination to survive. He builds a burrow and, when winter closes around him, he stocks it with turnips and a stolen smoked ham hock, and lets a kind of madness overwhelm him. Snowflakes fall fat and feathery, or small, hard and crystalline, as he plays Rosalind and Orlando, Phoebe and Ganymede, peopling his lonely Arden, spouting under a frozen greenwood tree that 'all the world's a stage'.

He knows nothing of the course of the war, of the King of Sweden joining the Protestant cause, of the turning tide, of the *Magdeburgisieren* when the whole population of Magdeburg – a city then the size of Paris – is put to the sword by the Catholic League. His body and heart remain numb with the cold.

But the world will not let him be. In the spring, when he sees smoke on the horizon, he runs, straight into a Swedish patrol. They are hunting Imperial stragglers, having driven away the occupation army. To the Swedes – with their jaunty victors' step and yellow and blue ribbons on their hats – he is quarry. They toss him between them as lions toy with their prey before the kill, pulling at his matted hair, yanking his tangled lovelock, plucking at the clothes which he'd ripped off a murdered farmer. Only his English saves him from a ball through the head. He is taken to their major-domo, to whom he relates his history. The man takes pity on – or at least makes use of – him, pressing him to be a horse-boy. He enters his service, and re-enters Berlin, as a soldier.

Yet liberation from the Catholics brings the city no relief. Like the Austrians before them, the Swedes rob, prod and abuse the Berliners. In their search for 'treasure' they batter widows and cut off boys' hands. In their eagerness for confession they pour raw sewage down throats in a torture known as 'drinking the Swedish draught'. Now it's Catholics who dangle from the trees like so many shrivelled fruit (Jews were hung indiscriminately by both armies). Sparks and ashes rise from the burning buildings as if to sow seeds of evil across the world.

A horse-boy's role is to follow his army, along with an unholy crew of sutlers, harlots and hangers-on. Albany grooms, polishes and serves table, receiving as his reward black bread and any peasant maid of whom his officer has tired. He takes the loaf but not the girls, for their whimpers cause him pain. Instead he stands with the soldiers at muster roll, and waits for action.

Albany is cast in a new role as a musketeer. He weighs out bullets ten to the pound, charges cartridge pouches with powder and shot, takes six weeks to build enough muscle to carry the heavy weapon. When the order comes to advance, he steps on that oldest stage, lying in wait with a dozen other guns, springing a trap. He is Henry and Coriolanus, charging forward into the fray, his blood summoned, his sinews stiffened, butchering the enemy as they cry for quarter. His light frame makes him quicker on foot than most, and he is ever in the front rank, imagining himself to be as feared as the plague itself.

Nevertheless the Austrian forces regroup, pushing them back into the shattered city, its scorched walls ringing with the crash of pikes, the rattle of harnesses, the terrible howl of guns, trumpets and the wounded. He is caught behind the lines. He is captured and taken to be shot.

Then Dandy Hohler, his faithful Anthony, happens on the scene. He had been forced to join the Imperial side and vouches for him. Albany is spared death so that they may play for his commander in the old palace, reciting Adam's speech on virtue. Afterwards they eat French pottage and swill malmsey until the wine and wit run out. Come morning he is still in service as a prop-hopper, although his shot flies in the opposite direction.

His first Imperial patrol has little purpose other than to make monkey-tricks. A counsellor of Cölln, a man who changes his banner more easily than he, has been tardy in voicing support for the Catholic League's return. Graf zu Schwarzenberg, Berlin's despised new master who torches neighbourhoods which the Swedes threaten to attack, desires the counsellor's support, or his head. Albany and Dandy call at his home with musket and blade, intent on a course of firm persuasion.

But another Austrian squad is ahead of them, and employing harsher techniques. As they enter the courtyard the counsellor's thumb is jammed into a pistol's pan and, with flint removed, the trigger pulled. When he does not relent, the mashed digit is shoved into the barrel itself. A girl cries out before the gun is fired, and the counsellor's daughter is flushed from a hiding place in the attic. Until that moment Albany believed that no young women remained alive in the hellhole and her discovery changes the scene's dynamic. The captain of the advance squad takes it upon himself to inflict a different sort of pain on the counsellor, and begins to pleasure himself with the child.

At that moment Albany recognises the rapist as the Croat trooper. The rogue who he thought he'd killed is now his comrade-in-arms. The Croat does not know him of course, as he wears no dress, and utters a short, malicious laugh as he looks at her father.

In the few years since the appearance of the angry comet Albany had seen families drowned, soldiers' severed limbs twitch on the battlefield, children sprinkled with gunpowder and set alight. Yet now he – a poor player – suddenly wants nothing more than to run forward, to rewrite the text, to stop the horror and to save the girl as he could not save his lost sister.

'Any one else?' calls the Croat before Albany can act. He gestures to him and the other patrol. 'It is rare to savour such sweet flesh in Berlin these days.'

He steps back but blustering Dandy, buoyed by the camaraderie and scuppered by woe, bellows that such a treat should be enjoyed by a young man, for his first time. The revelation catches the men's imagination and they pull him forward. Albany resists but the Croat himself unbuckles his belt, pulls down his trousers and presses him into the warm clinch of the girl's legs.

'Come on, lad,' he says. 'Time to prove yourself a man.'

There is a reservoir of malice, of poison, in his soul. He wished to be admired, to make an audience laugh, to grow into his own good self. Yet at the end he is but a playwright's puppet, stripped of his pretty clothes and smile, a pitiful gallows-bird.

That evening he finds the Croat, leads him to drink and then on their return to the billet knocks him unconscious. He knows of a hole dug for the building of the new Schloss chapel but abandoned because of the fighting. Now he shoves the Croat into it, burying him up to his neck. When the man regains his wits and fathoms Albany's intent, he makes to shout. Young Albany stuffs a cloth into his mouth and assures him, 'As you have so often enjoyed toying with Death I will not cheat you of your last amusement with him.'

He mounds the earth high around his head, taking his time, pausing so as not to attract the attention of a nightwatchman. When he is finished the Croat's skull sits at the bottom of a kind of funnel, into which he sieves the last handfuls of soil. The Croat's clear brown eyes take on an extraordinary beauty as his nostrils fill with dirt. Albany stares into them as if into his own, as he suffocates, as light and power leave him. He finishes his work well, packing down the earth in faith that their evil may be buried away under the Schloss for ever.

How full a man's life is of pain and misery. Albany returns to his dubious duties and is maimed in service. In time Dandy and he find a bolthole to the west of the city walls, in Johann Sigismund's hunting park or *Tiergarten*. Around him the war rages on, drawing in all of Europe. Poles fight for Germans, French garrotte the Dutch, Spaniards march with Austrians, and Scots (like the English) serve any side which will pay them. Together the armies roll back and forth over Berlin, trampling its life and crops, bringing starvation, heralding the plague. Albany becomes one of its walking shadows, stumbling through the ruins, blinded by smoke and tears, pausing at familiar doorways painted with yellow crossbones, stopping at plundered graves, awaiting the end of the world.

Look at him. Look at his life as a child, a lover, a soldier, a weeping old fool sans teeth, sans eyes, sans taste, sans everything. Look at him strut and fret upon the stage, then crash off it into the dark embrace of one of those emptied, welcoming graves. He is battered and spent. His freckled nose is flattened. His love and lovelock are gone. His spirit is weary. He looks around the Marienkirche churchyard and sees only broken bones, unearthed and scattered, their marrow sucked dry by the starving of this foul place.

He is of this cursed ghost town, and will remain of it, part of all these things which are so much greater than he. Look, I say to you. Look with him as he closes his eyes, as he dies, knowing that in the sleep of death no more dreams will come.

Etching of Frederick the Great and the Potsdam Grenadiers by Peter Haas, c.1755. (*akg-images*)

Sanssouci, 1762

Death wields his scythe in every corner of the globe. Cannae, the Somme and Stalingrad claimed him as their own. Hiroshima gave him his busiest single day. Siberia's gulags provided him with decades of regular employment. Both Genghis Khan and Mao Zedong worked him to the bone for a generation all across Asia. But over the centuries it is to Berlin that he has most often returned.

He was present in its earliest days when waves of Teutons, Huns and Slavs fought each other on the marshy plains. He picked them off one by one along with the Wends, the Slavic people who settled on the sandy riverbank in the seventh century, and who named it *Berl* after the Polabian word for swamp. He stalked their heathen wilderness as it resisted Holy Roman emperors and later Polish kings, making the Mark Brandenburg – *das Land in der Mitte* – one of the last parts of Europe to be Christianised.

Year after year Death visited through famine, plague and robber barons who tormented the provincial backwater until it all but drained away into the poor, unproductive soil. He marched alongside the Habsburg and Swedish armies as they scattered dismembered bodies on its muddy streets during the Thirty Years' War. Over those heinous decades, he saw more than half the settlement's population burnt alive, boiled in oil or simply bound with willow switches and tossed into the river. Thousands were lost to typhoid, their nostrils filled with the stench of their own rotting flesh. By 1638 Berlin had been reduced to only 845 houses, less than half the previous number. Old Cölln was totally destroyed. Death gathered up the broken settlers and abandoned souls, held them as they wept, and heard them cry out in despair for a strong leader.

In 1640 their prayers were answered with the accession of an austere and ambitious despot. Frederick William, a Hohenzollern elector and descendant of the wealthy burgrave of Nuremberg, was determined that Brandenburg-Prussia would never again be devastated by marauding armies. He harnessed its survivors' fear to transform the devastated borderland. He built massive new fortifications around their hungry hovels and branded Berlin with his Calvinist industry. The city expanded to the south and west, spartan Friedrichstadt rising on stilts and stakes on the boggy ground, with 300 uniform, two-storey houses completed in its first year. Within two decades the neighbourhood boasted 12,000 souls. Along Wilhelmstraße aristocrats and royal ministers like Samuel von Marschall, a descendant of Scottish nobles, sited their palatial manor houses.

In return for growth and stability, the Hohenzollerns demanded total deference to their authority, and the still-traumatised Berliners whispered not a word of complaint. They devoted themselves to duty – without question, with tireless labour – and were forged into a disciplined people at arms.

'A ruler is of no consideration if he does not have adequate means and forces of his own,' the Great Elector wrote in his *Political Testament.* 'That alone has made me – thank God for it – a force to be reckoned with.'

By the start of the eighteenth century Berlin – now ruled by Frederick William's fanatic grandson, the 'Soldier King' – had grown into a great garrison. It was the capital of Prussia, the state built by an army. Its youth were conscripted, issued with uniforms, marched in step to cutting-edge weaponry factories over the now solid-stone Langebrücke. Eighty per cent of the kingdom's revenue was spent on its fighting men and armouries. The Soldier King also reformed the civil service along military lines, prescribing the exact duties of public servants with minute precision. A minister who failed to attend a committee meeting lost six months' pay. If he absented himself a second time, he was discharged from service. Absolute obedience was demanded of every man.

Along pristine, battalion-wide avenues soldiers saluted baton-wielding officers, trooped across cobbled parade grounds, breathed in air which reeked of gunpowder and discipline. Martial music echoed down the orderly lanes, into ranked houses scrubbed and cleaned as if for morning inspection. Every noon on Schlossplatz a bizarre troop of giant Potsdam Grenadiers – recruited or kidnapped from across Europe for their size – drilled for the Soldier King's pleasure. 'The most beautiful girl or woman in the world would be a matter of indifference to me but tall soldiers, they are my weakness,' he told the French ambassador.

He never started a war, but war – and the phobic preparation for it – became the obsession of his dutiful and brutish capital of absolutism.

The Soldier King's three sons were to be raised as soldiers, awoken at dawn by cannon fire, trained in the fifty-four movements of the Prussian drill code. The first boy died at his christening when a crown was forced on his oversized head. The second child had life shocked out of him by the roar of guns fired too close to his cradle. The only surviving son was a thin and delicate rebel.

Prince Frederick had enormous blue eyes and a sensitive disposition, to his father's despair. To toughen him up, the king knocked him about. He beat him for jumping off a bolting horse. He whipped him for wearing gloves in wet weather. One wild winter night, when the wind howled in from Russia and a pitcher of drinking water froze at the dinner table, he ordered him to stand guard outside the palace. The child took to hiding under his mother's bed.

Young Frederick's education was strict and unimaginative, focused on mathematics, politics and warfare, bereft of literature and Latin. Why study the ancients, barked the Soldier King, as the Romans had been beaten by the Germanic race?

'The Prince is to rise at six,' dictated the king. 'As soon as he has his slippers on he shall kneel at the bed and say a short prayer to God loud enough for all present to hear. Then speedily and with all dispatch he shall dress and wash himself, be queued and powdered; and getting dressed as well as breakfast – tea, which is to be taken while the valet is making his queue and powdering him – shall be finished and done in a quarter of an hour, that is, by a quarter past six.'

To instil in him love for the military, the Soldier King gave Frederick – at the age of six – a regiment of 131 children to drill. The Crown Prince Cadets were reviewed by the visiting Russian Tsar and the King of England. When he was fourteen years old, he was put in charge of the giant Potsdam Grenadiers.

Frederick called his uniform his shroud. He craved a world beyond the parade ground yet conformed for fear of unleashing his father's rages. On clear summer nights he escaped into the palace gardens and lay on his back on the damp grass beneath the stars. Once he spotted the Great Bear and, taking aim with a pistol, fired at the beast in his fury, imagining the shot travelling across the Milky Way to strike its flank.

Frederick began to find other worlds through books. With his tutor's help he assembled in secret his own *Wunderkammer*, a rich library almost wholly in French. He sat for hours in his window seat memorising Aristotle, Rabelais and Bossuet. He lingered over a thin folio of courtly lyrics, written three centuries earlier by an unknown hand, and revelled in the literary joys of summer, love and young voices rising in song. He composed poetry as well as copious letters to family and friends. While overlooking the parading officers' plumes and the Marienkirche, he also penned essays on armed aggression and the state of Europe. Germany was fatally divided into small states, he observed; the Thirty Years' War had been its weakest moment; Russia was in perpetual chaos; England

– though rich and happy – had produced no notable painter, sculptor or musician.

As the Soldier King shamed condemned prisoners by dressing them in French clothes at the gallows, his son dreamt of being a poet in Paris or a troubadour. Young Frederick hid away his love of the arts, marching to drum beats by day, practising the flute in his locked room at night.

At the age of fifteen he was deeply confused and frustrated. His heart burst with desire, his mind sparked with curiosity, yet his life was shaped by violence, rigidity and duty. His first foreign trip fed his hunger. He travelled with his father to Saxony, the wealthiest and most scandalous German state at the time. In Dresden Frederick enjoyed plays, opera and a woman. He became infatuated with the Countess Anna Karolina, who was both a daughter and a lover of their host Augustus the Strong. Augustus – who had no aversion to incest – collected beautiful women much as the Soldier King amassed marching giants. Over the course of his life he sired 355 children.

Augustus could not resist tempting the Soldier King and his love-struck son. During a tour of the palace, a curtain was drawn aside to reveal a waiting, naked courtesan. The Prussian King puffed and fussed and excused himself from the bedroom so Augustus, having observed the Crown Prince's reaction, offered him the woman – in place of the Countess. Frederick may or may not have accepted the offer, but he did not give up Anna Karolina – at first.

On his return to Berlin Frederick found love of another kind. Hans Hermann von Katte was a young aristocrat, charming and handsome with high forehead and smooth, blond hair tied with a black bow. The two young men became inseparable and, like star-crossed lovers, hatched a plan to flee the barrack room for England. On the eve of their flight Katte stood on the threshold of Frederick's bedchamber, his foot against the door as if to hold it open, their faces so close that they felt the other's breath on their cheeks.

A wild white moon rode in the sky that night and the air felt fresh and free. But the young men were betrayed. In his fury the

Soldier King imprisoned his son, and forced him to watch his friend beheaded. Death plucked love away and Frederick collapsed into a two-day faint, his soul seared by the trauma, empathy driven from his heart.

Frederick was said to like women only while taking his pleasure, afterwards he despised them. In 1733 he married Elisabeth-Christine of Brunswick-Bevern, a Protestant relative of the Habsburgs. He 'paid his tribute to Hymen' and then – with no heir forthcoming – detached himself from his wife, making only a single formal visit to her each year, for coffee.

All his closest confidants were male. After Katte's execution he embraced his soldier servant Fredersdorf, who would serve him until his death. He befriended a debauched Scot named Keith, an Englishman called Guy Dickens and the flautist Quantz. The Venetian coxcomb Francesco Algarotti was an especial favourite. After his wedding Frederick had written to him, 'My fate has changed – I await you with impatience – don't leave me to languish.' In private the Crown Prince draped himself in an embroidered velvet robe, ruffled his hair like a Gallic dilettante and played his flute for friends with tears in his eyes. None were blind to his need to be noticed, to his appetite for fame.

In a report to London the British ambassador called Frederick's friends 'the he-muses', noting that females were banned from approaching his court. One night the Soldier King swooped on the clubby boys like a black bear, throwing their robes and volumes of romantic poetry onto the fire.

Music became Frederick's other means of escape, enabling him to hold back the shadows, helping to fill the bitter emptiness in his heart. It also thawed his icy self-control and brought solace from his father's unpredictable temper. The Soldier King's disregard for the arts appalled him. Before his birth, court intellectuals had been dubbed 'dog food'. A jester had been appointed to run the Berlin Academy, which was then closed to save money.

In 1740, when his father died, Frederick set about making Berlin a cockpit of ideas and music. He reopened the Academy, inviting

the French philosopher Maupertuis to be its president. He extended the old Schloss to rival Versailles. He built an Opera House,
redesigned the Tiergarten, ejecting its last squatters, and modelled
the Gendarmenmarkt on Rome's Piazza del Popolo, flanked by the
graceful French and German cathedrals.

His crowning construction was Sanssouci, an intimate, pink and
white rococo pleasure palace above Potsdam's cascading terraces.
He filled its colonnades and gilded halls with books, artefacts, dancers and thinkers. He walked his beloved Italian greyhounds in
its stately grounds, seemingly at peace with the world. Every night
at 10 p.m. there was a concert in the Round Room. One evening
he and Bach made music together, the king giving him a theme
and asking for its composition into a fugue in six parts. He invited
Voltaire to take up residence in the study.

Voltaire was the master wit of the century. Since childhood Frederick had admired him, claiming to champion his humanist ideals,
devouring his plays, novels and essays. The two men became correspondents. Frederick asked him to review his essays and erotic
poems ('The love which joins them heats their kisses,/And leaves
them ever closer entwined./Heavenly lust! Ruler of the world!').
He tried to lure him to Berlin for more than a decade. In 1750 his
persistence paid off, helped by the offer of an annual salary of
20,000 francs.

In the years before the French Revolution Voltaire believed that
only an enlightened monarch could bring social change to Europe.
His distrust of democracy, which he saw as propagating the idiocy
of the masses, pleased his all-powerful host. Both men considered
plebeians to be 'crows' that pecked at patrician 'eagles', to borrow
from Shakespeare's Coriolanus. The common man needed to be
kept in his place. Voltaire invested his political hopes in Frederick,
moving to the capital, editing the king's six-volume *Art de la Guerre*,
dazzling Berlin's dinner table conversation, debating questions of
civil liberties late into the night.

Prussians looked forward to a new, enlightened age. They believed that Frederick was a man of peace, an intellectual, a lover
of music and poetry. 'Peace cannot fail to make art and science

flourish', he assured them. On his grand European tour Boswell wrote that Berlin 'was the most beautiful city I have seen'.

But the capital was already a place where true identities were hidden behind masks. The young king was determined to use his inheritance 'to acquire a reputation', as he put it. His father had bequeathed him both a robust military and a cold, calculating heart. In his most ruthless and creative moment, he marched the country to war.

In those years Germany – 'the battlefield on which the struggle for mastery of Europe is fought', according to the philosopher Leibniz – was still a mishmash of more than 300 divided states and principalities. Prussia and Austria were its biggest rivals. When the old Habsburg emperor died leaving no male heir, Frederick spurred Berlin's metamorphosis from prey to predator.

'Having, as is well known, interests in Silesia, I propose to take charge of it and keep it for the rightful owner,' he announced. He took Austria's wealthiest province in seven weeks, twisting Prussia's neurotic defensiveness into naked aggression. He seized its mines and wheat fields, abandoned his allies, shocked Europe with his gall.

He learnt the art of warfare on the hoof, leading brazen attacks, earning a reputation as the most fearless commander of the age. Risk-taking made up for his inexperience, as did his care for no one. Frederick was 'full of fire . . . quick to pounce and take advantage of foibles . . . with no heart whatever,' bemoaned a defeated general. 'Your Majesty, do you want to take that battery on your own?' an aide called to him as he led yet another cavalry charge, fighting as if he had nothing to lose.

On sleepless nights before an attack, for over twenty embattled years, Frederick soothed himself by composing poetry and reading Racine.

In 1756 the Austrians – joined by Russia and France – sought revenge and attempted to squash the treacherous upstart. Frederick answered them by seizing fickle Saxony and laying siege to Prague. He was beaten back, retreated to his books, then advanced again to Rossbach near Leipzig, where he inflicted another humiliating defeat on his enemies.

For a year the tide turned against him. Silesia changed hands, a vital convoy of 4,000 supply wagons was captured and Frederick had to borrow money from England (London wanted to keep the Continentals fighting among themselves to check French ambitions in North America). Tens of thousands of his troops were butchered on the battlefields, paying for his cold ambition with their limbs and lives. Advancing Russians terrorised East Prussia, tales of their appalling atrocities preceding them to the capital as they would at the end of the Second World War.

But in 1762 the Russian Tsarina died and – in what became known as a Miracle of the House of Brandenburg – her successor, mad Peter III, ordered his troops to change sides and put themselves under Frederick's command. The Austrian alliance collapsed. The Habsburgs would never regain their lost territories. France surrendered the Rhineland to Frederick and Quebec to the British. Prussia, alone on the Continent, emerged victorious. As Voltaire wrote, the audacious Berliner changed the destiny of Europe.

On horseback Frederick circled the old walls, reluctant to enter the city, mortified by its ruin again. He skirted the deserted cattle market – once Berlin's Tyburn and 'devil's pleasure park', soon to be renamed Alexanderplatz after the Tsar's grandson – and the walled gardens of Friedrichstadt. Along its wrecked streets he found only wretched orphans and gutted buildings. In the broad Achteck parade ground at the Potsdam Gate – where Potsdamer Platz would rise one day – a lone, pony-tailed, temple-shaved fire juggler spat plumes of flame into the air and begged for coins. 'More fire, my lord?' he called through blackened hands on seeing the king. 'Do you want more fire?'

Frederick spiralled around the Fischerkiez's broken boats and trampled gardens, by his dark Court Opera and the baroque Zeughaus artillery armoury, with its stone busts of agonised warriors, and into the Schloss courtyard, hardly lifting his head. War was 'a cruel thing', he wrote by candlelight in the cursed and battered palace. 'Nobody who has not seen it with his own eyes can have any idea of it. I believe now that the only happy people on earth are those who love nobody.'

But what are the tears of heart-sick kings and widows if the state has been saved? he then asked in his essay *Discours sur la Guerre*. Frederick set about rebuilding his capital and nation. He gave 35,000 army horses to peasant farmers. He enticed skilled refugees to settle in the restored neighbourhoods. He commissioned new buildings with straight lines and in pure tones to emphasise order, precision and strength. To feed the growing population he encouraged the cultivation of potatoes, ordering that selected fields be planted with them, and sentries stationed around the perimeter. Word was spread that the potatoes were for the king's table only, but the guards were told to 'look through their fingers' and not apprehend trespassers. With their hard-earned instinct for survival, his hungry, plebeian 'crows' stole into the fields, unearthed the royal tubers and replanted them on their own land.

Finally in league with Russia, Frederick resumed making war, pushing his territory beyond Silesia into Poland, eating its undefended provinces 'like an artichoke, leaf by leaf'. By 1786 he linked Prussia's scattered, conquered parts together into a unified state.

At the end of his life, with his tattered uniform patched and stained by snuff, Old Fritz was feared more than loved. Neither thunderstorm nor hailstorm was said to be as terrifying as the 'honour' of the king's visit. He was isolated, alone and friendless, and no longer bothered with the pretence of humanism. Yet in their dread of disorder, in their fear of ever again being sucked into the vortex, Berliners allowed him – as other leaders before and after him – to direct and dominate their lives.

In 1806 – two decades after Frederick's death – Napoleon captured Prussia's capital, having destroyed its army at Jena and Auerstedt. Astride his white charger, the new emperor rode through the Brandenburg Gate, glowering from under his hat at the defeated Berliners. At the Garrison Church, he stood beside Frederick's tomb. 'Hats off, gentlemen,' Napoleon told his fellow officers. 'If he were still alive, we would not be here.'

The French Revolution had shattered the old hierarchical ways. The Ancien Régime had collapsed and its King Louis XVI had been executed. In most of Europe and America, citizens had rejected authoritarianism and put their faith in reason and progress.

But not in Berlin. German obedience – as well as faith in absolutism – had been fixed by the trauma of the Thirty Years' War and by the egotistical Hohenzollerns. For all his learning and debates with Voltaire, and his lip-service to radical ideas, Frederick had isolated his country from the full flowering of the Enlightenment.

Frederick had created Prussia by binding together the disconnected Hohenzollern lands. As Napoleon's troops stripped his palaces of their wealth, carrying away sculptures, paintings and a folio of medieval songs, passers-by heard the airs of a flute echo over Schlossplatz. Berliners remembered the lost king's music and – humiliated by the French occupation – grew nostalgic for the old certainties. Then, instead of embracing tolerance and universal brotherhood, they filled the vacuum in their lives with nationalism. Frederick wrote:

> Tadelt nie die Taten der Soldaten,
> Leuten, die da sterben sollen,
> Sollt ihr geben was sie wollen,
> Lasst sie trinken, lasst sie küssen,
> Denn wer weiß, wie bald sie sterben müssen.

> Never criticise the acts of soldiers,
> Those men who are destined to die,
> Give them all that they wish,
> Let them drink, let them kiss,
> For who knows how soon they must die.

Karl Friedrich Schinkel's design for the entrance to the Fürstliche Residenz, 1835 (not built). (*bpk/Kupferstichkabinett, SMB/Reinhard Saczewski*)

Lustgarten, 1816

Berlin is a place where men set their dreams in stone, or at least in brick. It is not an ancient city. It has no Roman remains like London, no catacombs like Paris. Its youth always spurred it towards the future. Yet at the same time it longed for a noble past, so created buildings to perpetrate its own myth.

For centuries Schlossplatz was its seat of power, its Westminster and St Paul's, its White House, Smithsonian and Pentagon. On the square stood palace, cathedral, armoury and royal gallery. Its monuments revealed Berliners' ambitions as well as their hubris. Here 'Irontooth' defined war as destiny, Frederick set out to glorify himself and in 1914 Kaiser Wilhelm aspired to rule Europe by sending a million men to their deaths at Verdun, Ypres and Passchendaele. Here after the 'War to End all Wars' Karl Liebknecht proclaimed the ill-starred socialist republic and Hitler promised a thousand-year Reich. Ten years later Communists levelled the Schloss as a hated symbol of Prussian aggression. In its place they erected a huge grandstand for massed parades and then *Erichs Lampenladen*, Party Secretary Erich Honecker's doomed 'light bulb shop'-cum-asbestos-filled people's palace. When it too fell the old Hohenzollern Schloss began to rise phoenix-like on the vacant lot.

In Berlin past and future have forever collided, in brassy marches, in utopian visions, in a bland and sorry limbo, in the construction, demolition and preservation of dreams.

The night air crackled with feeling and fireworks. Eager songs echoed off the old walls. Paper streamers braided themselves onto branches which, in the flickering light, gave the trees the look of willowy girls, dancing, hugging, tossing their tresses in the breeze.

Karl Friedrich Schinkel set down his lantern and gazed into the dark. At his back was the palace. To his left, at the end of the avenue, the Brandenburg Gate was surrounded by his victory decorations and cheering citizens. To his right stood Bouman's baroque cathedral, built on the site of the medieval Dominican abbey. But ahead of him there was nothing. No torches lit the poplar-lined parade ground. Not a soul stirred in the gloom of old canals, kitchen gardens and sprawling, ramshackle cottages beyond them.

At the age of thirty-two, Schinkel was Prussia's *Geheimer Oberbauassessor*, in charge of the design of all public, royal and religious buildings. In his elegant blue overcoat and whitest linen, he cut the figure of a steadfast civil servant. His chiselled mouth and fine-boned features were accentuated by the lamplight. Yet beneath his careful, tailored exterior he was a man tormented by his imagination.

In the darkness ahead of him Schinkel envisioned a colonnade of eighteen Ionic columns. Behind it he pictured a public portico with a vast hidden rotunda. He saw Berliners, in elegant frock coats and high-waisted dresses, mounting open flights of stairs, circling antique sculptures, contemplating Renaissance paintings in the galleries of a majestic, neoclassical temple to art. It would be a new type of building, he fancied, the world's first museum in both purpose and organisation, flanked by the Arsenal and the cathedral, facing the Schloss, asserting that culture was one of the four pillars of society.

His visions came to him like a fever, keeping him awake, forcing him to his drawing board almost every night. Often they overwhelmed him even in broad daylight, playing themselves out across his sight like a waking dream. In his mind's eye stone pediments and medieval façades rose and fell along Unter den Linden. City squares shifted their axis before his eyes. On a hill above the open barley fields south of the old city walls, he imagined a spired monument to Prussia's triumphant army surging upward out of the soil towards the blue vault of heaven.

Now at last, with the final defeat of Napoleon, Schinkel could channel all these wild fancies into his disciplined zeal for work. In his euphoria he conceived a new heart for Berlin.

Schinkel had been born into a changing world. At the age of six his hometown of Neuruppin had burnt to the ground. His father, a Lutheran pastor, had died as a result of the blaze.

Neuruppin was a garrison town twenty kilometres north-west of Berlin, reputed to be the most Prussian of Prussian settlements: conformist, conservative, reactionary. Its residents built their houses in the classical style. No adult missed church on Sunday. No child forgot to kiss their father's hand after Easter supper. Only when he ran alone into the fields did Schinkel – like the young Frederick – feel that he could breathe. On summer evenings he watched the swallows sail free, black against a frothy sky, turning and catching the sun on their sleek bodies, falling like dark, golden darts.

He was a shy boy, hungry for novelty, anxious to please yet prone to anger, once casting a soup bowl onto the stone floor when his mother would not explain why his father had died. She could not listen to his fears, closing her ears and eyes to him even when he cried out at night. In his dreams he was consumed by fiery phantoms, able to save neither his father nor the late, great king. Schinkel turned in on himself, drawing pen portraits of Frederick, of the Great Elector, of other legendary German heroes. He performed plays about honour and loss in his small toy theatre for which he made precise figurines, mounted on slender rods.

He was a child of his time, flush with romantic notions which found form at an exhibition at the Berlin Academy. In 1797 he gazed at plans for a massive Doric temple at the Potsdam Gate to Frederick, the leader who could have saved Prussia from indignity and the Corsican corporal. Even though the monument – raised on an enormous geometric plinth, flanked by obelisks, containing the king's coffin – was never built, its design fired his imagination, showing him a means of fixing for ever ideas in stone. At the age of sixteen he resolved to become an architect.

The shame of defeat had inflamed German Romanticism. Young artists seeking a way forward – especially in this city without history – reached back to a 'lost', mythical world. They embraced the Gothic, with its links to the German Middle Ages. They glorified ancient Greece, to distance themselves from Napoleon who identified with Imperial Rome. For them the Enlightenment was too utilitarian, too short on spirituality, too French. In its place these 'true' Germans celebrated the wonder of Nature. They aspired to unlock the mysteries of the soul. They took into their hearts the exaltation that theirs was a race morally superior to all others, as proclaimed by the German Idealist philosopher Johann Gottlieb Fichte.

Their champion was Goethe, in whose early works young men left home to journey into the unknown. On the road towards meaning and truth, they tramped through untamed woods, experienced love, confronted death and – if they survived – became masters of life.

In 1803 young Schinkel set off from Berlin on his own *Wanderjahr*, or footloose gap year. He summered in the galleries and studios of Dresden, Nuremberg and Vienna, then crossed the Alps.

'Suddenly I peered down on the vast surface of the Adriatic Sea which, its waves gleaming in the evening sunlight, encircled the steep foothills many thousands of feet below me,' he wrote home to his sister in Berlin, his pen racing across the page, barely able to contain his excitement. 'Vineyards clustered on the mountains, forming slopes; many hundreds of country villas, behind thick foliage, shone brightly out of the green or hid in the valleys.'

The Mediterranean light and life dazzled Schinkel, as it had both Goethe and Wordsworth on their Italian journeys. In his *View from the Summit of Etna* and a dozen later landscapes, travellers stood awestruck on the threshold of a new world, gazing down from the rocky heights to a harbour town which – in Schinkel's poetic imagination – symbolised both culture and eternal life.

Over eighteen months, under the bright sun and night skies wild with stars, he felt free again. His laugh became larger and more infectious. His brush and pen never seemed to leave his hand. He was always drawing. He filled a dozen notebooks with fluid sketches and excited comments.

In Bologna a dragonfly – terracotta red like the Piazza Maggiore's medieval brickwork – alighted on his sketchbook, too beautiful to be brushed away. In Sicily he drew Islamic monuments, re-working their proportions. In sweeping panoramas of Palermo and Messina he relaxed his stiff northern draftsmanship. At Girgenti he imagined an evocative utopia, fixing his vision on the page. He had little money and often went hungry, surviving on bread and grapes, but it mattered not for – like Goethe's heroes and in keeping with Fichte's theory – he was reaching for self-awareness.

On his return to Berlin – and reality – there was neither pride nor work. He reined in his joy as Napoleon's Grande Armée pillaged the city. He woke at night with the smell of smoke in his nostrils, fearing that his disgraced capital had been put to the flame. The cocksure conquerors promenaded along the boulevards, flaunting their *gloire* and revolutionary colours, bringing brisk business to the wine-sellers and brothels. They also showed off their taste for *sosies de vedette*, whores who dressed themselves up as famous women. He saw them beyond the Potsdamer Platz beer and cake stalls and in the back lanes near the milk market: Medusa, Cleopatra, even Queen Consort Louise herself waving from upper windows or waiting in dark doorways, offering themselves for sale. Schinkel turned away when they plucked at his tailored cuff, feeling as ashamed as he had when Berlin's cowed governor instructed citizens that their first duty was 'to be quiet. This duty I charge the inhabitants of

Berlin to perform.' In his anger and frustration his romantic fancies boiled into political nationalism. But he needed to be practical. He realised that there would be no architectural commissions until the return of the banished Hohenzollern family. He had to eat, to pay for his handsome finery, to keep up appearances.

In Italy he had developed a unique way of interpreting landscape, charging ordinary scenes with emotion, meaning and a magical sense of light. He'd paired natural illumination with an additional inner radiance, creating works that made the world seem larger and more hopeful than it was. Schinkel believed that art – be it painting, theatre or architecture – could transform life, that an aesthetic education could bring about social and political change. Like his contemporary Caspar David Friedrich, in whose romantic works Nature seemed to speak to the human heart, he set about to enlighten Berliners through painting.

As foreign travel was difficult during the French occupation, Schinkel painted a vast *Panorama of Palermo*, based on drawings from his Italian sketchbooks. The thirty-metre-long canvas was displayed in a specially built cylindrical theatre near Alexanderplatz. Spectators stood at its centre on a raised central platform, bewitched by the illusion of space and the voices of a hidden narrator and choir.

Its sensational success led to new 'optical perspective' dioramas of St Mark's Square, St Peter's, Constantinople and the Nile, Vesuvius and the *Seven Wonders of the Ancient World*. His paintings of beautiful and inaccessible parts of the globe enabled humbled Berliners to project their beleaguered pride onto 'the miraculous buildings of the Classical age'. To drive home his point, Schinkel portrayed the northern Prussian city of Stettin alongside Athens' Acropolis.

When in 1812 Napoleon's troops advanced on Russia, he created *The Fire of Moscow*, with coils of smoke billowing above the Kremlin, to celebrate the fighting spirit of their Russian ally. He worked in a kind of focused frenzy on a hundred additional stage designs, rediscovering his childhood love of the theatre, replacing bulky baroque sets with light, painted backcloths, an innovation which allowed for rapid scene changes. Spangled arches of stars swept up to heaven in his sets for Mozart's *Magic Flute* (Mozart had visited Berlin in 1789 and performed at the Schloss). Dawn broke above the pyramids at the Temple of the Sun, alluding to the struggle between the powers of light and darkness. Schinkel saw no paradox in creating 'genuine, ideal illusions' in the theatre so long as they sparked both the audience's 'creative imagination' and their patriotism, thereby turning their hearts and heads.

Napoleon's cataclysmic defeat in Russia – 422,000 French troops had advanced across the Neman River and only 18,000 returned six months later – was repeated at the Battle of Leipzig and, two years later, at Waterloo. France retreated, Berlin was liberated and King Frederick Wilhelm III, great-nephew of Frederick the Great, returned from exile. Immediately he commissioned Schinkel to design a Prussian medal for bravery, the Iron Cross. When the Quadriga – the four-horse chariot which Napoleon had carried off to Paris as a spoil of war – was restored to the Brandenburg Gate, Schinkel replaced the goddess's oak wreath with the same Cross, changing the figure from a courier of peace into a goddess of victory.

The end of the French occupation brought a year of crazed optimism. Democrats agitated for political reform. Students called for the creation of a unified nation. Schinkel caught the hope of the new age and embodied it in a pencil portrait of his young wife Susanne. She stood in a simple dress against a classical stone balustrade. Behind her a bright landscape of leafy trees opened onto the sea. Her downcast eyes brimmed with calm optimism. Her hand rested above her stomach. She was pregnant.

But the ruling elite had returned with no intention of surrendering once more their regained privileges. Schinkel's plans for a triumphant medieval cathedral, ringed by pinnacled spires, was rejected. The Gothic – with its link to German Romanticism – had become charged with notions of reform. The king wanted to stifle the voices calling for self-determination and political change. Like his predecessors he demanded continuity and conformity, and buildings which projected his authority.

So Schinkel abandoned the Romantic dream. He needed to build, to vent his restless imagination, to have a patron. Yet again he suffered from insomnia. At least once a month he cried out so suddenly that he woke his baby daughters. He was a father now, he reminded himself, a respected servant of the Crown. He was bound by duty, obliged to serve the authoritarian regime for the common good. Susanne took their children to a field beyond the Dom to collect camomile flowers, brewing tea for him every evening.

On that heady January night in 1816, as fireworks burst overhead in celebration of the French defeat, he stood at Schlossplatz – in the Lustgarten – and imagined Berlin as a capital of consequence. He looked into the darkness and knew that his real work could now begin.

The Neue Wache, or New Guardhouse, was his first major commission. He created a low cubic building next to the Zeughaus armoury on the tree-lined boulevard Unter den Linden, fronted by columns and a pediment, lined by statues of generals, to honour Prussia's victorious army.

Three minutes' walk away, the Gendarmenmarkt was flanked by the French and German cathedrals. When the National Theatre was gutted by fire, Schinkel placed between them a new playhouse, and created one of the most elegant squares in Europe. A fine, wide flight of steps rose up to a noble portico and into the temple-like auditorium. On the opening night the audience cheered his stage set panorama of Berlin, elated to see their city, their new theatre, themselves honoured in his splendid vision. After the performance, the crowd surrounded his house and serenaded him.

To diehard Romantics, ever hopeful of becoming masters of their own lives, he was a traitor. But the king was pleased. As he and other German leaders suppressed liberal groups with characteristic severity – introducing press censorship, banning Beethoven's opera *Fidelio* with its ode to freedom sung by political prisoners, ordering the public beheading of a student who had assassinated a reactionary playwright – he allowed Schinkel to create his masterwork.

The Königliches Museum – known today as the Altes Museum

– was to be pedagogic, exhibiting art both to educate and to aggrandise the nation. In London the British Museum was under construction. In Paris the Louvre had been thrown open to *les citoyens*. Berlin's ambitions were impelled by its ingrained insecurity, plus the return of its looted treasures from France.

Schinkel designed a two-storey structure with colonnade and open portico, linking the 'rough' outer world to a 'sublime' inner sanctuary. On the portico's walls murals depicted an idealised history of civilisation. The central domed room was modelled on the Pantheon. 'Beauty in itself and for the city,' he wrote, creating a haven for art in the bullying and belligerent garrison town.

Architects must balance function and poetry, firmness and delight. As so many of their decisions need to be justified and approved – materials, dimensions, cost – they are forced to rationalise their art. In the same manner they must work within the prescribed dimensions of their time. Schinkel was a tithed artist in an age of repression. When not bent over his drawing board, he was on the road, travelling by coach across Prussia from Pomerania to the Rhineland, advising on the construction of barracks, churches, lighthouses and an artillery school. He brought gas lighting to Berlin and introduced its first street signs. He planned the layout of Potsdamer Platz, sweeping away the cake stalls and tarts, giving it temple-like stone gatehouses in a nod to the unrealised mausoleum which had inspired him to architecture. On the southern hill of windmills and hollyhocks he raised his cast-iron monument to Prussian soldiers, renaming the hamlet Kreuzberg after the Iron Cross on its pinnacle. In a move that took him further away from Romanticism, he designed the *Pickelhaube*, the spiked helmet that would become another symbol of militant nationalism.

He also helped to establish a system of design education, worked on furniture, and in iron, silver and glass. Yet all the while the whirl of his teeming imagination, and riot of projects too abundant ever to be realised, left him feeling inadequate. In turn his ambition drove him to devise ever more utopian and fanciful designs.

'I am inwardly torn apart by work which draws me away from

my "real" purpose,' he confessed, fearful of compromise even as he produced his finest creations.

In 1826 Schinkel visited Britain. He wanted to study Smirke's unfinished British Museum, at the time the largest building site in Europe. As Italy had given him a view of a luminous and romantic past, England and Scotland now opened his eyes to the dark, satanic present. He saw London's docks, Telford's bridges and Brunel's Thames tunnel. In the Midlands he sketched iron foundries and factories. In Manchester he drew unbroken lines of spinning mills, seven or eight storeys high, which spread alongside the canals with no regard for aesthetics or workers' welfare. In Lancashire he wrote of filthy potteries and machine works 'where three years ago there were only fields, but these buildings are so black with smoke that they might have been in use for a hundred years'. He noted that labourers toiled sixteen-hour days for two shillings a week. To him the 'monstrous masses of building put up just by foremen, without architecture' created a bleak cityscape. He was shaken by the changes wrought by the Industrial Revolution, and by the street protests of striking Irish navvies. Yet he was astonished by British engineering innovation: fireproof vaulting, railways on raised tracks, above all the use of brick. After three months in Britain he took home firm ideas about what he did – and didn't – want to introduce to Prussia.

Britain and her workers seemed enslaved by utilitarian purpose. Its mills and gas plants were rigid and bereft of beauty. But Schinkel saw no reason why functional structures couldn't also be works of art, transforming the environment, illuminating lives. He set about making brick – the versatile building material of the industrial age – serve an artistic purpose. He began with a church and then, in 1832, built the Bauakademie.

Elegant in appearance, pioneering in construction, his School of Architecture was a revolutionary work. Its form, practicality and streamlined façade anticipated by a century the Bauhaus's minimal modernism. As with the Altes Museum, Schinkel clad the building in a cultural tutorial, its terracotta panels illustrating key moments in the development of architecture: Hercules embraced a Doric column, kneeling girls crowned with ears of corn symbolised the Corinthian and Ionic orders, a naked woman measured space with a plumb line. He both mastered historical forms and touched the future, only then to retreat from it.

The creative mind is not an orderly place. Ideas do not arrive in neat ranks, at convenient intervals, like soldiers falling into line on a parade ground. Superior notions do not stand apart from the rank and file, sporting regimental plumes to distinguish their quality. Nor does the enemy wait outside the walls. It lurks within the ranks, dressed in the same uniform, making it difficult to tell friend from foe. Light casts shadow and dark doubts can eclipse the brightest idea.

The imagination's caprice troubled Schinkel. He struggled to master its inconstancy, to order the world. At the same time he began to mistrust his instincts. He fell back on aged notions of hierarchy: 'The modern period, with its pressing enterprises directed to the existence of the individual, does not attain reflectiveness and is absorbed in anxious activity.' When he could not sleep he tramped Berlin's spreading factory district, watched the first soot-belching chimneys rise above August Borsig's iron foundry, saw workers crowd into cramped and airless tenements, and realised how much remained to be done. Beyond the centre Berlin was evolving without order, in the pursuit of profit alone. His fear that the city would grow as ugly as Britain seemed to be coming true.

In the last years of his life – while initiating dozens of civic projects – Schinkel made two last grasps at utopia. First, he designed a whimsical residence for the Greek royal family atop the Acropolis in Athens. It was never built.

Then he conceived a dream palace for the Russian Tsarina, sister of Prussia's Crown Prince. Schloss Orianda was to be a stupendous ornament with fountains, garden courts and a dazzling Ionic temple. Its terraces would overlook the Black Sea. Its classical sculptures of goddesses would wing along hallways decorated with gold and semi-precious stones. Marble caryatid figures would hold porticos aloft as in ancient Greece. Orianda was intended to symbolise, as Schinkel told the Tsarina, the endurance of Europe's great imperial dynasties.

It too was never built. After two years' labour on the commission, Schinkel was thanked for his efforts with the gift of a small mother-of-pearl box. He fell into a depression, suffered a stroke and slipped into a year-long coma.

'In my view the artistic sphere, which alone appeals to me, is of such a limitless extent that a man's life is much too short for it.' Schinkel had worked himself to death. All his life he – like Goethe's Faust – had strived without counting the cost. His unrelenting imagination had exhausted him. Like other Romantics, he learnt too late that culture would not lead his people to national enlightenment. Art could not defeat absolutism.

Autumn lime leaves crunched and crackled beneath ten thousand footfalls. The funeral cortège snaked across the Spree drawbridge, through old Oranienburg Gate and into the Dorotheenstadt cemetery. River boatmen doffed their caps. The king's own military band played a sombre mourning march. In silence Berliners – their heads dipped as low as the afternoon sun – lined the broad cobbled paths flanked by oaks and chestnuts. A white marble angel seemed luminous in the lengthening shadows. Their haunted architect's 1841 gravestone was inscribed with the words:

ALL THAT HEAVEN HAS GIVEN US
ALL THAT UPLIFTS US TO HEAVEN
IS TOO MIGHTY FOR DEATH
TOO PURE FOR THE EARTH.

'Finally the towers of Berlin,' a Viennese visitor wrote on arrival in the city a few years later. 'The collection of buildings are more beautiful than I have ever seen together; the streets are wide, the impression is kingly.'

Schinkel had transformed the aspirant capital, linking it to

Athens and Rome, giving form to the Lustgarten, Unter den Linden, Gendarmenmarkt and the Tiergarten. In buildings constructed as well as in designs never executed, he – and his student Friedrich August Stüler, who carried forward Schinkel's vision in the Neues Museum – left a legacy of the coexistence of beauty and function, tradition and innovation. His achievement was real yet he perceived himself as a failure, because he knew that he had compromised, and because reality could never keep up with all that he imagined.

But there remained something illusory – even disingenuous – in his gracious, neoclassical creations. Beyond the cultural temples and long stretches of noble residences, and the elitist society which held onto privilege, lay a future that would be brutal, bloody and not unfamiliar.

CHAPTER 5

*Lilli Neuss,
and the Owl*

Armaments factory worker, c.1858 (*Archive of Modern Conflict*)

Alt-Moabit, 1858

She watched him at the evening window, poised like a runner at the starting gate. He turned back into the room and she sought his eyes. She smiled, told him to sit, to wait until morning, but he didn't respond. His look was so far away. He glanced at their sleeping son, not yet nine, so biddable, so tired, then turned back to the window. Lilli looked down at her needlework and felt a shiver run through her.

One day a man may just walk away, she thought. A man may walk away and leave behind all those who were once dear to him, all those who rely on him. Those left behind stay behind and can do nothing but weep. A man can leave but not a woman. Women stay in the home, at their labours, with the children.

'I'm taking him with me,' he said, and started to wake the boy.

In the tiny room his sudden movement startled her. He was a large man, so broad that his wielding arms might glance the opposite walls in moments of anger. His head often brushed the smoke-stained ceiling. Beside their bed the plaster had been

smashed by his fist. But instead of reaching out to strike her, those
arms gathered up the boy, chiding him awake and into his jacket
and boots.

'Leave him be. Let him sleep,' pleaded Lilli, dropping her work.
The boy had stayed late at the forge, held back on the excuse that it
was pay day, and then not been paid. He needed rest, Lilli worried.
She always worried. But the man did not listen. He insisted that he
and the boy go back to the forge for the money.

'You'll be right back?' she asked, for there was something else.

'Before you finish the last piece,' he said with a surprising smile.
'Now get on with it.'

Lilli heard their feet descend the stairs and returned to her
labour. She had another seven pieces to finish before bed. Then
she sprang to her feet. She leant out of the window to catch sight
of them on the street below. Two figures turned at the new barracks on Straße vor den Thoren. My best friend, she thought. My
unhappy, only friend and son. But the two figures didn't stop at
the forge, rather they went on towards Weidendammer Brücke.
She pushed herself further out of the window to get a better view
and almost lost her balance. She could no longer see them in
the dark.

She sat back in the chair. She tried to focus on her work. There
will be an explanation, she thought. When they return he'll explain
why they went towards the station and we'll laugh and be happy
again. I'll fry potato pancakes crisp as he likes them. I'll borrow
some jam for the boy. She leapt up again. Women wait and worry,
she told herself. Wait and worry.

An hour passed and then two. She finished her piecework.
She turned down the lamp even though she knew there'd be no
sleep. She kept watch, listened for their familiar footfalls. In rooms
above and below she heard a baby cry and strange, nocturnal
groans.

When the sky began to lighten, the smell of baking bread rose
through the open window. Beyond the thin walls echoed the sounds
of couples waking and bickering, of men stomping out to work, of
wives slumping down to their looms. Pipe smoke mingled with the

smell of cooking onions. Tinsmiths' hammers tap-tapped in the courtyard. Sunlight strained through the lines of drying nappies and sorry underwear, catching the dirty faces of children at cellar doors.

As the factory horns howled, Lilli thought she spotted them in the press of brickies and metalworkers. She levered herself back onto the ledge, and felt another stab of disappointment. Her red eyes caught the attention of a neighbour, passing by with the other working women – milliners, dressmakers and laundresses – who followed the men.

'Husband still asleep?' the neighbour called up in a mocking manner.

'Yes, still asleep,' answered Lilli, her cheeks flushing as the women laughed.

The jibe made her duck back into the room. Now in the morning light she noticed that their suitcase was missing, as well as his suit. She reached into the niche behind the flour bin. He had always guarded their earnings as if Lilli were a child and might squander it on fripperies. The money was also gone.

A decade had passed since she'd come to Berlin. At the age of fifteen, in the second summer that the harvest had failed, she'd left her home in Silesia. In those hungry years few country people could afford to marry, and many chose instead to seek their fortune in the capital. They left in their tens of thousands on the new railway lines, clutching crisp paper passports and old dreams, carrying single rucksacks or heavy trousseaux. Lilli travelled with them, weeping as she leant out of the carriage window, letting go of her sister's hand only as the train gathered speed, waving farewell to her mother until a cinder lodged itself in her eye.

The man had come to her rescue then, coaxing the cinder out with the corner of a handkerchief, and she was so grateful for his help and the intimacy of his proximity that she let him ride beside her. He'd made the journey a dozen times, he said. He was from Silesia himself and had been back to visit relations. He told her that he wanted to earn enough money to buy passage to America. She fell for both his charm and story of the difficulties of a single woman finding safe accommodation in Berlin. His proposal that they pretend to be a married couple terrified her, yet he assured her it was only for her protection. But, as she found that evening in a small railway hotel, the arrangement was not without obligations. She didn't dislike him, and he was tender (or at least thought-ful) and they laughed when he twisted his black moustache in his fingers.

To his credit he did not desert her when she found herself with child, although the news wiped the smile from his lips. He landed a job at Borsig's foundry, making the locomotives which would bring more young people from the eastern provinces. She trusted the man even though he was often moody, lashing out at her from time to time. She laboured in their room at a small loom, training their son to help her before he was four years old. They were not unhappy, ate almost every day and enjoyed summer Sunday pic-nics in the Volkspark. Lilli would sit in the sun, her face turned up to the warm, bright light, as if storing it up against the coming darkness.

After the man and their boy had been gone a week she considered suicide. In the gloomy room she wound a skein of yarn into a soft noose. She thought of drowning herself in the Spree. She wondered about jumping out of the window until she realised that the fall might only cripple her, and from where would the money come for the doctor? And how could she then care for her man and son when they returned home?

Often he had told her that he hated Berlin. He hated the deep, sad streets, hated the puffed-up officials, hated the unkind, pig-headed Berliners and their alien humour. He had never asked her what she hated, or if she too felt trapped, or any question for that matter apart from why she had earned so little that week. He told her not to waste time in gossip with neighbours. He kept her from making friends. Yet at the same time he spoke to her less and less, vanishing for whole nights, never once explaining his actions. For every master there is a slave, for every victor there is a victim, and Lilli came to see submission as duty, especially after he beat her. She accepted the blows and loneliness, living only for moments of tenderness with the boy: his first haircut in the tin bath; the evening he learnt to clap his hands, and kept clapping them while falling asleep at her breast; his confusion at age six on being awoken for his second day at the forge. 'Don't be silly, Mother, I went to work yesterday,' he told her.

Now with her boy gone she slid into despair. She called by the forge but the proprietor abused her for her son's absence. She waited outside the corner *Kneipe* but no drinker admitted to having seen her man, or took pity on her. Berliners *were* hard people. Suffering seemed to have bled them of empathy. They mocked weakness.

But Lilli could not run from them and their solemn city. She knew of nowhere else to go. She couldn't return home, deceived, abandoned and robbed of all that she loved. The shame would be too great. She had to stay, and continue to live a kind of lie, and find a means to survive.

After a month her loom was seized for back rent and she was thrown onto the street. She managed to salvage her bedding, which she pawned to feed herself for a week. She slept under a bridge in the Volkspark, near to the spot where her son had once given his whole bread roll to a duck, and her man plunged into the pond to retrieve it. She found a bed in the Ochsenkopf workhouse and a job in a brickyard. But with no coat and the coming of winter, she soon needed to find indoor employment.

For three months she toiled at a Moabit wash-house, soaping and scrubbing clothes, turning and soaping them again. Then she found work in a basement laundry, starching cuffs and collars. In the constant rush of water from the faucets, she gazed at her raw hands under the white soapsuds and remembered that she had once been young.

Some nights she woke in a panic, unable to picture her son's face. Who would remember him if not she? Who would remember her, and so save her too from being lost?

As she waited and worried, waited and worried, Lilli remembered the first talk of emigration. Her husband and son had gone ahead to America, she began to tell the women who worked beside her. When they'd earned enough money for her fare they would send for her. She repeated the fantasy so often that it became her truth. She kept no room of her own, she told them, and lived as a *Schlafmädchen*, renting a bed by the hour, taking turns in it with two other women, as she might be off to New York any day.

Once every week at the Borsig factory gate she scanned the hard, tired faces until she ran into an acquaintance of her man, an under-manager at the canteen. He looked into her eyes, listened to her story, then touched her hand.

'So you know,' he said, leaving Lilli unsure if he really knew what had become of her family, or if he had simply accepted her story. 'Your arms are slender and fair but strong, Frau Neuss,' he went on. 'There is always room for a hard worker in the kitchens.' Lilli coloured, drawing her shawl around her shoulders, knowing at last to be suspicious of men. 'I could put in a good word for you, if you wish,' he said.

In March 1858 Lilli began work in *la terre Moab*. The vast Moabit factory north of the Spree was Berlin's new industrial heart. As huge as a city and as cramped as a cell, cinders rose red from its fifteen chimneys. Beneath them 2,000 men slaved as if in irons, forging boilers and wheels, hammering out spikes and track, building twenty-five locomotives at once in factory halls as ugly as Schinkel had seen in Manchester. Newcomers covered their ears to block out the noise. Coal soot lay thick on the narrow lanes. Footprints wound from foundry to shop floor as if across a blanket of black snow.

Sometimes during her working day Lilli paused for a moment near the glowing furnaces to watch the flames and massed men, feeling the touch of sparks on her skin, wondering if her lost son laboured in such a satanic mill. But usually she stayed in the kitchen, mincing pork, kneading dough, peeling potatoes. There was always food to eat, for which she was grateful, but rarely the time to eat. Bread needed to be in the ovens before dawn, meats boiled by ten, beer available from two. The men ate in shifts, at speed, unwinding only to smoke a bowl of their pipe. Pots, cauldrons and glasses were rarely washed and dried before nightfall.

In that scalding August, when there seemed not enough air to breathe in Berlin, the company completed its 1,000th locomotive. In celebration August Borsig himself, who only thirty years earlier had founded his one-man firm to make steam pumps for Frederick the Great's fountains at Sanssouci, opened his villa to the public. Thirty thousand Berliners wandered through his princely gardens, wondering at his free-roaming peafowl and peacocks. Gruff-accented workers ate raw, open-face *Hackfleisch Brötchen* and drank their fill at long oak tables. The sausages, buns and beer were his gift, and his employees – flushed with pride for their industrial mission – danced the Polka around the flower-bedecked locomotive *Borussia*, the Latin name for Prussia.

In Borsig's workshop Prussia had been cast in iron as Germany's saviour, destined to unite the fragmented states. In the works kitchen Lilli's destiny was to peel and scrub and rinse until, around midnight, she retreated to a storeroom. She dropped asleep on the sacks of potatoes. It was there that the under-manager found her.

The man had never been far away throughout her time at the factory, monitoring deliveries, disciplining tardiness, watching the sway of her hips. In a way he saw the taking of her as his due. She submitted herself in silence, in recognition of his power, fearful of being beaten again. Women can never trust men, she repeated to herself. Women can only bow to their will, and dream that there might be a different way to live.

The owl fell into her life on the night she discovered she was pregnant again. It was a fledgling, not yet able to fly, and rolled out of an unseen place under the roof. She rescued it from the flashing seconds before it would have dropped to its death. She scanned the gables for its nest but neither saw broken tiles nor heard a hissing parent. She made it a home, lining a washbasin with grass and moss gathered in the park. The bird ate maggots and, in the days and weeks that followed, Lilli fed it on mice which she caught in the kitchens. She loved to stroke its mottled buff feathers and its downy white chest, and to gaze into its heart-shaped face. At night its snores comforted her when she slept.

One Friday evening Lilli returned from work to find the bird had flown. The new *Schlafmädchen* who shared her room had left the window ajar, perhaps on purpose, and the owl had hopped onto the sill and out of her life. Lilli searched the street below and its stinking, muddy margins but found not a feather. Her old neighbour spotted her and her condition. 'In the gutter again are you, Frau Neuss?' she called out. 'Time to hurry away to America.'

Lilli's shame caused her to slip in the mud, soiling her skirt. At the pump she rinsed her hems then retreated to the room, chased by mocking laughter, trapped within the four walls. Only that morning the under-manager had asked her if she could bind her waist, so as not to cause herself embarrassment.

Sometime after midnight she walked out into the dark. Gas lamps had not yet reached her neighbourhood and – until her eyes grew accustomed to the gloom – she trod through the sombre, brick alleys with her hands stretched out in front of her like a sleepwalker. When she found herself at the Hamburger Bahnhof, she paused beneath its twin towers, hardly seeing the night freights steam through the high arches to the station turntable. A police *Schutzmann* spotted her and drove her back into the shadows. She kept to them along the canal and looping Spree, skirting both Charité hospital and the artillery garrison, crossing the river at Weidendammer Brücke, as her man and son had done twelve months earlier. At its apex a cast-iron Prussian eagle seemed to mock her.

At first light a cold, light rain began to fall and, lost in the unknown avenues, she took shelter in a long, odd building open at its side. Above her the portico was decorated with murals. They were the largest paintings that she had ever seen. In them, caught by the rising sun, Jupiter rode an eagle out of the heavens, angels and harpists processed towards earth and Pegasus alighted next to an exotic pool. Before her in *Entwicklung des Lebens auf der Erde vom Morgen zum Abend*, men and women moved from dawn to dusk, from youth to death. Children frolicked in Arcadian woods, naked lovers embraced, old soldiers and crones crossed a raging sea on their final ferry ride.

Lilli was awed by the frescoes, by the story of the span of human life, by the journey away from Eden and innocence. Above all she was shaken by the quiver of five archers who – in an upper panel – aimed their arrows at a bird staked to a tree. The poor creature had a strange, heart-shaped face and in that moment Lilli thought she recognised her little owl. She shivered, in part from the cold, and reached out as if to touch it.

At the entrance to Schinkel's great museum she wept. When the bronze portal opened she timidly entered the Altes Museum. In its sky-lit rotunda, surrounded by a gallery supported by twenty Corinthian columns, she gazed at colossal statues of heroes named Augustus and Germanicus. She stood before gods of antiquity called Apollo and Venus. Her dress dragged up the curving, double staircase. In the upper hall she stopped before a painting titled *Leda and the Swan*. In it Leda – the daughter of an ancient king – cradled a swan between her open legs. The bird's long neck was pressed between her breasts. Its bill pecked at her neck. Lilli felt as if her eyes were pressed open, as if her heart swelled with a long-forgotten dream, until a museum guard, disturbed by her dishevelled state and disarrayed dress, asked her to leave the building.

In those days a common remedy for inducing a miscarriage was to swallow phosphorous match heads. One hundred was thought to be too few. Two hundred was too many. The correct amount depended on the woman's weight, and the stage of her confinement.

In her room she emptied the owl's nest from the basin, filled a jug with fresh water and barred the door. She took off her tight clothes and wrapped herself in a kind of loose sheet, in the manner of the king's daughter in the Correggio painting.

Lilli then counted out 150 matches and at the last moment, to be sure, added another ten. She sat herself by the open window and began to suck off their heads, one by one. The taste was foul – like rank garlic and acid – but she pushed on.

The burning sensation in her throat took her by surprise. She'd expected to feel pain only in her abdomen. But the luminous, red-flecked vomit strangely reassured her. That is my old life dying, she thought.

Then her head started to swim and her ears began to ring. She rose to shout at the barrack's tinsmiths, to tell them to stop their racket and give her peace, but she couldn't unbar the door. She couldn't even find the latch.

Lilli called out but no one seemed to hear her. No one came to her rescue. No one had remembered her. Women suffer and survive, she repeated to herself. Women suffer and survive. She slipped on the sodden floor and banged her head on the metal bed frame. In her last moment of consciousness, she saw a vision of herself as a strong and flawless Leda, forever young, forever beautiful, and beholden to no man, awaiting the love of a winged god.

In those mean *Hinterhof* courtyards the facts of Lilli's fate were remembered for no more than a week. By then the kernel of her history had spread and mutated through Moabit as if on a whispering breeze. In one version her man came home wracked with guilt, full of repentance. In another her son – suddenly older, wealthy and freed of time's confines – arrived from America to pay for doctors and to buy her a cottage in her Silesian home. In a third version the owl – which it seems may never have existed – perched on the window sill all night to watch over her prostrate body. Each version of the tale, in its distillation of Berliners' fears, hopes and values, was a reminder that life had to be given meaning, and that they – like us all – were creatures of narrative, earth and time.

In fact, as far as anyone can now know, Lilli's *Schlafmädchen* returned on Sunday. The landlord helped her to break down the door. On the bed the bruised young *Berlinerin* was marble cold. Yet her body glowed with such otherworldly radiance that the landlord – an unsentimental man never troubled by his emotions – could not tear his gaze away from her.

As the *Schlafmädchen* gathered up her few possessions and scrubbed away the stains, the small, brown owl remained motionless at the window. Only when the men came to take the corpse did the bird drop away in a sweeping, soundless flight, vanishing into the dark, as much a myth as Lilli.

Walther Rathenau, Weimar Minister of Reconstruction, at Wiesbaden conference, 1921. (*Topfoto*)

Chausseestraße, 1881

What is beauty? he asked, turning the petite Degas dancer in his hands. Schiller had called it the gateway to knowledge. Goethe considered it a manifestation of secret natural laws. Keats thought it synonymous with truth. Kant said it was purposive without purpose, finality without end.

Walther Rathenau held the small bronze under his desk lamp, cupped the figurine's lifted head, ran a finger down her spine. He'd read that beauty led to a quickening of the heart, that it enhanced one's ability to feel. He flicked the dancer's cotton skirt, toyed with its blue silk bow. But the sculpture stirred no emotion in him, however much he wished it would. He sensed no heightened desire, no longing for youth, no hint of redemption. To him the bronze was only a pretty doll, as it would have been to his father before him. Yet he knew he should like the piece, want it, buy it. He had to do the right thing. He had to compensate for an absence in him. He'd ask the dealer to send an invoice in the morning.

Rathenau – industrial tycoon, artists' patron, dinner jacket

philosopher and Weimar Foreign Minister – picked up his pen.
'What was once the pride and beauty of the city is today stifled,
old, out of place,' he wrote, unaware that his words would far out-
live him. 'The Athens of the Spree is dead, and a Chicago on the
Spree is emerging in its place.'

Berlin was never an ethnic German city. Its poor land and isolated location had made its survival dependent on incomers. In
the Middle Ages plague increased the elbow room. 'Die Pest hat
Raum gemacht', ran the old proverb. Tens of thousands of Franks,
Flemings, Rhinelanders and Danes settled in Brandenburg during
the twelfth and thirteenth centuries. The oldest surviving Jewish
gravestone dated from 1244. The Dutch drained its marshland.
The Huguenots developed the woollen and lace industries. In
1685 Frederick William, the Great Elector – desperate to replace
the thousands lost in his wars – had offered sanctuary to religious
refugees. Fifteen years later more than a third of the population
were French. Poles, Silesians, Swedes and more Scots followed
them. Frederick even mooted building a mosque to attract Muslims,
250 years before the arrival of the first Turkish *Gastarbeiter*.

But conformity, and the rub of historical trauma, ground down
the immigrants' differences, reshaping the gems of diversity, flat-
tening the mosaic into a duller, dutiful, stony archetype.

Hence the 1848 liberal revolution – which transformed much of
the rest of Europe – came to nothing in the city. The army had
surrounded the upstart National Assembly and ordered its deleg-
ates to disperse, which they did in orderly ranks, never to return.
Demands for universal male suffrage, parliamentary democracy
and individual rights based in natural law were denied. Criticism
of the king – even the expression of 'unhappiness or discon-
tent' with the government – was forbidden. Authority remained,
as ever, firmly in the hands of the military and the monarch. As
Lenin noted later, the Prussians – both cowed natives and incomers alike – were incapable of sustaining a revolution as they'd
never disobey the 'Do Not Walk on the Grass' sign at the palace
gates.

Otto von Bismarck – who served as prime statesman and Chancellor for almost thirty years – told them that Prussia's strength was not 'determined by its liberalism but by its power . . . by iron and blood'. He was a self-centred, unprincipled, despotic opportunist who harnessed Berliners' ambitions. He championed army and industry, mobilising blood and iron to provoke strategic wars against Denmark, Austria and France. Borsig's locomotives pulled the troops to victory at Königsgrätz and Sedan. Artillery shells milled in Moabit fell on Paris, killing 400 besieged Parisians. Thirty thousand Prussian soldiers marched down the Champs-Élysées, bristling with contempt for their half-starved rivals. Bismarck defeated the Reich's enemies and united German lands, pounding his desk and shouting, 'I have beaten them all! All!'

In victory Berlin became an industrial giant. The spoils of war poured into state coffers already swollen by the economic successes of Borsig, Bayer, Krupps and Siemens. Broad, ostentatious avenues arrowed out from the centre towards Warsaw and Paris. Grand, ranked apartment blocks marched alongside them, reinforcing the sense of uniformity. Strips of asphalt ran parallel to the tramlines, from home to factory and destiny. The whole city seemed designed for function, its single-minded people asserting that order could banish chaos. In 1871 Wilhelm was proclaimed *Kaiser* – Caesar – at Versailles, a venue chosen to humiliate the French and avenge the shame of Napoleon's occupation of Prussia sixty-five years earlier. Bossy, belligerent Berlin, which 'fed itself by war and became fat through war', boomed with aggressive, industrial nationalism.

In his wealthy suburban Grunewald villa, Walther Rathenau lay down his pen. His speech was written, the hour late. Beyond his study window the night – his last night – was black and still but for the hooting of an owl. Most people find beauty in nature, he told himself, or in works of art like the little sculpture on his desk and the Klimt portrait which hung behind him. Others – he thought – find it in poetry, Persian ceramics or even aesthetic English coffee pots. To him beauty was not to be found in objects but rather in

clear thinking, in self-belief, in success. He wanted to burn with a
hard, jewel-like flame. He wanted to embrace the beauty of being
alive. He understood the importance of emotions, but he could not
feel them.

Walther Rathenau had been born to the ring of hammers. As
a small boy he had toddled around his father's first workshop on
Chausseestraße, around the corner from Lilli Neuss's former tenement. He loved to watch molten metal run into moulds, find its
form, cool iron hard. He always asked questions of the old Berlin
engineers and braziers. He was curious and clever, with large, dark
eyes and a sensuous down-turned mouth.

In 1881 his engineer father Emil had travelled to the first International Electrical Exhibition in Paris. There he'd seen Edison's
new incandescent lamp, recognised its potential and bought the
patents. At Chausseestraße young Walther had flicked the invention's switch off and on, off and on, filled with wonder until his
father pushed him away, knocking him to the ground, telling him
it wasn't a toy.

The German Edison Company for Applied Electricity – or AEG
as it was renamed – outgrew the old works at lightning speed.
Within a few years Emil launched a 'galaxy' of light bulbs, built
colossal generators near the Borsig factory and engineered a system
to deliver electricity to individual houses, winning the contract to
light Berlin. In its advertisements, AEG's goddess of light raced
towards a brilliant future.

With his galloping success Emil Rathenau expanded the business by investing in aluminium plants and long-distance power
transmission. He took to manufacturing cars, trucks and trams. His
Technical Flight Department began building aeroplanes for the
War Ministry, improving on the Wright brothers' design. By 1914
AEG had expanded into a ten-billion-Mark commercial empire
with 66,000 employees.

Emil worked seven days a week. He never took more than half an
hour for lunch. At breakfast, business was discussed. After dinner,
factories were inspected. He established – along with competitor
Werner von Siemens – the fundamentals of mass production a

decade before Henry Ford. He invented new forms of co-operation between banks and industry. His energy and example helped shape German industry.

Rathenau's father may have been a pioneer of large-scale capitalism, and one of the wealthiest men in Germany, but as he grew older Walther came to see the constant absences from home as a surrender of personal freedom, as weakness. Emil subordinated himself to a purpose which lay outside himself, young Walther believed. He thought in things, not in ideas and words, and took for granted the traditional structure of the world. His father was neither master of his life nor of the empire which he had created. He was its slave, and there was no beauty in that.

Walther Rathenau's own defence against weakness was money. Money 'which is obtainable by industry, brains and strict economy', according to his biographer, the diplomat and diarist Harry Kessler. Money 'which protects like golden armour the all-too-thin and tender covering of the soul'.

On the ride to university, when his driver wheeled the Benz *Motorwagen* through Schlossplatz, young Rathenau stared at Berlin's old buildings – the palace with its ever-cursed chapel, the ungainly Neue Wache and Altes Museum – and wondered why his father so admired them. He wanted to get away from the city's neo-romantic façades, stifling parlours and massed tramp of regimental parades. He felt no love for the sprawling, stone golem. As soon as he was able, he moved to Switzerland to work as a chemist. There in the AEG laboratory he discovered how to obtain alkalies and chlorine through electrolysis. He then moved on to Bitterfeld where he built and managed an electro-chemical factory and a power plant, working his way up the firm.

In 1899 his father invited him to join the board and – at the age of thirty-two – he returned to Berlin as a rich and elegant bachelor: cool, persuasive and independent with a gentle sorcery to his conversation. Rathenau had an ability to adapt himself to those he met, taking their measure swiftly, never revealing his feelings, leaving them with the desire to meet him again. 'It's strange,' he confided to his brother. 'If I have been with people for a long time,

I believe that they begin to become like me. They see things with my eyes and speak with my language and all have the feeling that I can see through them.'

The Kaiser invited him to the Schloss to hear his views on science and industry, at the same time recognising their shared trait of insecurity masked by brilliant talk. At the palace, Rathenau behaved as the dutiful courtier, entering the throne room between rows of pages dressed in pink, standing below him on his dais. But in private he observed that Wilhelm II had 'a nature unwittingly directed against itself'. He 'is an enchanter and a man marked by fate . . . on the road to disaster'.

He could have been speaking about himself.

'Your Highness,' Walther Rathenau said in his baritone voice, bowing before Prince von Bülow, one of the arrogant chancellors who followed Bismarck. 'Let me, before I am honoured by the favour of being received by you, make a statement that is at the same time a confession.' He paused for effect, giving time for his poise and evening dress to be appreciated, playing the part of both conformist and non-conformist. 'Your Highness, I am a Jew.'

Rathenau – as the new AEG chairman – was one of the first Jews to be accepted into Berlin's aristocratic circles. By 1910 he headed eighty-six German and twenty-one foreign businesses including ten metalworks, three aircraft manufacturers and the car maker NAG as well as half a dozen African mines and all of Chile's electric railways. He was a patron of the arts, supporting poets and the painter Edvard Munch (who during his four years in Berlin created the earliest version of *The Scream* – initially titled in German *Geschrei* – and evoked bitter controversy with his shows). Max Liebermann, the head of the Secession art movement, was Rathenau's cousin. On the evening of the Feast of St Martin he walked from the Dom with singing children, the candlelight from their paper lanterns dancing across their faces and along Unter den Linden. Every Christmas he took a box at the Staatsoper and invited the great and good to hear *The Magic Flute*. His connections, charm and astute diplomacy would have won a high state appointment, had he been a Christian.

'In the youth of every German Jew there comes a moment which he remembers with pain as long as he lives; when he becomes for the first time fully conscious of the fact that he has entered the world as a second-class citizen, and that no amount of ability or merit can free him of this status,' said Rathenau.

To him, the German language, history and culture were of far greater importance than blood. His people were the German people, his home was Germany, his faith was 'the German faith which stands above all creeds'. The Jews had been part of Germany for 1,500 years, prospering under Charlemagne, suffering during the Crusades and Middle Ages, and Rathenau considered them as native as the Saxons, Bavarians and Wends. In articles and books he argued for assimilation, telling fellow Jews to stop acting like Jews. He advised them to become 'a living part of the nation', not 'a strange and isolated tribe, glitteringly and ostentatiously decked out, hot-bloodedly mobile of expression . . . an Asiatic horde on Brandenburg sand'.

Nationality was not a matter of blood, he stated. Diversity can be a strength, he argued. No nation should be defined by ethnicity, as the race theorists propagated, but by common values. Jews and Germany are strongest together, he wrote. His books sold in their hundreds of thousands.

In the first decade of the twentieth century Germany's population swelled by almost two million souls. Its industry raced to dominate Europe. After the 1870–71 Franco-Prussian War and the unification of the states, Bismarck had claimed that the Reich was a 'satiated' power. But Greater Germany – like Prussia before it – had no natural boundaries, apart from the Alps. Nine neighbours encircled it, containing both its people and its economic ambition.

In 1914 Germany went to war with the declared aim of defending the Fatherland. But the true objective was to expand its territory and market, seizing raw materials by annexing most of

Belgium and eastern France. After a short period of consolidation, Berlin's plan was to attack and bankrupt Britain, its most dangerous competitor. 'The question is one of victory or extinction,' trumpeted an editorial in the *Süddeutsche Monatshefte*. 'If we win – and anyone who doubts we shall is a dog – we can impose our rules on the conquered world and give things the shape necessary for our own development and for the good of the small neighbouring peoples that flock around us and look to us for protection and salvation.'

To industrialists like Thyssen, Stinnes and Kirdorf, all of whom had influential connections with the *Kaiserreich*, victory meant profit. Defeat meant material loss. Alone among them, Rathenau recognised the real danger. He saw that the Allies had all but inexhaustible resources. He knew that America would support Britain and France. He pressed for a negotiated peace, proposing 'an industrial customs union' – a precursor to the European Union – to save Germany. 'Fuse the industries of Europe into one ... and political interests will fuse too,' he advised.

But disaster could not be averted. The howitzers began to howl and a generation of young men marched into the hail of steel.

The cosmopolitan Berliner slipped on a nationalist mask, hiding his fear while outwardly supporting the war effort. Rathenau discovered that Germany's stockpile of raw materials would last only six months. In response he – like Lloyd George in Britain – organised a War Materials Administration, creating hundreds of special companies to supply the military. Scrap metal, park railings, even the copper roofs of churches and town halls were melted down. Chemists like Fritz Haber were urged to use science to enable Germany to fight on. Moabit and Spandau – once villages where Konrad von Cölln had sung of love and honour – sprouted yet more factories and chimneys, becoming the roaring centres of the armaments industries, employing 120,000 people.

As the dead fell in the deep Flanders mud, the fog of war began to cloud Rathenau's clear judgement. He felt compelled to do the 'right thing', and approved the deportation of Belgian labourers. He supported Field Marshal Hindenburg's 'silent dictatorship'. He even changed his mind about an early armistice. Yet rather than ingratiating himself with the High Command, he was kicked out of the administration. There was no room for Jews at the top.

On the eve of defeat in 1918 Rathenau wrote to a friend, 'I am like someone in the middle of packing for a journey. My father and brother [both of whom were dead] are waiting for me in that neutral country to which no railway leads. They cannot understand why I am delaying.'

At Versailles the victors imposed their terms on the defeated. France asserted that there were 'twenty million Germans too many' and demanded the return of Alsace-Lorraine. Poland snatched Upper Silesia. The Saar was to be occupied for fifteen years. Germany lost thirteen per cent of her territory, ten per cent of her population and all her colonies. The Kaiser fled to Holland and lifelong exile, weeping as his train pulled away from Berlin. His army was slashed from 800,000 to 100,000 men. His General Staff was abolished. All aeroplanes and tanks were scrapped, destroyers were scuttled. A 'War Guilt' clause saddled Germany with sole responsibility for starting the war, obliging it to pay crippling annual reparations of about seven per cent of national income. Berlin bewailed the injustice, forgetting its declared intention – if Germany had won – to ruin its industrial competitors and subjugate its neighbours.

But despite the appalling losses, Germany's myopic leaders lacked the vision or courage to break with their belligerent Prussian past. The first President of the Weimar Republic, Friedrich Ebert, hailed the return of the 'unconquered' army at the Brandenburg Gate. Hindenburg refused to take responsibility for the military failure, blaming it on 'saboteurs, Socialists, Communists and Jews'. General Schulenburg went further, declaring 'German soldiers will claim . . . that they were stabbed in the back by their comrades-at-arms, the navy, together with Jewish war profiteers and shirkers.' Over 12,000 Jews had died in the trenches fighting for Kaiser and Fatherland. Rathenau's War Materials Administration had helped support the country at war. Yet in the public's desperate need for scapegoats, he and other Jews were now accused of cowardice and

racketeering. The seeds were sown which would make them a race
apart.

In 1919 Rathenau was a 'man of false notes and circumstances gone
awry – the Communist in a damask chair, the patriot out of condes-
cension, the avant-garde music-maker on an old harp,' according to
diarist-diplomat Kessler. And yet he was 'a virtuoso'.

The new government was interested in his economic ideas.
Rathenau found a political role in the middle ground between
strict socialism and rapacious capitalism. In 1920 – as the country
teetered on the edge of bloody revolution – he was invited to join
the Socialisation Commission and National Economic Council. He
served as a private adviser at conferences with the Allies. Within a
year he took control of the Reconstruction Ministry.

The broken Reich could never meet the demands of Versailles.
Full payment of reparations would have meant political and economic collapse. Berlin used the Reconstruction Ministry, which
had been formed to administer compensation for the Allies, to
evade its bitter obligation.

Rathenau had always evoked the strongest emotions. Now he
became all the more provocative for heading a ministry which was
at best ambiguous, at worst a lie. He worked to build a construct-
ive relationship with former enemies, at the same time as pushing
for inflation to dilute Germany's debts. He became Foreign Minister, charming the French, blunting their jagged vengeance, then
slipped on yet another mask to initiate a secret military alliance
with the Kremlin.

In violation of Versailles, Germany acquired facilities for the
building and testing of weapons in Soviet Russia, far away from
the Treaty inspectors. Junkers began to assemble aircraft outside
Moscow. The artillery manufacturer Krupp built a factory near
Rostov-on-Don. In time Luftwaffe pilots would train near Vivupal
and the Reichswehr would establish a tank school at Kazan. A chemical weapons facility would be built in Samara Oblast. The German
Navy would even be loaned a port near Murmansk. In return, the
fledgling Red Army gained access to German technology. The

clandestine military collaboration enabled Germany to begin to rearm itself. The two international pariahs – 'comrades in misfortune', according to Churchill – worked together to overthrow the system established by the First World War's victors.

Yet in public Rathenau – with his successes guarded as state secrets – was perceived as a traitor, surrendering the assets of the 'undefeated' Fatherland. In Munich Adolf Hitler incubated the idea of ghastly revenge. In protest against reparations, jackbooted Nazis attracted their first large crowds. In the radical nationalist press a sinister rhyme was circulated, 'Strike down Walther Rathenau, the goddamned Jewish sow'.

Rathenau sat at his desk in the dark. Over the last days an ominous air, both real and imagined, had hung over him. With morbid vanity he had told the British ambassador that he was sure to be assassinated. He had dismissed his police guard. He had refused to carry a pistol. He had written to a friend, 'Do not worry about my life. If an honourable life is to end, then let it happen not arbitrarily, but because that life has found its conclusion.'

Next morning – 24 June 1922 – Rathenau stepped into his open-top car. He was late for work, having been up for much of the night writing his speech, negotiating a reduction in reparation coal deliveries and turning the bronze dancer in his hands. His driver accelerated away from the Grunewald villa on the daily commute to the Foreign Office. Beneath the old oaks and chestnuts of Königsallee, at the point where the road snakes to the right, a dark grey car pulled up beside them. Its passenger, a former right-wing Freikorps soldier named Erwin Kern, blasted Rathenau with a machine-gun. Kern's companion Hermann Fischer then threw a hand grenade into the minister's car.

'It is not true that a murder is just a murder,' the Austrian author Joseph Roth wrote later. 'This one was a thousand fold murder, not to be forgotten or avenged.'

On the day of the assassination, one of 350 political killings in the tremulous Weimar years, the German Mark lost ten per cent of its value. Two weeks later it halved. By the end of the summer its crashing devaluation could not be stopped. Inflation turned into hyperinflation, ruining the economy, national politics and the lives of millions. Eleven years later the Great Depression helped to lift the Nazis into power. Kern and Fischer were declared heroes and the day of Rathenau's assassination was designated a national holiday. In 1933 AEG donated 60,000 Marks to the Party after a secret meeting with Hitler. Later, in a bitter twist of irony, the company was contracted to provide the electrical equipment for Auschwitz.

The strange alchemy of Berlin's air and soil, its dark melancholy and severe winters, its anger and regret, has created a people who are often locked away in their inner selves. In such a place what makes life worth living? Love? Spring sunshine? Diversity? Ideas? Or beauty? With beauty, one can find the point of being alive. Beauty can stir and engulf us. It honours those glad, good things that are larger and more interesting than us, yet are for ever part of us. Rathenau knew it. But he could not see it. He could not feel it.

All his life Walther Rathenau had kept watch over the inner workings of his soul 'as though it had been the Holy Grail'. Like Berlin itself, he found himself both trapped by and at odds with the past. He struggled to grasp a new identity yet he could not tear off his masks. Even when he had seemed to be most frank, even in the middle of an intimate conversation, he hid himself away.

Rathenau never married. He enjoyed the company of blond Aryan youths but was too fastidious to have relationships with them. Once he was spotted with a 'servant girl' and word spread that he had sex with lower-class women, and conversation with ladies. No one knows for sure. Even his closest female companion, his 'platonic mistress' for more than a decade, said after his murder, 'I have no idea *what* his love life was like. He never had any real feelings. He just had a longing for feelings.'

Rathenau was a paradox: an industrialist who dabbled in the arts and philosophy, a pacifist who kept Germany at war, a utopian who practised *Realpolitik*, a Jew who helped to arm Hitler. There was a deep loneliness in him, as there remains in his city, an absence which blocked an understanding of beauty, no matter how hard one tried, no matter how often one turned the lamp on and off, on and off.

CHAPTER 7

*Else Hirsch, and
the Illusion*

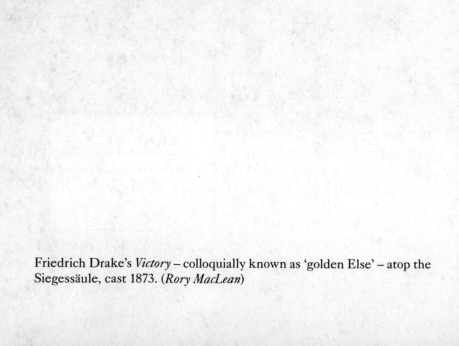

Friedrich Drake's *Victory* – colloquially known as 'golden Else' – atop the Siegessäule, cast 1873. (*Rory MacLean*)

Kronprinzenufer, 1873

How does one imagine? By asking how something could be. By reaching into the dark. By wondering how living might be at another time, in another life, with a different wife. By daring to be their other.

She is their maid, slave, nun, goddess and mother. She acts the part of victor, villain and choreographer. She is both player and play. Her bedroom is the theatre. The bed is her stage. Every encounter is a show. She stretches the span of a single event to its climax, to its natural conclusion. That's her secret, to manipulate the energy, to grasp the moment, to never let go, yet to leave space for the invisible. She always leaves that magical margin for her audience to fill with their imagination. A woman can play so many roles and she does them all, if it pleases her. For a price.

Her life before Berlin isn't much of a story, but then as ever it's how one tells it. At the Kaiser's *Ordenfest* and embassy parties she might allude to a noble Swedish childhood, and an estate lost in a game of cards. She'd hint of a decorated officer, a jealous heart and a bloody duel. With a wistful gleam in her mahogany-brown eyes she'd insinuate that she was cruelly abandoned. She'd talk of wild flight and feminine need, enticing with innuendo. She'd lift her lowered eyes, and win over men who should know better.

In truth her parents were born into service. When they married, their employer – a kind-hearted dowager charmed by their devotion – gave them a small house as a wedding gift. It stood at a crossroads on the edge of her property and her father and mother turned it into an inn, serving the *Jäger* who came to hunt in the forest.

Her father was a woodsman and a natural entertainer. In the evening he stood by the high table, spinning tales and sparking his customers' good spirits. Else loved to listen to him, and to the stories of the visiting huntsmen. She longed to experience first-hand the wonders which were described: city nights, torchlit carriages at the opera, elegant ladies glittering with jewels.

From her mother she learnt the kind of looks which would open that world to her, as well as earn extra coins. She also discovered that the manner in which she wore her pinafore, or gathered her girlish hair, brought pleasure to the guests. 'Give us a smile and another jug, Else,' teased the *Jäger*, taking liberties with her real name Elisabeth. Her father would pick up his fiddle and she'd dance with them, as child then maid then young woman, their faces flushed with excitement, their skin glowing, their hands reaching, touching, reeling across the rocking, wormy floor. At the end of the evening, when her mother collected payment, her apron would be full of money.

Their modest success enabled her to be schooled in French and book-keeping, and to leave home for a *Pflichtjahr* of service at another Brandenburg Schloss. In those green days she imagined herself as a dancer, turning heads as she spun across lime-lit boards, although a more likely future was as a housekeeper for a guardsman in a fine Tiergarten apartment. Else imagined that he would have an eyeglass and she'd bask in his reflected glory, organising crystal dinners for the *noblesse*, watching him stride, ivory-topped cane in hand, along Kufürstendamm, the city's great new boulevard. His limp – a fashionable battle wound – would be disguised from all but her.

But her father really did have a weakness for gambling and the family's savings began to bleed away. He was also a poor judge of character, agreeing on a whim to act as guarantor for too many 'noble' friends. When it fell on him to settle their debts, he could not pay. Else offered the little that she could, and all was taken, but still they lost the house. The shame cost her her *Pflicht-jahr* post. She watched poverty grind down both her father's health and her mother's love for him. He laid down the fiddle, picked up his old axe and disappointment rooted them to the spot.

Yet trees have roots and humans have legs, a feature which she viewed as a great advantage. On her sixteenth birthday she walked away from her past, from service and dark woods, towards Berlin's lights. The old dowager arranged for her to go *en pension* with a clergyman's family on Lützowstraße. His holy house may have been in the heart of the capital but it turned out to be a place of many privations. Her days were regulated by morning prayers, 'edifying' sermons and Bible study with hymns. The curate never allowed her the pleasure of staring out of the window at promenading couples, or walking the streets unchaperoned. He squashed every chance of liberty.

The only escape from his dreary penitentiary was for good works. Twice every week, on Tuesday and Thursday evenings, Else and his two other prisoners (Toni and Gisela, girls like her who'd come to Berlin to make something of themselves) loaded the carriage with tureens and pamphlets and made for the 'lair of the fallen', as the clergyman called it. In the places they visited, along Oranienburgerstraße and at the edge of the damp, black Tiergarten, they were expected to dish out soup and prayer sheets while trembling with virginal modesty. Else performed her part to the curate's satisfaction, nodding as he spoke of God's benevolence, yet she was fascinated by the raw life which she saw before her: gamesome, rackety women gulping down the food, squatting behind trees to relieve themselves, adjusting their dress in the open and in a manner that suggested their bodies wanted only to be free of wraps and petticoats.

At the pulpit the clergyman's sermons rang with pious arrogance, so confident was he in his world of certainties. God saves! God damns! There was no knell of doubt in his voice. Yet away from church, when he preached to the 'lost' women, his speech assumed a different tone, becoming loud and shrill. As she watched him Else realised that – in their company – a note of fear entered his heart.

She'd learnt from the 'noble' *Jäger* how money, or the illusion of it, bought power. She'd seen how it could be a tool to possess a man, and how its lack destroyed virtue and happiness. Now the visits opened her eyes to another revelation. At the edge of the Tiergarten she glimpsed a means of freeing herself from the curate's restrictions, and taking charge of her own life.

A decade on, Else stands in front of the glass and throws off her clothes, one garment after another, to gaze at herself. She sees strong shoulders, generous breasts and skilful hands. Her mahogany eyes come from her father. The short-sightedness is like that of her ninety-year-old grandmother (who at the inn stuck newspapers over the glass to stop her staring at herself). More than once she has been told that her snow-white skin is the softest thing any man ever caressed. Her hair is long and thick. When she plunges both hands into it and spreads it out, she looks as if she has wings.

Her other features may not be regular – her smile is too big, her teeth too small, her nose too bold – but she veils these deficiencies with lavish movement, direct glances and a free and fluid touch. Only her hips displease her and, for a time, she wished to be petite, or at least slim, but a taste for sweet *Kranzkuchen* hindered the attainment of that goal. At home a slice of cake, a glass of wine and a cigarette became her favourite treats, especially when counting first wrinkles.

The journey from preacher's prison to the palace's White Saal opened out like a series of interconnected rooms. One Saturday

afternoon, while at work in the parlour embroidering monograms
on hassocks, she lost her thimble. She searched for it in vain, then
decided to borrow one from her fellow lodger Toni. The preacher
was out at a christening and the house was as quiet as the grave.
She climbed the stairs to the attic and – thinking that Toni was also
away – opened her door without knocking. On the threshold she
stopped short for Toni was in bed, with the curate astride her. The
wretched man covered himself, shook Else by the shoulders and
ordered her to hold her tongue. She felt both shock and outrage.
Yet with his bare knees knocking and his eyes filled with fright,
she could not help but laugh.

The next morning both Else and Toni were ejected from the
holy house. But for all his hypocrisy the preacher was not without
Christian charity, or at least a sense of duty to her dowager. Their
new quarters were in the apartment of an unmarried parishioner
who supported herself by doing massage. She was a welcoming
soul, and judging from the quality of her clothes, successful at her
trade. She provided the young women with a bedroom with velvet
curtains and did not stop them from sitting by its open window –
indeed she encouraged them to walk in the leafy square. Else found
irresistible its strolling officers, the sailor-suited children launching boats in the circular fountain, the tinkling of water and bicycle
bells. Cabs bumped across cobbles, beneath balconies bright with
red geraniums, along their street so full of promise.

Their hostess enjoyed entertaining and – as a way of settling
them in – arranged an excellent supper of pies and clear soup
followed by pheasant. They had red wine and champagne, after
which the woman began to play the piano. Else felt no surprise
when one of the gentlemen guests seized her waist and danced
her around the room. Berlin arouses powerful emotions in people
and she wasn't born yesterday. But when his friend, an elderly Jew
named Bernbaum, caught Toni around the neck and started to
kiss her, Toni took up her glass of champagne and poured it down
his shirt collar. The man leapt up and bellowed his displeasure in
no uncertain terms. Else took Toni aside and told her not to be
a fool.

'I fancy he can give you diamonds on your garters,' Else whispered.

'I wouldn't be seen dead with his old diamonds,' Toni replied with a sniff. 'Anyways, he's married.'

'So was the clergyman,' she told her.

Else knew what was at stake and saw no reason not to take the upper hand.

'Toni, we have the chance to support ourselves,' she said. But Toni would not have it and left the room. The next morning she was gone.

Else, on the other hand, let the piano play on. She let the man put his arm around her waist, kiss her, draw her to him. She felt she was in control. She knew that she had an asset of real value. She wanted to drink champagne and revel in life. And Bernbaum did have diamonds.

Love promises that a perfect partner exists for every one of us. Love portends everlasting happiness with a single soulmate. Perhaps the dream is true – certainly the Romantics believed it – but Else had seen it founder for her parents as soon as the money was lost.

In the course of three months she went from maid to lover, from single bed to hotel suite, from plain frock to silk petticoats, from man to men. They wanted adventure, and the illusion of a romantic seduction, and she gave it to them. She enabled them to imagine themselves into another life, with a different wife. In return they paid her, and she satisfied their need for attention in their stares, in their reaching hands, as the unattainable object of their desire.

She had her guardsman, with aquiline nose and no war wounds, and an English lord who threw his money away with intoxicating abandon. Every morning his suite at the Angleterrre was filled with roses. She loved to wake to their perfume, and his insistent attention. The Jew Bernbaum remained sweet and unpossessive, introducing her to his cultured, tailored and close-buttoned acquaintances. Her name was passed between them like a bottle of finest port.

All of the men were married. All were rich. All needed to remain respectable. Yet at the same time they wanted to display Else as evidence of their success. As they stepped from carriage to ballroom, gallery to opera box, her pearl necklace and fox stole told their friends that they could afford her.

The exchange was not unfamiliar. To Else, bourgeois marriage was also based on money, not love. She gave men what they desired and in the transaction found her own pleasure. In her bedroom theatre the creation of the illusion thrilled her. Also she liked to look into their eyes and know – for all their wealth and bravado – that they were afraid.

She never counted numbers, especially during those initial weeks with the masseuse. She never stood on a street corner like the ruffle-feathered swallows who flew in from the eastern marches, nor joined the ranks of 'brides and grooms' at a *Tanzlokale*. Her intention was not to labour at the *maison de rendezvous* until her breasts and income withered. Instead she worked with the sole intention of becoming a *Baronisierte*, a woman kept by a noble. She would become his devoted wife in every sense, except for the absence of responsibility and a wedding ring. She would stage the play.

Else had acquired the habit of frequenting the Academy of Arts on Pariser Platz. Next to the Brandenburg Gate, the Akademie der Künste was a cultured place where a woman could venture alone, and its exhibitions attracted a certain class of leisured gentleman. One Monday afternoon she was dawdling in front of a small Schinkel drawing of a winged female figure when she felt a man's eyes on her. As soon as she returned the gaze he stepped forward.

The man introduced himself as an Academician and talked with animation about the show. Suddenly he confessed that he had noticed her on an earlier visit to the galleries. He stared at her without timidity or self-consciousness, glancing away only to look at the drawing. 'It is Victoria,' he told her, nodding at the Schinkel. 'The Roman goddess of victory. A virago. She is special to me.'

To her great contentment Else noticed that his interest in her increased as they spoke, although something in his manner so disarmed her that she missed half of what he said. She guessed that he was more than twice her age, perhaps even as old as sixty years. He had a full, scruffy beard and eyebrows which curved around the corners of his eyes. His hair was swept back from his bare pate to gather on his collar in a thick wave. She was glad to have worn a simple, white dress with cinched-in waist, and to have applied a playful brush of rouge.

Would she permit him to visit her some afternoon between six and eight o'clock? Else heard him ask. She gave him her card, and like a punctual schoolboy he came the next day.

Men like to believe that they are in control, that their wit and gestures of affection charm a woman, and lead her to surrender herself. Else was paid to sustain the illusion, with deference, soft lighting and token resistance. But Friedrich didn't play by the rules. Instead of flowers and champagne, he arrived at Kronprinzenufer with a satchel. In the front room, with its pretty view over the bowing Spree, he accepted the offer of tea and, as Else leant forward to pour it, neglecting to adjust her scarf, he stared with such intensity that she smiled in real pleasure. When she sat beside him he asked her to undress. She did as requested, although she was in favour of at least a gesture of courteous foreplay. He directed her to the stool and told her not to move. Then he took a leather-bound sketchbook from his satchel.

Friedrich would not be drawn into conversation as he worked. Only forty minutes later when Else tired of the pose did he lay down his charcoal. She moved towards him again and he rose to his feet, beginning to pack away his materials. Men are all the same, she thought. His hesitation is probably due to the formality of his age. She placed herself before him and lifted her eyes to his, expecting to see what she always saw. When she didn't, she felt a shiver run through her.

'Next Tuesday at the same time?' Friedrich asked, and gave her ten Marks.

Never before had she so looked forward to a visit. She couldn't explain it to herself. For years she'd refused to be passive, yet now she wanted nothing more than to be still, to be looked at, to be drawn.

On Tuesday evening he arrived in a carriage with a peculiar frame fashioned from wood and leather. He assembled it, placed Else in it and again she misunderstood his intent. He explained that the device (which was of his own design) enabled a model to hold her position for long periods. Friedrich adjusted her stance and the frame, guiding forward her left foot, lifting her right arm and – as nothing else to hand seemed suitable – placing in it a ring-shaped *Kranzkuchen* which she'd bought that morning. Again his intensity excited her. He gazed at her without blinking then bent over his sketchbook. He drew in silence for over two hours until the light faded from the room. When he could see no longer he disentangled her from his device, and left twenty Marks on the dresser.

On the third visit he dressed Else in full skirt and tunic. While adjusting the sash he brushed her breast, and apologised. He pulled the white cotton material against her knees, fanning it out behind her as if blown by the wind. The sound of marching men rose through the window, Prussian soldiers tramping off to one front or another, but Friedrich told her to hold the pose, not to look, saying that war had no place in her rooms.

A timelessness took hold of their encounters, even though he came to her no more than half a dozen times. Beyond the window the weather and light changed, the Spree turned inky blue then black, history unfolded, but indoors Friedrich concentrated on the curve of her thigh and tilt of her chin. Once he sat at her feet for a whole hour, drawing the temper of her heel and spread of her toes, letting his fingers rest on her ankle.

In his company Else relaxed and one evening began to talk. Friedrich had never asked about her past so she volunteered that she had been born in a Swedish estate. In response he said, 'Is that so?'

She knew right away that he didn't believe her.

'As a boy my bed was made of straw and wood shavings,' he confessed, not looking up from the pad. *Ein Bett von Hobelspänen.*

Slowly, and for the first time since her arrival in Berlin, Else spoke to a man about her true self, about her sadness for the collapse of her parents' world, of her anger at the 'noble' hunters who had deceived her father and taken advantage of her, about earning a living by creating illusion.

He laughed and asked, 'But does it make you happy, Victoria?' He always called her Victoria when he worked, after the little drawing in front of which they'd met.

'I am all that I want to be,' she told him, then paused to correct herself. 'I am all that I can be in a world where women are possessions.'

Only once did he speak of himself, telling her that he had fathered six children and his first wife had died, that his second wife was a *Gräfin*. He said that his sculptures stood in Berlin, Wittenberg and even Philadelphia, and his work had been shown at the world exhibitions in London and Paris. He'd even made the bronze statue of Schinkel outside the Bauakademie. None of this was told to impress her. She supposed he simply wanted her to know a little something about his passions. She was curious of course but at the same time, strangely, she didn't want to see his sculptures. She wanted to imagine him as hers, to have the fantasy that he knew her alone, to cherish the illusion that he had drawn and modelled only her.

Else wept after Friedrich's last visit, and again a year later when his gilded Victoria was unveiled. The Siegessäule – Berlin's great Victory Column – had been built to commemorate Prussia's defeat of the Danes but, by the time the monument was finished in 1873, Austria and France had also been humbled. Atop it, soaring over the city, his winged goddess of victory was part angel, part Borussia, part whore. She wore a helmet adorned with eagle's feathers. Her cloak flowed behind her as if in the wind. In her right hand – where Else had held the ring-shaped cake – was a laurel wreath. Her left arm lifted a battle standard crowned by the Iron Cross.

People said that his model had been his daughter Margarethe, and discretion kept Else from suggesting another possibility. But both women took exception to critics calling the figure 'all too massive and clumsy'.

She last caught sight of Friedrich at the Königsplatz inauguration, shaking Bismarck's hand, bowing to the emperor, beneath the fluttering banners and gusty September sky. His wife, the *Gräfin*, stood beside him, looking elegant in her formal silk skirts and bustle. Her bonnet was trimmed with patriotic streamers. Else was at the back of the crowd, with another man. Friedrich did not see her, except perhaps when he lifted his hand to his forehead and gazed up at the statue.

She never met him again, never went back to the Academy. In part it was Else who was fearful, of something she never had and would never imagine into existence. She could have found him, could have pleaded with him to return to her rooms, to sit with her in silence as the sunlight moved across the parquet. She could have hoped that he might lay his cool, beautiful hands on her wrist, on her knee. But she never did.

It's said that you can live in sin, not on it, but Else found the maxim to be untrue. She rode in torchlit carriages, slept on Egyptian linen, dined on Meissen porcelain and gold-plated cutlery in the Schloss's White Saal. She managed to acquire the Kronprinzenufer apartment with its pretty Spree view. Every spring she watched the pollen fall on its banks as thick as snow. Some days she even walked to the Tiergarten where she'd first seen those poor, proud, quick and gamesome women. The sun shone brightly on her beauty, until it faded, and her jocund step lost its lightness. Her hips continued to broaden too much for her liking. But despite the flight of time she liked to think she retained the same glint in her eye, the same will to please, the same hunger to imagine and to elicit imagination.

We all are mortal too soon and, eight years later, Friedrich died. His funeral was open to the public and, on the way home that evening, she asked the driver to stop at the Siegessäule. She dropped the carriage window and stared up at his Victory. In the evening light the setting sun enfolded her in a halo of burning gold. She no longer saw herself in the statue. Instead the structure itself seemed to embody an idea, making it so much more than an architectural curiosity, shifting the way one looked at things. The idea was an illusion, of course, of power, of heritage, of invincibility, but then Else knew all about the power of illusions.

Often she thought of writing down her story but there was never time. Then another Margarete came into her life. They met at the Hotel National – through a mutual acquaintance, over tea – at her favourite table by the fountain. She was a plain woman with frizzy, upswept hair but nevertheless Else was moved by her ambition, and her hunger. Margarete told her that she was raising a child by herself, having divorced her publisher husband. She said that she was an author and wanted to tell Else's story, or rather a story based on Else. But Else hadn't read her work and replied that she could not help her. There were confidences to be respected.

'The book would appear to be a diary,' said Margarete Böhme. 'In truth it'd be a novel with all names and details changed but it'd be based on real stories, on a real woman.'

Else smiled and shook her head. But when she rose to leave the restaurant, two gentlemen at the next table threw a couple of coins into the fountain, as if to make a wish. Immediately a young woman sitting alone stretched out her arm and fished them out. With a laugh the men set about amusing themselves, throwing Marks, Groschen and penny bits into the water. As many as a dozen working girls now stood up from their tables, streamed forward and grabbed for the money. The larger man roared until he shook like a jelly while his companion ordered the waiter to bring more change. As the new coins fell beyond their reach, the girls took off their shoes and waded into the pool, pushing in front, pulling at each other's hair. One woman slipped and fell into the water, pulling down her assailant, soaking them both from neck to hem.

Margarete and Else stared at the scene in fascination, in repulsion and in sorry recognition. As other male diners joined in the juvenile game, showers of coins fell into the fountain as if in a sudden downpour.

Else sat back down in her chair, and started to talk.

Interior of Café Passage, 1909. (*akg-images/Arkivi UG*)

Roennebergstraße, 1905

Where to begin Else's story? At the beginning. With inno-cence. In Margarete's head.

At her garden table under the willow tree, Margarete Böhme reaches away from Berlin, back to her own childhood home. She sees herself playing in the orchard, hears herself laugh-ing in the square, feels the disapproving stare of her stern and bothersome aunts. Her thoughts turn like a leaf in the summer breeze, in the airy mixture of memory, imagination and obser-vation. At her wooden table she uncaps her pen and writes, the old town's streets 'are very, very narrow and extremely clean. No grass grows between the stones, and the cocks and hens are not allowed to run about on the pavements. The houses look as sleek and smooth as men who have just been shaved by the barber.' She pauses, picturing herself as a girl in those houses, then adds, 'Not much goes on in this Godforsaken hole. It's desperately dull. If a carriage drives through the street, everyone rushes to the windows.'

Böhme lays down her pen and glances from herb bed to

rhododendrons. In Berlin she loves to write outdoors whenever the weather is kind, the light air ruffling her loose pages.

Her new book will be neither biography nor autobiography, or no more so than any other novelist's work, so Böhme needs to name its narrator. Over the years she has collected hundreds of names, most often from gravestones. She picks a notebook from the bench beside her. She reads that Amsel means blackbird and Trocken-brodt is dry bread. Another favourite is Kronjäger, named after a man skilled at catching cranes. *Haas* is the old German word for both rabbit and coward. She loves the Christian names Dagobert, Hedwig and Guntberta. She runs her finger down the list – Gottschalk, Butterfass, Teufel – lingering over them, and settles on Thymian, meaning thyme, the purifying herb which the ancients believed gave courage, which was placed beneath pillows to ward off nightmares. Thymian will be Else Hirsch, as well as Böhme herself.

'I am called Thymian,' jots Böhme and then, with a smile, 'What a mad name my mother picked out for me. It often makes me very angry. The other children say that it sounds like medicine, and the boys say something even worse which I can't repeat . . .'

During the morning in the garden, Böhme warms to the diary form, and to her Thymian. She writes, 'My aunt brought me this daily journal yesterday as a belated Confirmation present. "Such a nice thing for a young girl," she said. "And such a cheap one," thought I. But as it's here I may as well use it, and perhaps I shall discover that I have some literary talent.' This is how Böhme likes to begin her books: in character, open to wind and fancy, with a memory or a feeling, moving towards empathy, fear and dramatisa-tion. Without character she isn't engaged. She can't write from the heart, or imagine.

Imagine. That's a slippery fish. She isn't able to define the word. She can't pin down its meaning. All Böhme does is draw an anecdote or a news report into herself, feel her way around it, then dash it back out in a rush, from heart to head to hand to page. Two thousand words per day. Twelve thousand in a week. Three months to finished manuscript. Of course, she couldn't have started this book without Else. Else is the key. Without her, she'd have no raw material, no veracity.

Fiction can be so much truer than non-fiction, she thinks, based on real characters, with reality reworked to show its significant side. Hence Thymian's parents cannot be in service as were Else's people. Böhme wants to draw them as affluent yet flawed, easing them up the social scale for her well-to-do readers, as well as for dramatic effect. Maybe she'll make Thymian's father the town chemist, and her mother dying of a broken heart.

'My mother was always delicate as long as I can remember her,' writes Böhme in a diary entry, breathing her own memories into Thymian, giving her thirteen-year-old narrator a voice, a life. 'I never heard her laugh, and when she smiled she looked sadder than when she was grave. When I noticed her at the window, I was almost afraid to look at her. I don't know why. It always gave me a pang when I caught sight of her dear, pale, sad little face.'

Böhme sketches the father as a womaniser who seduces house-maids. When they fall pregnant he sends them away, paying 'their expenses plus 1,000 Marks indemnity'. His wife is so inconsolable that she takes to her room, losing the will to live. On her deathbed she strokes Thymian's cheek and asks, 'My sweet Thymi, my poor girl, what will become of you?' In the family house, now as quiet as a church, the child chokes back her sobs.

'One night they came and awoke me, and when I opened my eyes, the nursing-sister was standing beside my bed. "Dress your-self, little Thymian, and come with me," said the nurse. "Your dear mother is going to heaven and wants to say good-bye to you."'

In the dappled garden sunlight, Böhme is filled with anger. She deplores the dependency of women on men, rails against weak-ness and the expectation of submission. She bends over the table, sweeping the tendrils of loose hair off her apple-round face, pour-ing emotion into her scratching pen.

Her first half-dozen books had been populist pot-boilers, a genre that was then considered bereft of both substance and beauty. For twenty years she had kept herself by writing them, as well as by churning out hundreds of articles to augment the derisory pay.

Now – with the collapse of her marriage – she wants to break free
of tear-jerkers and prudish *Gartenlaube* 'gazebo' journalism. For
her, the diary form demands honesty, triggers immediacy, permits
social comment. On the grass at her feet her own little daughter
plays with her dolls.

As the nurse leads Thymian away from innocence so Böhme takes
hold of her reader's hand and says, 'Come with me on a journey.'

On Sunday Berlin is warm, sensual, with clouds high and the sultry
air tingling the senses. Böhme loves the intimacy of her modest,
moneyed Friedenau neighbourhood, under its old trees, surrounded
by beds of lilies, beneath red-tiled roofs baking in the sun. Onto
her garden back turreted apartment buildings with ornate façades,
grand entrance halls and four-metre-high ceilings; the homes of
contented families, commuting husbands, secrets. There's not a
breath of breeze all afternoon in her *Kiez*. The weather vane stands
stock still atop the advertising kiosk, unlike the local boys who
swarm around the ice cream stall.

Böhme walks to nearby Schöneberg cemetery (Städtischer
Friedhof Stubenrauchstraße, where Marlene Dietrich will one day
be buried). She listens to her footsteps on the cobbles, collects
names, pauses to watch a family burial, takes notes. She pictures
Thymian among the mourners, an agile, fragile figure in black beneath the lime trees, and writes, 'At four o'clock we took mother
to the churchyard. In the middle of his discourse the clergyman
turned to me, and told me that I must always be good, and never
forget that mother's last thought had been a prayer for me. I didn't
hear him very well, for suddenly it all went black before my eyes,
and then I knew nothing more until we drove up to our own house.
I had fainted in the churchyard, they told me.'

Böhme builds her plot through character. As character is action
so Thymian returns to the churchyard at dusk. 'The limes are in
flower and the narcissus smell so sweet. I shut my eyes and dream
that mother floats down to me dressed in white, and kisses me.'

In the manuscript Thymian is told that she will only see her
mother again in heaven. But how can a child understand this when

she's seen her buried in the cold ground? Böhme sets about haunting Thymian at home with nocturnal visions, both of her mother and of the housemaids ruined by her father's lechery.

'All of a sudden it begins to thunder. It sounds like a wild animal growling in the distance. Then there comes a great flash of light. I leap up and the whole room seems ablaze with blue fire. In the corner my poor, dead mother appears in her white nightgown, with staring eyes. I give one wild, piercing shriek and the light is gone, but that figure still stands there and stares at me as I shriek. Shriek.'

Every story needs a touch of evil, and in the diary it is Meinert, the dispenser at her father's pharmacy who lodges in the family house. '"What on earth is the matter, Thymi? What are you screaming like that for?" Meinert calls through the door, and as I don't stop, he opens it and comes in and bends over me. I cling tightly to him with both arms. I am speechless at first, pointing to the corner where the spectre is standing. Then I stammer out an attempt to tell him what I see.'

Meinert calms her, reassures her, pretends to drive out the ghost. He puts his arm around Thymian and the vulnerable girl feels better with 'a warm, living being beside me'. Then while her cheeks are still wet with tears he confesses that he loves her. He 'takes my head in both hands and bends down, close, close over me, so that even in the dark I can see his glittering blue eyes. I don't know what comes over me. My heart pounds against my side. I am terrified of Meinert. Yet a curious sort of thrill runs through me – the strangest, most mysterious feeling which I never before felt. I let him kiss me. I let him hold me closer and closer. It is as if I am stupefied. I try to get out of his embrace. I try to push him away. But I haven't the strength . . .'

How did Böhme find Else Hirsch? How did she step from parlour to boudoir? Divorce had opened the door. A day before Böhme's husband had left, he had told her of a widowed acquaintance who kept a *Baronisierte*. Perhaps he said it to shock her? Or to hurt her by showing what no man need ever be without? But when he'd gone, as if to blunt his power, Böhme had written to the widower requesting an introduction. It was granted with an amused smirk. Then serendipity played its part, as it always does in the arts, for the meeting would have come to nothing if the diners at the National hadn't thrown coins into the fountain, and the girls not rushed forward. Without it Else Hirsch would have walked away, and Böhme would have lost her source.

All that first evening the two women had sat together, parting only when the restaurant closed. The next day they met again at Café des Westens on the Kurfürstendamm. As they talked Else turned to face the window, gazing away beyond the horse trams and plane trees on Auguste Viktoria Platz. Böhme noted Else's manicured fingers curving around the teacup as if nestling a baby bird. Her smooth and supple forearms brought to mind the neck of a swan. Her lips were so full, so red that it seemed an affront for a man not to kiss them. Böhme touched her own small mouth and counted the months since her last kiss. She looked down at her own hands, clamped around the pen, and wished her veins did not stand out so.

Later, at Else's apartment near the Tiergarten, Böhme had sketched a gesture portrait, laying her pen on the page, not looking down, trying to capture in a few strokes an impression of the older woman: the strong shoulders, the direct gaze, the mahogany eyes outlined in black kohl that seemed to burn, to beckon, to live. The drawing would lie on her table throughout the writing of the book. To be honest Böhme felt envious, not of Else's life but of her confidence, her freedom, her power over men. At the same time she found Else's figure to be too plump for Thymian, so Böhme thinned her out, making her as slender as a cypress. She gave her long black hair and a great-hearted nature. She also gave her a child, nine months after the rape.

In the diary Thymian becomes pregnant and is sent away to the city and into confinement. Thymian's father then arranges for the baby to be sold to a wealthy local family. As Böhme watches the maid take her own child out for a walk in the Volkspark, she tries to imagine her feelings if she were never to return. She tries to fathom the agony and writes, 'I cry and scream and plead but nobody will listen to me. They arranged it all behind my back. I feel as though I have suddenly grown very poor. I know now that there is one thing in my life to fight for. I must get rich, so as to be able to have my child again, for with money one can do everything.'

Action must unfold like a wave making for shore, small at first, swelling higher and higher, crashing at its peak against the land. Böhme finds herself crying over her text and loneliness. She tears the pages from her notebook and throws them into the bushes. Then after a pork and *Knödel* supper she plays with her daughter all evening.

But at dawn she is in the garden again, upending the bushes, then on the street in her housecoat and slippers in a panic. She had woken with a start. She needed to rescue the pages. The gardener had tended the beds and cleaned them away. At last Böhme finds them beneath broken eggshells and coffee grounds in the compost heap. On the kitchen table she spreads them out, and is struck by their look of authenticity. She realises that the diary's impact will be greatest if it is believed to be true, if she is seen not as its author but as its editor. A handwritten page or two could even be reproduced in the book. The more readers who accept her fiction to be fact, the stronger will be her sales.

'Fräulein Thymian, you are fetching! You are exquisite! If you are clever too . . . you could live like a princess,' says the madame masseuse, related Else, writes Böhme. 'But you act too much the fine lady,' continues the masseuse. 'All very well if you were a little white lamb and had no experiences. I wouldn't say a word then. You would only be showing your sense in playing the game of perfect respectability and good conduct. Then you might marry a post office clerk, and have half a dozen children, and cook and darn, and have a beautiful sermon preached over you, and the epitaph – "Here lies an honest, plain cook and wet-nurse".'

Madame masseuse is a retired actress (sixth-rate, thinks Thymian), tall and vivacious with 'enough adventures to fill three novels'. As she warms to her subject's performance, Böhme makes her lean forward and advise Thymian, 'But you! A beautiful creature with a past already behind you, clever and cultivated, and no novice at love-making . . . No, no; hold your tongue! Anyone can see it. It's all very fine. But you carry it too far, my girl. Gentlemen don't mind for once being drawn on and then given the cold shoulder. They'll even stand it twice, perhaps. But after the third time, off they go. One isn't young for ever and when you're old and can't get it, you'll be sorry you were such a fool.'

Thymian is dead to her old society. She had a child, and has a history. So the masseuse invites her to join that 'other world where no questions are asked and people are free to enjoy life in their own way'. Into her mouth Böhme places a promise once made to Else, 'With us, you never hear the everlasting refrain, "Who is she and where does she come from?" We play fair and fear nobody.'

The diary's next dozen pages are said to have been ripped out during Thymian's 'mental and moral struggle'. In an explanatory 'editorial' note, Böhme knits her anger together with Else's salacious details, threading through flaring strands of melodrama, writing, 'She who in later years would chronicle the most shameful and terrible events of her ruined life had found too painful for preservation the record of this period, in which with faltering feet she crossed the last crazy bridge between two worlds.' The artifice of the missing pages was designed to excite the reader's imagination, and lend greater credibility to the diary.

Böhme needs to place her narrative, making it credible by locating it on authentic streets. The next Saturday afternoon she ventures along Kurfürstenstraße, with her daughter in hand so as not to be propositioned herself. She notes the brittle Linden leaves, the smell of scorched macadam, the air 'like a puff of flame'. Her eyes shine as they always do when her fantasy takes on a semblance of truth. Under the onslaught of midday sun, the working girls cast off what clothes they can, collapsing in the shade like panting dogs. Once they cool off at a slender green public pump, dousing each other with water, howling, until a passing constable herds them back onto the long, uncut grass. To Böhme the women appear to be both promiscuous and proud, renting out their bodies while never being more than fantasy possessions. Yet none of them will talk to her.

On Monday she returns alone and pretends to want to sell her engagement ring to a pawnbroker. Later on Zimmerstraße – dressed in a scarlet blouse and black skirt – she climbs pitch-dark stairs covered with shabby linoleum and rings a bell. Three visiting cards are nailed above the nameplate: masseuse, manicurist, French teacher. She is shown the best room in the house. It's a poverty-stricken chamber with dirty curtains, threadbare carpet, and a separate entrance. A dusty grey fur rug lies on the bed behind a Spanish screen. The rent is 180 Marks inclusive.

'Monthly?' asks Böhme, shocked by the cost.

'Do you think I mean for a year?' replies the landlady, catching her eye and grinning as if a particular understanding exists between them. When Böhme turns away in awkwardness, she adds, 'Come on, Fräulein. Think of the risks I run. Such a stylish lady as you won't make a fuss about a few Marks.'

'I am so utterly wretched that I can't think at all,' confesses Thymian in the diary. 'The stove smokes in my room. The bedclothes smell of chloral. I hear people coming and going all night. I am feverish and feeble, so enervated by this heat. I lie, half dressed, on the chaise longue. I look awful, like a perfect skeleton. Once or twice I try to take a "business walk" for customers but nothing comes of it.'

Like Else, Thymian's knowledge of languages then proves useful. She places her own card above the nameplate, as well as an ad in the *Berliner Tageblatt* which reads:

Fräulein Thymian

desires to give lessons in English and French.
Also Russian and Italian.

The double space between name and text alerts men that she is more than a linguist. Rich foreigners respond and begin to pay her. 'Last night I had a Russian who couldn't speak a word of German. He gave me 300 Marks.'

But as she works she thinks to herself 'that I really am dead, and that the people among whom I now live and work are corpses. They have breathed away their souls, they have expired. In this world of corpses, the stink of corruption fills the air. One has simply to get accustomed to it. The nausea gradually leaves one.'

Despite her secret envy, Böhme pushes the reader to ask how a woman like Thymian can survive, given society's hypocrisy? How can she retain love, given that men abuse her? At the same time as tapping Berlin's rising sexual heat, she wants to affirm the redeeming power of human goodness. Else related to her an anecdote about a prostitute who was offered a cemetery plot as payment, and the novelist latches onto it, giving the story to Thymian.

At a Ku'damm dance café a penniless geriatric propositions the *fille de joie*. 'I take him in at a glance – an old retired aristocrat, a worn-out rake, nothing more and nothing less,' writes Böhme in Thymian's diary. 'Leave me alone, you old ass,' Thymian tells him. 'You're spoiling my market.'

But the geriatric persists. He tells Thymian that he once owned an estate in Silesia, a country seat in Westphalia and a villa in Steiermark. He claims to have enjoyed Europe's 'rarest beauties' in St Petersburg, at the Moulin Rouge and along Dresden's Jüdenhof. Yet all that remains of his wealth and past are memories, and a Berlin grave plot.

'Then you have something to offer me,' says Thymian.

'What? The burying place?' asks the old man.

'Why not?' she answers. 'We too like to know where the worms will eat us.' She lights a cigarette and orders champagne on her own account. 'I'll make you a friendly offer. I'll give you five free goes if you sign over the deeds to me.'

The aristocrat grins, calls it a crazy idea, but persists with negotiations, first in jest and then in earnest. In the end a bargain is struck: the Schöneberg plot, with new iron railings, is exchanged for ten carnal encounters. With good grace he also pays the property transfer fee.

'My acquaintances laugh at me and say I must be mad,' Thymian reflects later. 'But it amuses me. The grating is handsome and a pretty willow weeps over the waiting grave. I'll have a seat put in, and a stone. I'll plant ivy and flowers. I'll spend hours there next summer.'

Fallen ochre leaves cushion the ranks of cobblestones. Bakers and newsagents turn down their lamps, lock their doors, close up shop. Children collect chestnuts off the pavement, their bell-like voices ringing along the Friedenau street, before their mothers call them in for supper. In the windows silhouettes watch, wait, pull down the blinds and look away. As the last light drains from the sky the canopy of trees becomes the roof of a cave. The street is transformed into a canyon. Even at the corner there is no clear view of the horizon.

Indoors Böhme steals writing time. Her daily life clamours – her daughter's tears, the maid's moans, the grate of tardy alimony payments, the scuttle of mice in the pantry – and she must drag herself away from the noise, into the calm of her study or the garden to write. She loves her child, yet also resents her. She resents how the child traps her, how marriage came with expectations, how hard it is to be a working woman and single mother. At her table, in those stolen moments, she vents her frustration and anger. She'll write six books in two years, and still barely cover her expenses. Her ex-husband usually pays the rent, although never on time. He isn't a bad man, he simply expected her to run his home, to give up her 'dabbling' in writing. Either she changed or he'd leave. There was no question of him being the one to change.

'It's really a relief to pour out my whole heart into these pages,' she concedes in Thymian's voice. 'It feels exactly like talking to a confidential friend.' Böhme likes to write in sequence, allowing her stories to develop a natural chronology. But sometimes – if her feelings are strong enough – she'll follow her mood. She decides to give Thymian a man even older than her own husband, exaggerating his status and prejudices, milking her own experience again.

Her fictional Count is a wealthy widower with grey beard and blue eyes. He takes Thymian to Nice, Monte Carlo and Paris. He showers her with gifts: a diamond and sapphire Secession belt buckle, a tea service from Raddatz, a sumptuous white opera cloak and an extra 1,000-Mark note. Yet she – like Böhme and unlike Else – is often alone. At night she lies awake, feeling 'the longing for love rise in me like some heavenly being with quivering, wide-spread wings'.

'The Count is thirty-three years older than me, and he doesn't manage well. Despite his cleverness and his knowledge of the world, I often find him dull and tiresome. He is a staunch Conservative and very proud of his noble birth, though he's too tactful to show it. But he can't hide anything from me, and I notice it in all sorts of ways,' relates Thymian in the diary.

'Once we were dining at the Matschakerhof and happened to get onto the subject of a reigning European house which certainly has no reason to pride itself on its offshoots. I gave expression to my opinion that a republic is a far healthier form of government than that of a royal house with an unalterable succession. In a monarchy it doesn't matter whether the heir to the throne is stupid or intelligent, evil or good, capable or incapable, he inevitably becomes King or Kaiser . . . and the fate of a whole nation is in his hands.

'The Count smiled ironically and observed, "You are well aware, Thymian, that I hold quite the contrary opinion." Then he spoke about a costume which I had bought that morning at Zwiebeck's. His dismissal of my opinion made me so boundlessly angry that I could hardly control myself. I wished that I could have thrown my glass of wine in his face. If at that moment he had asked to marry me, even if my whole future maintenance depended on it, I should beg to be excused. For to live year after year, day in day out, with such a wearisome man, would drive me crazy.'

Then a tall, dark stranger materialises in Chapter Thirteen. Thymian's white knight is a doctor who wants to understand her, and to whom she finally loses her heart. 'It's the old story, isn't it?' he says. 'An unhappy affair and then one step after another, down, down, down until you were stuck fast in the mire and couldn't get away.'

On their last walk together the real Else Hirsch makes it clear that she doesn't like Böhme's romantic subtext, snorting out loud when asked if love wipes away all sin, along with the follies and misdeeds of mankind. In Königsplatz, where leaves layer the footpaths golden brown and orange, Else mentions a special man – an artist of some sort – but she will say no more about him. Instead she gazes at the Siegessäule and asks – in a voice skewed with surprising vulnerability – 'You don't think Victoria is big and clumsy, do you?'

But the love story – for all its naivety – helps to secure the book's success. In 1905 *Tagebuch einer Verlorenen – Diary of a Lost Girl* – is published as a genuine memoir, and becomes the bestseller of its time.

'Berlin doesn't suffer from a superfluity of loveliness,' wrote Böhme, her words exposing both the capital's dark underbelly and the pervasive double standards of Wilhelmine society. 'There's always at least one door open to a man,' she raged. 'His whole existence is not ruined by one false step as is ours. The world belongs to men. We women are only suffered as a means to an end.'

The 'diary' sold over one million copies, spawned a play as well as half a dozen confessional, copycat imitations and two movies. In her preface, Böhme stated that the 'slight and unadorned narrative' is 'nothing, and pretends to be nothing, but an authentic contribution to a burning social question'. Until her death in 1939, she maintained that *Diary of a Lost Girl* was a work of non-fiction, edited by her but written by 'Thymian Gotteball'.

Of far more importance than the fact or fiction debate was the book's influence in changing both Berlin and Germany. For centuries conservative forces had used the old stereotypes to control womankind: girls had to submit themselves to the cult of purity, women were to be passive and to procreate, prostitutes were both victims and destroyers of the family.

But over the coming decades painters like Kirchner and Grosz, writers like Brecht and Irmgard Keun, actresses like Dietrich and Brigitte Helm used prostitution as a vehicle for redefining female sexuality. A tragic minority of women had been (and would always be) forced into the trade, of course, but in Berlin more and more sex workers became emancipated, aware of their worth and trading

on it. In books, on the stage and on the silver screen, they meta-
morphosed into exemplars of sexual liberation, becoming the
personification of the irreverent and rebellious capital. Through
them – and their portraits – women came to see that they were not
bound to be either angels or whores, daughters or wives, but rather
that they were free-willed individuals, able to express their active
desires, at the dawn of the new century.

CHAPTER 9

Fritz Haber, and the Geography of Evil

Opening of the Kaiser Wilhelm Institute of Physical Chemistry and Electrochemistry, 23 October 1912. Following behind Kaiser Wilhelm are Adolf Harnack, Emil Fischer and Fritz Haber. (*akg-images*)

Dahlem, 1915

In Berlin evil has postcodes. At 10117 in Göring's Air Ministry on Wilhelmstraße, the bombing of Guernica was planned and the results (number of deaths per kilo of explosive) analysed in preparation for the Nazis' Blitzkrieg of Europe. At 10178, where Schinkel had dreamt of a new kind of museum and Lilli Neuss awoken a long-forgotten dream, thousands of Berliners gathered to hear Goebbels speak, crying out on cue, 'Hang them! Hang the Jews!' Across Unter den Linden on Opernplatz, students wearing green and purple fraternity caps piled thousands of banned books (*Diary of a Lost Girl* among them) and set them alight, watching the half-burnt pages whirl in the night air like inky moths.

Evil slid out from the city centre like a cold and oily vapour, from the Schloss to the old gallows in the east beyond Alexanderplatz at 10249, through the Brandenburg Gate to Friedrichstadt and Prenzlauer Berg where, in 10415, V-1 rocket guidance systems were built by slave labourers in underground prisons. In a Tiergartenstraße house at 10785, patriotic scientists designed the T4 euthanasia programme which led to the execution of 70,000 mentally ill and handicapped '*Untermenschen*'. At 14109 the 'final solution' was drafted in a western lakeside villa beside peaceful Wannsee. On Platform 17 of Grunewald S-Bahn station, 14193, some 50,000 Berlin Jews were loaded into cattle cars and shipped east to their deaths. At the Reich Railway Office, hundreds of obedient *Schreibtischtäter* – 'desk perpetrators' – calculated individual bills for the one-way journey. Adults were charged four Pfennigs per kilometre. Children under ten paid half fare. Infants travelled for free.

In every Berlin postal district the bombs fell, tongues of red and yellow flames flared into the sky and Soviet soldiers raped tens of thousands of women. And beyond Margarete Böhme's comfortable, middle-class Friedenau, evil slithered unseen into leafy suburban Dahlem, 14195, where Germany's finest chemist – who would later be awarded the Nobel Prize – became the father of chemical war.

The evening breeze unfurled the sallow green cloud. Six kilometres long and fifteen metres high, it rolled in silence across the sodden Belgium plain. The Canadians watched it approach their lines and then, with a shift of the wind, drift to the east. It engulfed the neighbouring trenches and pooled in dugouts, suffocating the French and Algerians at their posts. Soldiers who tried to outrun it stumbled in agony. Fluid gurgled in their burnt lungs, spewed filthy green between their lips. The men tore at their clothes, clawed out their eyes, choked in the poisoned air, then died by the thousand.

Back at the German lines the 'gas troops' signalled that the 5,700 steel cylinders had released the last of the pressurised chlorine. Within minutes columns of masked Reichsheer soldiers moved forward towards the undefended trenches, a distinctive pepper smell lingering in the air. They met no resistance.

As he watched the advance, Fritz Haber's heart pounded like a drum. Pride swelled in his chest. The Kaiser's chemist had opened the Western Front. His innovation had created a military bridge across the enemy positions. There was no obstacle now between Berlin and Paris.

At that moment in 1915 Haber became – in his own words – 'one

of the mightiest men in the German Empire'. He felt himself to
be 'more than a great army commander, more than a captain of industry'. He was 'the founder of industries', his creation essential for
the economic and military expansion of the Reich. He had proved
his patriotism. He had devised 'a higher form of killing'.

Half a lifetime earlier, a shaft of sunlight had fallen on Haber. He
was nineteen years old, on leave in the capital in 1887, at a loss what
to do with the afternoon, and his life. His duties in the field artillery regiment were tedious. His two years at university had bored
him. Like his country, he longed to find a purpose, to catch hold
of an endeavour that would give meaning to existence. Idleness
was unbearable but what in God's name was he to do? Then fate
had drawn him into the Altes Museum, placing him in front of the
vast painting at the very moment that the clouds parted high above
Berlin.

   In the gilt-framed canvas before him, Kaiser Wilhelm I – hero of
the Franco-Prussian War and dressed like a deity in luminescent
ceremonial uniform – led a pageant of historical and allegorical figures through the Brandenburg Gate. A Teutonic knight on a black
charger flourished the eagle-blazed Prussian war flag. Exulting
soldiers and comely maidens strutted behind them. Cherubs and
angels circled overhead, carrying crowns, sounding trumpets. An
ancient woodsman gestured the way forward to destiny. German
civilisation was on the march, proclaimed Ferdinand Keller's epic
painting, and in the sudden flood of sunlight young Fritz Haber
shivered as he envisioned himself joining the patriotic procession.

A first, shadowy photograph captures him as a lonely three-year-
old, gripping a wooden chair, clutching a toy rifle. He cranes
himself forward, widens his worried eyes, craves the approval of
an unseen figure behind the camera. His mother had died when
he was three weeks old. His grieving father, a Breslau dye merchant, had closed his heart to the child. The boy's birth had stolen
his wife away from him, and he could never forget it. A whole
decade would pass until the man showed any emotion, when he

remarried, showering years of frustrated affection upon his new wife and her daughters.

As soon as he was old enough, Haber moved away from home. He joined the army because of his hunger for attention, for the status which came with rank. He passed the tests for a commission but was rejected as an officer because of his Hasidic background. So, like 10,000 other German Jews between 1890 and 1910, he converted to Christianity.

Haber wore pince-nez spectacles. He had a thick head of curly hair. He loved to discuss and debate, drawing people into arguments, developing ideas as they talked. He had a quick mind and an ability to clarify a matter in a few precise sentences. Only the shape of his future seemed to elude him. He was unable to settle on any single subject or place, moving from Berlin to Zurich and Jena, barrack room to factory, industry to academia.

Then in 1894 he landed a job as a lab assistant at Karlsruhe's Technical University. Almost immediately he decided that science was superior to other human endeavours. To his mind science was never regressive; discovery was built on discovery, knowledge on knowledge. Its march of progress – like that of the nation – could not be undone, and it gave him a sense of certainty, of purpose.

At Karlsruhe, Haber focused his energies on chemical technology. He worked hard, initiating a frenetic research programme. He studied the combustion of hydrocarbons and the loss of energy in engines, invented the glass electrode and linked chemical research to industrial processes. He travelled to America to observe New World innovation, obsessed with science's power to shape society. He became a professor by embracing technological progress, convinced that his work would both strengthen Germany and better mankind.

At the start of the twentieth century the world was running out of food. Over thousands of years mankind had fed itself by converting wilderness to farmland. But with the settlement of most available virgin land, food production was no longer determined by geographical expansion.

European and American farmers already relied on expensive, imported, nitrogen-rich guano to increase soil fertility. Like every chemist, Haber knew that the atmosphere contained inexhaustible reserves of nitrogen. But the airborne atoms were inert. If he could break their atomic bonds, he reasoned, the gas could be converted into a form which would be available to plants. It was a chemical problem, and the challenge fired his imagination.

In the lab he mixed nitrogen with hydrogen at a temperature of 1,000 degrees Celsius. The fierce heat did synthesise ammonia, the raw material for the production of fertilizer, but only in minute quantities. He gave up the work, until a rival dismissed his calculations as inaccurate. In response Haber redoubled his efforts. His quest became an obsession and within twenty months – through the use of pressure as well as heat – he succeeded in producing synthetic ammonia, creating *Brot aus Luft*. Bread out of air. In time half of the world's crops would be fertilised by the Haber-Bosch process. Yet his synthetic ammonia also had a darker, deadlier use.

In 1910 the new Kaiser – grandson of the 'luminescent' Wilhelm I in Keller's jingoistic painting – called for wealthy industrialists and financiers to fund an elite research institute. He wanted to link science with industry and the military. He had already amassed the most powerful army in the world and launched a blue-water fleet, second in tonnage only to the Royal Navy. He had laid claim to French-occupied Morocco and pushed a railway line from Berlin towards Baghdad (to gain access to the Persian Gulf and the oilfields of Iraq). Now he wanted to use scientific innovation as a weapon.

At the Berliner Schloss, surrounded by sycophants, Wilhelm II proclaimed, 'To say that Germany should cease its *Weltpolitik* is like a father telling his son – if only you would not grow up, then I would not need to buy you long trousers.' His grandmother Queen Victoria called him a 'hot-headed, conceited and wrong-headed young man, devoid of all feeling'. His vanity and arrogance would bring about the end of five centuries of Hohenzollern rule, and – in his demand for unswerving, unquestioning loyalty to his authority – all but destroy Germany.

*

Ripe green buds swelled on Dahlem's lime trees. Thickset women swept the first fallen blossoms from the steps of solid farmhouses. Beyond the slender, swaying birches, in the open fields on the western edge of Berlin, rose the imposing stone and stucco buildings of the 'German Oxford'.

Fritz Haber plucked a bright bud from a sapling, turned it in his fingers, eased apart its carpel. History is a matter of determination, he told himself as he watched the working carpenters and bricklayers. We make our own story, picking and pushing the facts, choosing who we become.

With the 'fixation' of nitrogen, Haber had become Germany's top physical chemist. He had outgrown modest Karlsruhe. When the emperor had invited him to Berlin, asking him to be the founding director of the Kaiser Wilhelm Institute for Physical Chemistry and Electrochemistry, he couldn't – and wouldn't – refuse. He gazed across the building site, planning, scheming, dissecting the lime bud without thinking, destroying it between his fingers.

'The only deplorable thing about Haber was that he was a bit power-hungry,' recalled James Franck, a young researcher who would later serve in Haber's 'gas troops'. 'He knew his own intelligence and wanted power. He knew what he was capable of, and his fingers were itching to do it.'

In Dahlem Haber began to amass his own empirical empire, drawing around him Germany's finest scientists and researchers. He supervised the design and construction of laboratories and offices. He named neighbourhood streets after famous chemists and physicists. He convinced young Albert Einstein to move from Switzerland and join him 'to do for physics what I did for chemistry'. His arrogance and ambition mirrored that of Germany's leaders.

With his bald head, thin lips and smouldering cigar, Haber cut a distinct figure as he hurried between grave, grey ministries and the pompous Prussian Academy. He was driven by a need to do, to change, to create. He fought for the Institute's independence yet at the same time he believed the duty of every citizen was to serve the nation. Common purpose took precedence over individual interests.

Einstein saw things differently. He was a truly independent thinker, in service to no man or authority. To prove his point he renounced both Judaism and later his German citizenship. He was on the cusp of writing his new theory of the universe. 'Haber's photograph unfortunately is to be seen everywhere,' he grumbled on his arrival in Berlin from Zurich. 'It pains me every time I think of it.'

Einstein considered Haber to be a kind of genius civil servant, blinded by patriotism, crippled by insatiable personal vanity. Yet the two men became friends, due in part to the difficulties of their marriages. Haber helped to draft Einstein's marriage separation agreement. Einstein tutored Haber's son in maths. Einstein also planned to settle in the capital, leasing a *Schrebergarten* allotment which he called his 'Spandau Castle', planting vegetables while pondering relativity.

But as Germans convinced themselves once again that they were threatened by encirclement, a chasm opened between the men. Haber rallied loyal scientists around the Prussian battle flag, placing absolute faith in German honour, inventiveness and power. He inspired them by quoting Horace: *Dulce et decorum est pro patria mori*. How sweet and fitting it is to die for one's country. In response Einstein observed, 'Our entire much-praised technological progress, and civilisation generally, could be compared to an axe in the hand of a pathological criminal.'

In the heady, halcyon days of August 1914 the Deutsche Reichsheer marched towards destiny, cheered on by Berlin's euphoric crowds. University students massed outside the Berliner Schloss singing 'Deutschland, Deutschland über alles'. The Kaiser promised that the troops would 'be home before the leaves have fallen from the trees'.

'Every face looks happy – we have war!' cheered the actress Tilla Durieux. 'Bands in the cafés and restaurants play "Heil dir im Siegerkranz" and "Die Wacht am Rhein" . . . People line up to offer their motorcars for service . . . Soldiers at the railway stations are given mountains of buttered sandwiches, sausages and chocolate. There's a super-abundance of everything – of people, of food, of enthusiasm.'

Berlin wanted a short war. Its plan was to trap and annihilate the French Army in a great encircling movement. At first the strategy seemed flawless. Within thirty-five days of mobilisation the Kaiser crowed, 'Rheims has been occupied, the French government has moved to Bordeaux and the advance-guards of our cavalry stand fifty kilometres from Paris.'

But the Tsar mobilised his troops with unexpected speed, invading East Prussia. German reserves had to be drawn back from France, enabling the Allies to halt the Reichsheer's western advance at the Battle of the Marne. Paris did not fall in six weeks as planned. Belgium did not submit to annexation. The rival armies dug in along a 650-kilometre line stretching from the English Channel to the Swiss border. The swift, mobile campaign faltered into a grinding war of attrition. Two million men faced each other across the barbed wire and mud. The Kaiser's plan failed, and Germany had no alternative strategy.

Within months Berlin began to run out of ammunition. The Royal Navy's blockade of German ports starved its enemy of both munitions and food. Bread was rationed. Queues formed outside butchers' shops. In time baking cakes was forbidden in parts of the city to preserve flour stocks. With its ships stranded in harbour, Germany could not import nitrate. Without nitrate its factories could not make bullets, shells and TNT.

Walther Rathenau took the lead, summoning military and business leaders to the War Ministry, mobilising the nation's industrial resources. Haber joined them, offering his knowledge as a means to overcome the desperate shortages. He proposed modifying his process of ammonia synthesis to produce nitric acid. The man who had produced bread from the air, giving life to millions, now turned airborne nitrogen into an explosive tool of death, to feed the machines of war.

A scientist belongs to the world in times of peace, and to his country in war, said Haber. His innovation allowed Germany to fight on, rather than surrender in December 1914. In Berlin he and

Rathenau forged an alliance of soldiers, scientists and businessmen, creating the world's first military-industrial complex. But rather than prolong the war, Haber was determined to win it swiftly. Like all Germans he believed that the nation had embarked on a moral crusade, fighting under God for survival and honour. Moderation, never a German strong point, had been drowned out by rhetoric. Arrogant nationalists clamoured, 'Every shot, hit a Russian! Every stab, kill a Frenchman!' Victory had become the only acceptable outcome, and victory meant breaking the deadlock on the Western Front.

The 1899 Hague Convention – which had been signed by all the warring parties – had banned the use of poisoned weapons. Yet each country was developing them in secret. As Berliners went hungry, Haber enjoyed a luncheon of fillet of hare with cherry sauce, washed down with a fine Rheingau Riesling, in the officers' mess at Kummersdorf, the artillery range where Wernher von Braun would later launch his first rockets. That morning Haber had witnessed the test-firing of experimental 'T-Shells'. Named after chemist Hans Tappen, *T-Granate* contained both explosive and the poisonous organic compound xylyl bromide.

Over cigars and Asbach brandy, Haber argued with Tappen that the large-scale use of xylyl bromide would be ineffective on the battlefield. He wanted to find both a cheaper chemical and method of dispersal. Later that day his Opel stalled on the drive back to town. In a cloud of exhaust fumes he had the idea of engulfing the enemy in gas.

The Minister of War, Erich von Falkenhayn, approved Haber's wind-borne 'blow' attack. His scheme was to dig pressurised bottles of liquid chemical into the German front line. On its release the liquid would vaporise. A favourable breeze would carry it across no man's land and into the trenches opposite. German troops could then seize the abandoned positions. If enacted on a wide front, and executed with surprise, the weapon could clear the way for a dramatic military advance.

Haber's institute – founded for the promotion of all sciences

– was now ordered to serve the army alone. Guards were stationed at its entrances. Barbed wire secured its perimeter.

The High Command wanted a chemical that killed and Haber offered them chlorine. It cost almost nothing. It could be sourced from existing manufacturers. The iron gas cylinders needed for dispersal were available, the chemical giant BASF having supplied liquid chlorine to the dye industry since the 1880s. Above all, it asphyxiated in seconds.

Haber marshalled his scientists, among them future Nobel laureates James Franck, Gustav Hertz and Otto Hahn. In February 1915 they tested the world's first weapon of mass destruction, with Haber's wife at his side.

Three dozen dogs were leashed to stakes hammered onto a frozen plain. As the yellow cloud rolled towards them the animals howled in terror, straining against their leads. When it enveloped them a pitiful wail filled the hollow of the sky. Clara Haber seized her husband's hand, digging her nails through her gloves and into his skin. Within a minute both gas and sound dissipated, and the corpses of the dead animals lay on the slashed earth, the heat of their bodies melting the surrounding snow. Haber checked both his shock at the speed of death, and his euphoria for the ghastly triumph.

Three days later Haber and his 'gas troops' moved to the front line near Ypres. Over the next month, working under the cover of darkness, they dug thousands of cylinders into the earth along a ridge called Hill 60. The British and French spotted the unusual activity, tunnelled under the hill and blew it up. They shelled Haber's positions, fracturing one canister and gassing twenty German soldiers. Still they didn't appreciate the danger. Only on 22 April 1915, when the wind shifted to the south-west and the cloud of death, six kilometres wide, rolled towards the Canadian trenches, did they understand that a new era of warfare had dawned.

Over the next fortnight four more gas attacks were launched along the Western Front, killing over 10,000 Allied soldiers. But the Kaiserreich commanders never pressed home the advantage. No massed concentration of troops marched through the devastated lines to Paris. No bridge was thrown across the silenced trenches. The opportunity was squandered. For all its lethal power and the enemy losses, Germany gained less than a mile of no man's land.

Yet Haber won Berlin's respect. He felt himself to be a Prussian officer, a master over life and death, autocratic and ruthless in his drive to victory. His 'gas troops' were heralded as heroes. His work was called 'a triumph for German ingenuity'. Death-making was his art. He was summoned to appear before the Kaiser.

At home in early May he held a party to celebrate his success, wearing for the first time his new, ceremonial uniform and gleaming medal. Soldiers, chemists and industrialists – including executives from Rathenau's AEG – lifted their glasses and toasted their new alliance. Bombastic speeches were made about innovation shattering the enemy's strength. After the guests left, Haber went to bed. His wife Clara – who had condemned his work as 'an abomination of science and a sign of barbarism' – tidied her hair, stepped out into the garden and then shot herself with his service revolver. Their thirteen-year-old son Hermann found her dying beneath the tall trees.

The very next morning, unwilling to defy orders, Haber left Berlin for the Eastern Front. He had to direct a gas attack against the Russians. His obligation to duty far outweighed any sense of loss or personal culpability. In any case, he had always thought that a family confined a man, sapping his energies. He called fatherhood 'the murderer of talent' and likened women, whom he had never understood, to 'lovely butterflies'. 'I love their colours and glitter but there it ends,' he once said.

'Now I am at the front again,' he wrote to a friend, puffed up with self-importance, busying himself to keep conscience at bay. 'Working through all the complications of war, I have no time to look left or right, to reflect or to sink into my own feelings. The only thing that lives in me is the fear that I won't be able to carry on, or bear the enormous burden placed on me.'

Over the next three frenetic, murderous years, Haber's oily evil spiralled out from Berlin and Ypres, seeping across Loos, engulfing

Rawka and Riga. Haber rushed from trenches to field headquarters, War Ministry and laboratory, devising and applying new weapons of terror. Within months of the first grim gas attack, the Allies had retaliated with their own chemical weapons. In response Haber and his fellow chemists developed new gases and methods of delivery, his Institute growing into a military installation which employed 1,500 people.

In Dahlem he conceived variegated shelling, a hateful two-stage procedure in which *Maskenbrecher* shells – containing arsenide irritants which penetrate filters and force the removal of masks – were followed by bombardment with mustard gas. Unlike chlorine, mustard did not blow away with the wind. It was a persistent poison that clung to clothes and soil, blinding and choking its victims as well as those who touched them long after the attack. Haber considered the technique to be 'a fabulous success'.

As the war reached its climax, the Reich fired some 100,000 chemical shells, propelled by Haber's explosives, filled with his gases. By September 1918 the British developed their own mustard variant, unleashing it on the Belgian front against the 16th Bavarian Reserve Infantry. Among its many victims was an obscure Austrian corporal, temporarily blinded by an attack.

No sense of impropriety or immorality troubled Haber. In some ways he differed little from French and British war chemists like Frederick Donnan and William Pope, men who also put aside morality to embrace the technological imperative, convinced that whatever could be invented would be invented. But Haber stood apart from them because of his vile vanity, his bloated egotism and his tireless inventiveness.

Wunderwaffen – wonder weapons – did not bring victory. Instead the iniquitous gases and industrial explosives only extended the suffering, bringing hunger and hastening economic collapse. Almost two million Germans were killed in battle while a further 750,000 died of malnutrition at home. All the country's nitrogen was fed to the insatiable arms factories, leaving farmers without fertilizer and the country to starve.

In its final defeat the German Empire ceded Alsace and Lorraine rather than gaining iron-rich Briey and Longwy. Instead of annexing Belgium, she surrendered Eupen and Malmédy. At Metz Cathedral, seized by the Germans in 1871 and returned to France in 1918, stonemasons decided not to remove the Kaiser's face from a medieval knight's statue. Instead they inscribed around it the words *Sic transit gloria mundi*. So the glory of the world passes away.

Fritz Haber – who contributed more than any other individual to German power in the First World War – grew a beard and went into hiding in Switzerland. His certainties had been shattered. Germany had not marched to greater glory. His sun-blessed leader had not donned a luminescent uniform. His science had impoverished not bettered mankind. But instead of being arrested as a war criminal he was awarded the 1918 Nobel Prize in Chemistry. In his laudatory address the President of the Swedish Royal Academy described in detail the significance of ammonia synthesis for agriculture. No mention was made of Haber's contribution to the explosives industry, or of his involvement in chemical warfare.

The honour enabled Haber to return to work in Berlin. He turned his mind to a new way of empowering his benighted, bankrupt country. When the Mark collapsed after the assassination of Walther Rathenau, Haber tried to extract gold from the sea. Twenty years earlier a Swedish scientist had found tiny amounts of the precious metal in sea water. According to his calculations, every ton of ocean contained about six milligrams of gold. Haber steered the Institute towards the project, and the hope of relieving the Fatherland of its debts. But four years' work and numerous sea voyages came to nothing. The Swedish figures were grossly optimistic, and the failure plunged him – like the country – deeper into despair.

'I brood over the purpose of life,' he wrote at the age of fifty-six. 'The only thing that is worthwhile for a man of my years and my nature is action, doing things, being useful. But I don't know where I can find a place that would make the necessary allowances for my damaged nerves and my diminished strength.'

With no sign of repentance Haber focused on his administrative responsibilities. He hired researchers, supported pioneering work in fundamental physics, quantum mechanics and even physiology. He continued to dismiss the critics of chemical warfare as outdated, and began to develop domestic pesticides based on knowledge acquired during the war.

By the late 1920s another evil was uncoiling in Germany. Romantic, tribal notions of superiority were used to blow away the humiliation of defeat. Haber remained true to Germany, even as Germany discriminated against his Jewish colleagues. Jews came to be banned from being judges, from serving in the civil service, from breathing the same air as gentiles. A quarter of the scientists at Haber's institute were of Jewish descent. Einstein, who had remained his friend through the war, deserted both him and Berlin, moving to Belgium, Britain and finally the United States.

In 1933 the obscure Austrian corporal, whose terrifying exposure to gas had driven him into politics, became Führer. Carl Bosch, the engineer whose factories had produced Haber's fertilizer, explosives and poisons, appealed to the new leader for an end to discrimination against Jewish scientists. He argued that Germany needed men like Haber. 'Then we'll just have to work for a hundred years without physics and chemistry,' replied Hitler, unwilling to save the man whose iniquitous genius had helped spur him to power.

Haber's unquestioning patriotism, his inventiveness, even the Nobel Prize, could not protect him now. He submitted his resignation and left Berlin for a scientific conference in Spain, never to return. His heart and spirit were broken, his identity lost and his status in Germany reduced to that of a second-class citizen. He was – as Einstein wrote – like a man who had worked for his whole life on a single theory, and then been forced to abandon it. A glimmer of hope came with the offer of an honorary post at Cambridge, arranged by his former adversaries, England's own poison gas chemists. He accepted the offer but – as an obedient Prussian – he felt obliged to complete matters with the authorities, settling his tax affairs and requesting permission for 'an honourable separation' from Germany. No permission was forthcoming. In its and his absence, he asked that a note from him be posted on his Institute's bulletin board.

'With these words I depart from the Kaiser Wilhelm Institute . . . which under my leadership for twenty-two years was dedicated to serving humanity in times of peace, and the Fatherland in times of war. As far as I can evaluate the result, it was good and useful for science and for the nation's defence.'

Not even at the end of his days, as he pondered the capacity of science to both nourish and destroy life, did the Kaiser's chemist understand that morality and patriotic duty could be wildly at odds with each other.

But Fritz Haber's twisted legacy lived on: in the million men who were scarred and blinded by his weapons; in the physicist James Franck, one of Haber's gas troops, who helped to build the atomic bomb; in the amoral linkage of science and military which continues to devise ever more deadly weapons; in the use of poison gas against civilians in Morocco, Libya, Ethiopia, Vietnam, Iran, Iraq and beyond.

Hitler also kept his work alive. Far from abandoning physics and chemistry as he had threatened, the dictator advanced Haber's quixotic quest for *Wunderwaffen*. First he financed the production of synthetic petrol. Then he approved the use of Zyklon B – the cyanide-based pesticide developed under Haber in a leafy corner of 14195 Berlin. In the Nazi extermination camps, the chemical would claim the lives of some four million people, among them all of Haber's nephews and nieces, and tens of thousands of other Berliners.

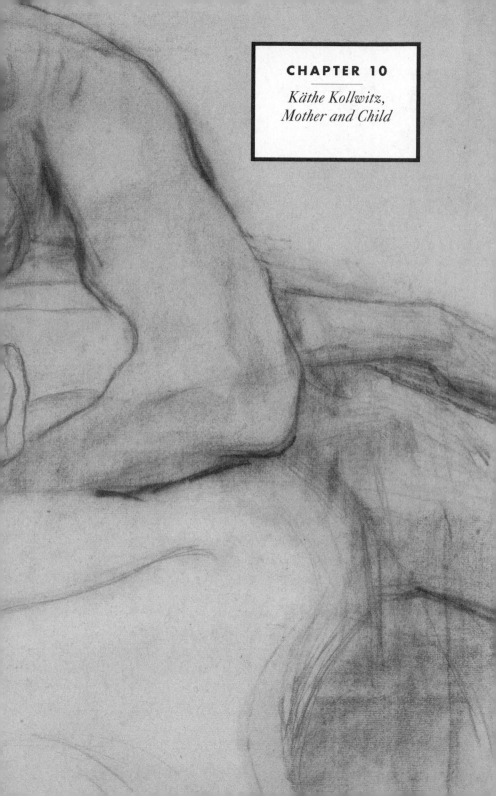

CHAPTER 10

Käthe Kollwitz,
Mother and Child

Woman with Dead Child (*Frau mit totem Kind*) by Käthe Kollwitz, 1903.
(*bpk/Kunstsammlungen Chemnitz/May Voigt*)

Wörther Platz, 1903

The child's head falls back. The mother grips his frail flesh, buries her face into his stilled chest. His hair is as soft and warm as feathers in the sunshine. Hers is patchy and thin. In her great, strong hands she clenches the boy's delicate shoulders in a fierce grip, folding him towards her. She aches to breathe life into him again, or to absorb him back into herself.

'Live!' the woman cries at the corpse. 'Stay!'

But the boy will not return. The dead leave us alone with thoughts of what was and might have been, to face the bleak void of life and love for ever lost.

Mud: formless, unshaped, unmodelled like the clay wrapped in wet rags in his mother's studio, waiting for a form to be released from within, waiting for a story to unfold.

In 1914 Peter Kollwitz is eighteen years old, slogging through the mire with other fresh-faced volunteers. Ranks of engineers drag up the artillery. Horse-drawn ammunition columns are whipped towards the front. Officers in staff cars stand ramrod tall and bark orders for *die große Schlacht*, the great battle which will punch through the Allied lines. The Imperial Fourth Army clicks its heels, snaps to attention, stands poised to seize Calais and swing south to Paris. A shrapnel shell bursts overhead, two bivouacs catch fire, a week's rations go up in smoke, yet wave after wave of young men run on into the thunder, singing as they reach for victory.

Peter's regiment – Infanterieregiment 207 – is only ten days out of Berlin. Less than two months ago he was on holiday in Norway, trekking between blue fjords and high glaciers in the company of German, English and French hikers. In the northern wilderness the young travellers heard about Sarajevo. When they parted at Bergen they shook hands, wished each other well, and declared, 'We need to go home. It's supposed to be war.' Now he and his companions advance and dig trenches, hunker down to face the 11th Belgian Line Regiment.

Yesterday the first letter arrived from his mother.

'My dear boy! No news of you from Belgium so we have to assume you are in France. Perhaps you are already under fire. My love! Although your life may now be in danger and although I im- agine the hardships you must now endure, I do not feel as weighed down with sorrow as in the past. Perhaps it is because I have been drawing and so have moved the pressure away from my heart and onto the paper. I think of you with a firm confidence. And with love, you beloved faithful boy.'

The letter is tucked into his breast pocket. The regiment lays down its shovels. At midday there are sausages, beans and barley malt coffee. Peter swears he can taste cordite.

'Better than Aschinger's at Alexanderplatz,' jokes Jürgen, a new friend. The lad is always joking, despite his bad boots and blisters, despite the sudden howl of the Tommy heavies which cuts short their meal.

A burst of flame roars through the cookhouse. The earth leaps and Peter falls back. Clods of mud rain on him as he stumbles for cover. Another bellow and the ground splits open. High explosive blows apart a field mortuary tucked behind the trees. Peter drops into a crater, away from the dry spurts of machine-gun fire, into the wreckage of torn coffins, blood, bones and shit. In terror, corpse rats scuttle across the dead and dying. A fist reaches out of the soil, clawing at the earth, until its buried owner suffocates in the mire. Beyond the broken black crosses, Jürgen is crawling, white-eyed, writhing in pain, clutching his mess tin, missing a leg.

In response to the bombardment, a breakthrough is ordered across the Yser River. Peter's regiment is to advance through the mud before the Belgians flood the lines.

Late that Thursday afternoon Peter takes cover in a ruined farmhouse in Esen. He is breathless, nervous but not a coward. The dipping sun glows orange through the smoke. Beneath the hissing shells he and two others squeeze through a shattered window and crawl into a depression in the ground. Their position is protected only by a stack of newly cut turf. They catch their breath. They make to move on. Peter lifts his head, and a bullet whistles into his mouth, stopping his heart.

In a handful of days the German losses are so heavy – more than 25,000 young, ill-trained volunteers slaughtered at Diksmuide alone – that the attack is nicknamed 'the Massacre of the Innocents'. Despite the sacrifices, the Belgians succeed in opening the sluices at Nieuwpoort, creating a mile-wide floodplain, arresting the German advance, turning the low-lying fields into a mass grave.

The morning after Peter falls a second letter arrives for him.

'My dear boy! Are you receiving our cards? It's a strange feeling that everything we write may never reach you. Father and I are well. Father has a lot of work. I am drawing. Where might you be? It is as if one thinks in the fog. Farewell, dear boy! We send regards.'

The letter is returned unopened to Berlin, stamped simply 'Return to Sender – Killed in Action.'

Käthe Kollwitz, Peter's mother, is forty-seven. It's a Tuesday morning at the end of October 1914. She has come out of her studio to stand in his room. She places her hands on the iron bedhead, the metal cold against her palms. She looks at his easel, his bookcase, his skis leaning in the far corner. A guitar hangs on a nail. Once he listed for her his reasons for living: billiards, mountaineering, Expressionism, the sky at night, Tuscany in May. He loved to linger over a beer at Aschinger's, to watch flickering Danish *Kintopp* movies at the Prenzlauer Berg summer fair, to walk and sing with friends in the woods. Peter had been a *Wandervogel*, a member of the student movement which wanted to be free of strict Prussian *alte Moral*. He often skipped school. He hoped to be an artist like his mother. A year earlier he started painting classes at the Decorative Arts Museum but he didn't stick at it. He went on playing truant, trekking instead through the Grunewald, celebrating the solstice with friends in Köpenick in the forest where Colin Albany had once wintered. In the summer before he left for Norway, Käthe critiqued his work harshly, too harshly.

Now he is in the ground, wrapped in tarpaulin and buried in a crude wooden box in the mud behind the trenches. Twice the boy was cut from the umbilical cord; the first time to live, the second time to die. Käthe squeezes the iron bedhead until her knuckles go white. She hears a voice, and realises with a start that she's speaking out loud, to herself, to him. She cries suddenly, sobbing and sobbing with her broken face in her hands, unable to stop, all but unable to go on.

'The children. The children,' she gasps. But she means the child. The child.

Death. Käthe's dialogue with death begins almost four decades earlier in Königsberg on the Baltic. She is just nine years old, the third surviving child of a progressive family in the philistine East Prussian port. Her father is a free-thinking solicitor who refuses to serve the authorities, reads Marx and joins the nascent Socialist Party. Her grandfather is a dissident Protestant minister who champions the martyrs of the 1848 revolution. But their utopian vision does not inure them to tragedy.

Käthe sits with her siblings at the kitchen table in 1873. Their mother is ladling soup. Their old nurse wrenches open the door and cries, 'He's vomiting. He's vomiting again.' Their mother stands rigid by the oven, lets no sound pass her lips, then goes on ladling.

She will not be comforted when her one-year-old baby Benjamin dies of meningitis. She locks away her emotions as two more infants are taken from her. Yet all the while timid, tender-hearted Käthe gazes at her, feeling her anguish. Soon she begins to suffer from violent tantrums, as if drawing the woman's grief through herself.

Käthe likes to explore the working port with her sister, roaming across the Königsgarten to the cathedral, wandering down to the docks. The girls stand for hours on the wooden pontoons, their scarves waving in the wind, watching the longshoremen unload puffing steamers and laden barges: bacon and timber for Berlin, dried cod and wool for Leipzig and Dresden. The men swing heavy crates ashore, cast off for other harbours. They are Russians, Latvians and Lithuanians, dressed in sheepskin and leather, and their hard labour stirs a longing in Käthe.

'Beautiful to me are the Königsberg dockhands,' she writes as if of a first love. Ribbons and bows, fancies and fashion hold no charm for her. Instead she's stirred by the workers' taut muscles, by their pure action, by the 'beautiful bold outline of the movements of ordinary people'.

Here on a levee Käthe also sees a drowned girl washed ashore, and watches the corpse being carried away by mourners, her heart moved by the wails of fishwives and the silent torment of a father.

On Sundays after church Käthe and her siblings lie on the carpet in the minister's bright front room, the air heady with the smell of lilies and furniture polish, gazing at his books of copper engravings. They fall quiet to catch the conversation around them. The minister believes that God's gifts bring responsibility, that talent obligates duty. He tells her parents that a son who can tell stories should become a writer, that a girl who can sing is obliged to join a choir. Every individual has a duty to develop his or her talent, and then to share its fruit to nourish society, without regard for personal profit. The gifts that we are given must be given away again, not kept, thereby enabling the creative spirit to transform the world.

Some days the minister, tall, thin and dressed to his chin in black, sits Käthe on his knees to talk about the Gospels, or quote Lessing and 'Song of the Shirt'. When the old man reads Thomas

Hood's poem about the urban poor, his stern, steady voice breaks and Käthe stares in wonder as his tears fall upon his shaking hands.

Käthe is eleven when her parents recognise her gift for drawing. She is fourteen when she takes her first lessons with a Königsberg copper engraver. At sixteen, her sex barring her from attending the city's art academy, she studies under the naturalist painter Emile Neide. After her seventeenth birthday her father sends her to the Women's Schools in Munich and then Berlin, annexes of the cities' male-only art academies. He wants to distract her from romance as much as to advance her studies. By now she is falling in and out of love with stonemasons and dockhands, plunging herself into states of longing for she knows not what.

In the large, bare studios she learns to draw from life, developing her craft through application rather than inspiration. She cuts her long hair, puts away her pretty blouses, pulls on a rough painting smock and – like other bohemian women – embraces work and celibacy, as sex means marriage and enslavement.

In her first, scalding Berlin summer, Käthe stands at her dormitory window. In the same neighbourhood where Walther Rathenau was born and Lilli Neuss died, she peers at the labourers lingering under archways, and at their wives who ease fractious children to sleep, two, three or more to a bed. She sees whole families camping on balconies or dossing in parks, unable to find a room. At the Anhalter Bahnhof she watches them arrive by the thousand: farm workers, groundsmen, *Ortsfremde* serving girls with starched butterfly bonnets, wet-nurses who leave their own babies at home to sell their breast milk in the swelling capital. The incomers pour off the land and into tyre and torpedo factories, or join the snaking dawn queues outside Borsig's, Siemens and AEG. In the fifty years to 1890 the population of the *Feuerland* – the industrial 'fireland' of Moabit – increases twenty times. Berlin itself all but doubles in size. On dark and icy winter mornings, when the frost sticks to the soles of her shoes, Käthe sees labourers' wives staring into bakery windows, counting out small coins, their barefoot children clinging to their skirts and wailing in hunger and cold.

To Käthe, colour is bourgeois. Colour is used in the prosaic portrayal of the beautiful. But drawing is like poetry, in that it is both suggestive and subjective.

That first winter at the Women's School Käthe discovers the work of the graphic artist Max Klinger. Klinger uses monochrome etchings to create 'epic' narratives. His series *A Life* traces the story of a young Berliner's ruin, mirroring and mocking the ruling elite's moral hypocrisy, as the woman loses her virginity, is abandoned by her lover and thrown into an open sewer. In stark, Expressionistic images, he declares that the world should not be this way.

His passionate example liberates Käthe, freeing her of the obligation to imitate the appearance of the world. Her draftsmanship grows more expressive, her line expansive and fluid. She finds the confidence to be an artist advocate, devoting herself to both feeling and speaking for those who cannot do so for themselves.

Her first cycle is *A Weaver's Rebellion*, a series of six images inspired by Klinger and Gerhart Hauptmann's play about a Silesian uprising, *Die Weber*. In the first lithograph, *Poverty*, a despairing woman leans over the skeletal head of a dying boy. The father and another child huddle beside an empty loom in the dark, low-ceilinged hovel. In the second frame Death himself, having dispatched one child, brushes the mother's arm and takes her as well. In the subsequent images the workers rise up in revolt, provoked by the loss of the mother and child.

A Weaver's Rebellion takes four years to complete and scandalises officials at the 1898 Great Berlin Exhibition, the city's annual art fair. *Poverty* – which Käthe calls 'the child of sorrow' – sells for 500 Marks. Adolph Menzel, the leading painter of the day, proposes awarding her the exhibition's prestigious Gold Medal. But the Kaiser vetoes the nomination. Artists who criticise with their stylus are to be snubbed.

Käthe is now twenty-eight years old. She has abandoned celibacy to marry Karl Kollwitz, an open-minded *Kassenarzt* doctor who cares for the poor. Their home is in Prenzlauer Berg, one of the working-class neighbourhoods which has evolved around Berlin's

wealthy heart. Its gloomy tenements and stinking courtyards make
it a place bereft of air and light. Three out of four of its children
have never seen the sunrise. Half of them have never heard birdsong. A third are below normal height and weight. Tuberculosis
rages through the human warrens which Christopher Isherwood
will call the 'barracks' of the poor. Crowded, pestilent Prenzlauer
Berg is a place that can kill a man, joke local residents, as easily as
if one uses an axe.

The Kollwitzs' apartment is large in comparison to their neighbours, with four tidy rooms and a small balcony overlooking Wörther
Platz, the only open space in the neighbourhood. Käthe stands on
the balcony gazing across Berlin and asking herself, 'What can I
give?' Since her graduation she has borne two sons. She has helped
her husband to establish his practice. She has equipped her studio
with an oak worktable, copper plates and tools. Her fine, long face
has grown heavier, her hands are red from the caustic soda with
which she scrubs the surgery floor. But her dark, downturned eyes
retain the girlish brightness which Karl so loves. He is devoted
to her, Käthe knows. He supports her, encourages her work and
never asks her to adjust to his needs. Motherhood hasn't sapped
her strength, rather it has stimulated her. She feels more creative
because she is more in touch with her senses.

She looks across the rooftops south to the glittering domes of the
cathedral and Schloss, west to the welter of grimy factory chimneys, the monstrous engines sparking and puffing in the service
of capitalism. She holds to her breast – and against her heart – her
sketchbook, the morning's drawings. Every day in Karl's waiting
room Käthe registers the patients, drawing them out as she draws
them: the cloth-cutter with severed fingers, the fierce tiler crippled
by a fall, a battered tanner-woman recovering from her third miscarriage, the bow-legged twins wheezing with consumption.

'When I meet the women who come to my husband for help and
so, incidentally, come to me, I am gripped by the full force of the
proletarian's fate,' she records. 'Unsolved problems such as prostitution and unemployment grieve and torment me, and contribute to
my feeling that I must keep on with my studies of the working class.'

Karl's patients become her models, as do her sons. Käthe labours to capture in her images 'things seen and experienced from the soul'. At her studio table she works as if possessed, sleeves rolled up, hair falling into her eyes, as if to get her visions out of herself. 'I have never done any work cold,' she confesses. 'I have always worked with my blood.'

But the Kaiser does not want artists to speak from their heart, to break from tradition or to be free. He wants to own them. For him, the purpose of art is to reflect the greatness of the state. Prussian artists are of value only if they glorify Germany's heroes, as his ancestor Kurfürst 'Irontooth' had believed with the medieval *chansons* and *Minnelieder*. During his reign, he fills the capital with pompous nationalistic monuments flanked by busty angels and exulting, armour-clad demi-gods. He drives through the Tiergarten an avenue – the Siegesallee – lined with thirty-two dour statues of Hohenzollern rulers. His crass 'Victory Boulevard' is a gift to the city which will enable 'even the lower classes, after their toil and hard work, to be lifted up and inspired by the force of ideals'.

His art magnifies and intimidates to keep citizens in line. 'Art which transgresses the laws and barriers outlined by Me ceases to be an art,' he proclaims in 1901. 'When art, as often happens today, shows us only misery, and in a manner that renders it uglier than misery itself, then art commits a sin against the German people . . . it descends into the gutter.'

His Siegesallee is dubbed *Puppenallee*, or Dolls' Avenue. Rathenau calls it a feudal folly. Max Liebermann advises that dark glasses be worn when looking at 'this crime against good taste'. Karl Baedeker, the travel guidebook publisher, refuses to award a single star to it, or any other of the Kaiser's monuments. The dancer Isadora Duncan – a frequent visitor to Berlin – urges citizens to demolish the avenue.

The Kaiser's 'sinners' are the Berlin Secession, a breakaway band of painters and sculptors who champion modernism and introduce Berlin to Monet, Manet, Munch and Cézanne. Käthe takes part in their first show and its success makes heavy industry and its victims an accepted subject. Even military men slip into the garden of the Theater des Westens to see it, although anonymously, in civilian clothes, as the Kaiser threatens to punish officers who visit the 'subversive exhibition'.

Käthe touches the needle to the copper plate. The noise of the street below – the high calls of the rag merchants, the deep, boozy laughter from the wine cellar – seems to fall away. She loves the sensation of steel on copper, the feeling that the lightest touch cuts something solid, real, hard. With her nib she strokes the plate, scores it, attacks it. She draws out ideas, brushes away minute curls of wax, forgets about the lentil soup simmering on the stove until the smell of burning wafts in from the kitchen. A raw emotional urgency infuses *Raped*, an engraving in which a ravaged girl is left for dead in the undergrowth. At her table beneath the window Käthe moves on from rebellion to *Peasant War*, her second cycle based on an uprising during the Reformation. In *Outbreak*, one of its prints, an enraged woman – of Käthe's age and build – urges the serfs into revolt. In another, the haunting, premonitory *Battlefield*, a mother searches through stacked corpses for her dead son. Her characters are historical yet alive to Berliners as she models them on the men and women who wait and weep in her husband's surgery. She pulls so many prints, discards so many plates, but Karl never complains about the expense.

Käthe is fascinated by the rhythm of creativity, by her emotional highs and lows, by the long months of deep despair when she stares at the blank page, clutching her head, appalled by her lack of talent. She tries to discern a pattern, plotting her creative periods on a chart. She calls artistic strength her 'potency', linking sexuality and fertility with imagination. But she can find no bond between daily life and inspiration, other than her enduring dread of loss.

In the bitter winter of 1902 both her boys fall ill. Peter has a weak lung. Hans contracts diphtheria. She and Karl nurse their sons through the long, anxious nights. In the unheated bedrooms a chill grips Käthe's heart, wrenching up memories of her mother's bereavements, bringing the anguished nightmare that at any moment her children's lives may be cut off, that her sons might vanish for ever. She feels timidity seep into her soul, the dread of loss making her cling to what she has, undermining her courage.

When the pale spring sunshine finally falls across their sickbeds, and the boys begin to recuperate, she gives those fears outward form. She takes Peter in her arms. She asks him to drop back his head, to relax his muscles, to stay as still as the dead. She draws herself and the boy in the mirror until the pose becomes too much of a strain and she lets out a groan. 'Don't worry, Mother,' Peter consoles her in his birdsong voice. 'Your picture will be beautiful too.'

Her inks mix with her lifeblood. Sketches, intaglio plates and grief-stricken etchings haloed in a gold wash gather in piles in every corner of the studio. The image of a mother cradling a dead child will obsess her through the rest of her career. She confesses, 'All these prints are extracts of my life.'

It is death which animates life, by limiting it. Death vitalises Käthe, driving her to live to the full, not to waste her gifts. She is devoted to her husband Karl but – as the years pass – she feels no passion for him. His ordinary, domestic needs begin to infuriate her. She cries out for space to breathe. She shuts herself in her studio or storms off into the streets. As the boys grow older she travels to Paris and Florence. She meets the art critic Hugo Heller, a Hungarian Jew. Heller is dynamic, erudite and an enthusiastic social democrat. When he moves to Vienna to open a gallery, he and Käthe become correspondents. After his wife dies in 1909, they become lovers.

No written record remains of their liaison – Käthe burns all their letters before her death – but six explicit drawings survive from that year. In *Sekreta* rapid, sensuous strokes of charcoal give form to a breathless intimacy. A man rises above the woman, she opens herself to him. In *Liebesszene 1* he grasps her from behind. The woman is always Käthe, always wracked by her feelings, always haunted by leave-taking.

Käthe uses an identical pose in *Death and Woman*. In it the woman's lover is replaced by Death, who pins back her arms and locks her legs with his skeletal limbs, dragging her away into the darkness. She both resists and surrenders to his fatal embrace, throwing back her head, yet held to life by a naked child clinging to her breast.

'After people love one another something very sad is left behind,' she writes. 'Life remains always life to live, and so is earthbound. Perhaps, for that reason, life is all the more beautiful, for it is always permeated with this sadness. Why do tears run down people's faces when they see the most basic, human sights? Because to become one with the earth is the most frightening reality.'

She is forty-seven on the declaration of war in 1914, sitting on her bed and 'weeping, weeping, weeping'. Eight weeks later Peter is dead, and her greatest fear has come true. Like so many parents, Käthe and Karl accepted that Germany needed to defend itself. But as their children are shot, shelled, gassed and ground into the bloody earth, they come to realise that 'we were betrayed then, at the beginning. Perhaps Peter would still be alive had it not been for this terrible betrayal. Peter and millions, many millions of other boys. All betrayed.'

The killing leaves an empty space, an absence which Käthe tries to fill with work. She draws and draws to distract herself, to numb herself, to leech her pain. She plans to carve a memorial to Peter, the largest sculpture she will ever undertake, which will occupy her for the next eighteen years. At first he is its subject, then it becomes a relief of mourning parents and finally a granite mother and father, Käthe and Karl themselves, crumpled in grief, arms clasping themselves, alone, bereft and betrayed. Together in 1932 they unveil the work at Vladslo War Cemetery in Belgium, their sentinel forever gazing across the graves of 25,644 German soldiers, among whom lies Peter.

Käthe is convinced that art can – and should – change the world. She wants her work to stir emotion, to incite action, to serve the people. As German youth is slaughtered, and the Kaiser calls for under-age boys to join the fight, she challenges him in an editorial, pleading, 'There has been enough of dying! Let not another man fall!'

At the same time she turns away from historical subjects, no longer approaching the present from the past. She wants to effect her own era 'in which human beings are so much at a loss and so in need of help'. In *War*, a cycle of haunting woodcuts as moving as Picasso's *Guernica*, a naked woman offers up her newly born child for sacrifice, Death's drumbeat drives frenzied volunteers into battle, and a ring of mothers form themselves into a defiant circle, determined never again to give up their children. Käthe feels the burden. She cannot stop being an advocate. It is her duty to voice the sufferings of people, the sufferings which will never end.

'My dear Peter,' she writes to her dead son. 'I intend to try to be faithful to you. What does that mean? To love my country in my own way as you loved it in your way. And to make this love work. I ask you to be around me, to help me, to show yourself to me. I know you are there, but I see you only vaguely, as if you are shrouded in mist. I pray that I can feel you so close to me that I will be able to make your spirit live in my work.'

Käthe is now fifty-two years old. Beneath her balcony the defeated and despairing city reels in drunken stupor. A crab-like war cripple begs in Wörther Platz, battle medals clinking against his metal limbs. A pair of adolescent veterans – their uniforms filthy as if from the dirt of the trenches – cling to the arms of a starving, red-lipped whore, singing, taunting, ready to murder her at the slightest provocation. Beyond them an elephant from the zoo draws a coal cart as so many horses have been butchered and eaten by the hungry. Defeat has stripped away the city's gaudy imperial skin, revealing beneath a twisted and ugly skeleton.

Into its streets Lenin sows world revolution. From Moscow he sends millions of Marks and 300 skilled agitators, disguised as Russian Embassy staff. His activists energise the 1919 Spartacist Uprising, in which workers seize government buildings and bring Germany to the brink of a Bolshevik coup. The Communist leader Karl Liebknecht parades through the streets in a phalanx of armed trucks and prepares to take power. But the savage, reactionary Freikorps – from which Hitler will later draw his storm troopers

– crushes the uprising, hacking through the massed strikers with bayonets, machine-gunning unarmed demonstrators outside the Reichstag. Battle smoke rolls across Pariser Platz, driving bystanders into the Academy of Arts with stinging eyes, engulfing the goddess of victory. Hundreds of broken bodies are strewn in the gutters. Rosa Luxemburg, the movement's radical idealist, is shot in the head and dropped through the ice into the Landwehr canal. Karl Liebknecht is murdered and dumped by a Tiergarten lake.

Käthe is not a Communist – she describes herself as 'evolutionary' rather than revolutionary – but she accepts his family's request to sketch the corpse. She makes six drawings of Liebknecht's painfully distorted body, his head wounds concealed by red flowers. In her heartbreaking *Memorial Sheet to Karl Liebknecht* she gathers a frieze of proletariat mourners around their fallen, Christ-like martyr. Yet all the while she is tormented by doubts of her ability to express herself.

'Will the woodcut do it?' she agonises. 'If that too doesn't, then I have proof that it lies only within myself. Then I simply can no longer do it.'

'It' is both her vision and her perfectionism.

'There is a nothingness in me, neither thought nor feelings, no challenge to action, no participation. Low. Low. Touching bottom.'

The Weimar Republic was 'born in defeat, lived in turmoil and died in disaster', writes historian Peter Gay. Nightmare inflation eats away Kollwitz's life savings, like those of millions of other Germans. The 1929 Crash and rampant unemployment are exploited by the Nazis. The government's timidity ten years earlier, in empowering the Freikorps and making few reforms to the imperial system, enables the military to retain its grip on power. The arrogant soldiers who 'liberated' Berlin now march under the swastika.

Like the Kaiser before him, Hitler hates Käthe's work. Once again art must serve the state. She responds from her studio with a last cycle of eight stark lithographs. In them Death, with dramatic flying cape, swoops upon a group of children, then on a girl, a mother and on Käthe herself, offering his disembodied hand and drawing them out of life.

In turn the dictator condemns Käthe – along with contemporaries like Dix, Grosz, Chagall, Kandinsky, Kirchner and Mondrian – in the 1937 'Degenerate Art' Exhibition. Germans are shown which forms of expression are – and are not – acceptable in the new Reich. Her prints are removed from public museums. An exhibition to mark her 70th birthday is cancelled. Even her small sculpture *Tower of Mothers*, in which women defend their children from sacrifice in war, is removed from an obscure neighbourhood group show.

Twice the Gestapo call at her home, inspecting her studio, peeling back the damp drop cloths which protect her unfinished clay figures. They threaten her with arrest unless she retracts her antifascist statements. They warn her that neither her reputation nor her age will save her from the camps. Expecting the worst, she and Karl take to carrying vials of poison with them. But a return visit never comes. The Gestapo let fear do its work, in the Kollwitz household as across Germany.

'There is a curious silence surrounding the expulsion of my work from the Academy show,' she notes. 'Scarcely anyone has anything to say to me about it. I thought people would come, or at least write – but no. Such a silence around us.'

An artist needs an audience. For all her professional life Käthe worked in service of the people, acting as advocate and producing affordable prints for the poor. Now she can no longer reach them. She is isolated, forbidden to participate, unable to alert others or document the unfolding tragedy.

Now, at the end, Käthe is seventy-seven. She will not live out the Second World War. Nor will Karl, who dies after being prohibited from practising medicine. Nor will their grandson Peter, named after their own lost son, who is killed on the Russian Front. Berlin – her home and canvas for more than half a century – is in flames, destroyed by the punishing air raids which finally, brutally shake Germans out of their delusions.

Much of her work burns in the bombings. But among the survivors are a hundred self-portraits, drawn, etched and engraved across the course of her life. In many of them the artist seems to balance her head in her hands, as if moulding her own cheeks and chin, as her eyes gaze into the distance, picturing a world that should be otherwise.

Käthe Kollwitz took life as it was and, charged yet unbroken, captured in her art the pain suffered in this place by its mothers and children, giving Berliners a first, true, unadorned portrait of themselves. 'All my work hides within it life itself, and it is with life that I contend through my work.'

Fifty years after her death, on the reunification of Germany, Schinkel's Neue Wache guardhouse became a national memorial to the 'victims of war and tyranny'. At its centre was placed Käthe's *Pietà*, her sculpture of a grieving mother and son. Buried beneath it lie the remains of two other boys – an unknown German soldier and an unknown resistance fighter – as well as soil from nine European battlefields and from Auschwitz, Buchenwald, Dachau, Mauthausen and Natzweiler. Today it is one of the most visited spots in Berlin, and the mother's bronze limbs, which cradle her dying child, gleam from the touch of countless living hands.

CHAPTER 11

*Christopher Isherwood,
in a City of the
Imagination*

Christopher Isherwood, 1935. (*photograph by Humphrey Spender/Topfoto*)

Nollendorfstraße, 1927

The English actress dipped her head like a bird. Her companion – the seedy club's handsome pianist – whispered, proposed and the woman fluttered back as if startled, perching her head on her hands, all but covering her cherry-red beak. Then she laughed, touched his hand and chirped into song. At the bar the proprietress signalled with her cigar and Jean Ross soared through the hot smoke, into the spotlight and onto the tiny stage.

Across the room Christopher Isherwood – with boyish blue eyes and a flop of auburn hair – watched the busy bird, jotting details in a slim black notebook. She had a small dark head and a finely arched nose. Her plumage was black silk with white collar and cuffs. Her fingernails were painted emerald green. Her short bob seemed to emphasise the length of her neck, leaving it lank, exposed, boldly naked. When she darted forward to kiss the piano player, her large brown eyes crossed in concentration, in need of glasses but unwilling to ruin her sleek, avian profile.

Beside the stage an UFA studio bit player with plucked eyebrows ignored Ross's song, concentrating instead on a sultry waitress. At the next table a pale woman stroked the cheek of a powdered matron, turning to her husband only when he winked at the barman. Two lovers, with hands on thighs and heads pressed together, cried beneath a framed headshot inscribed 'To the one and only Lady Windermere'.

Ross sang badly, almost without expression, but she didn't seem to give a damn. Her take-it-or-leave-it grin made Isherwood laugh out loud. She had an extraordinarily comic quality, he thought, and he had to get it down on paper.

He had met Jean Ross two days earlier. He and the poet Stephen Spender were living in Berlin, visiting a friend, when Ross had stopped by to use the telephone. Ross was nineteen years old, a dropout from the Royal Academy of Dramatic Art and – so she said – shy with strangers. To compensate she hijacked their conversation by detailing her lovers' attributes and then pulled a diaphragm out of her handbag with smoke-stained fingers.

'I think that woman's absolutely repulsive,' Spender said later.

'I think she's really a little girl,' replied Isherwood in his teasing, plummy voice. 'Next time I see her I'm going to throw a cushion at her.'

In Berlin myth has always spawned myth. In 1843 Balzac had called it the capital of boredom. 'Imagine Geneva, lost in a desert, and you have an idea of Berlin,' he wrote, damning its citizens as dutiful, industrious and phlegmatic. The novelist Theodor Fontane had agreed with him, considering it bereft of the chic and elegant. 'All there is in Berlin is imitation, decent ordinariness, respectable mediocrity, and all Berliners feel so as soon as they get out of Berlin,' Fontane had written in the 1890s. The Marxist revolutionary Rosa Luxemburg wrote once in a letter, 'Berlin makes the most unfavourable impression on me in general: cold, tasteless, stolid . . . I already hate Berlin and the Germans so much that I could kill them.'

But by the start of the twentieth century a new Berliner had made his debut on the wooden stages of the *Lokale*. He was a savvy

Aryan *gavroche*, dressed in coarse woollen stockings and peaked cap, charged with irreverent wit and suspicious of authority. His girl, the typical *Berlinerin*, was sharp and amoral, vivacious rather than beautiful, more crass than Else, more vampish than the angelic Thymian, flaunting her sexuality like a dog on heat. The caricatures caught the popular imagination, spread from cabaret to vaudeville, and soon real Berliners were refashioning themselves in their image. Foreigners also embraced the myth, accepting it as reality, letting fiction reshape the city.

German youth had lost faith in the future on the First World War's Western Front. Now they grasped the present with febrile, sexual energy, dancing to the rattle of jazz bands and machine-guns, gorging themselves on warm flesh, drawing into their open arms foreigners like the painter Francis Bacon, novelists Vladimir Nabokov, Paul Bowles and Djuna Barnes, the composer Aaron Copland, actresses Lilian Harvey and Greta Garbo, as well as Spender, Auden and Isherwood. Berlin's young women didn't want to be kept like pretty butterflies, to be *baronisiert*. Its men felt no joy waking in a cold, empty bed. All wanted to live their one and only life, now.

By 1930 more than two million visitors a year poured into the licentious capital, many of them to mingle in the bedrooms and boy bars, to live out their fantasies at its masked balls and revels. Along 'the Passage' near Friedrichstraße hungry young men – struggling to find enough to eat – sold themselves for ten Marks and a glass of beer. Every evening behind the elegant department store KaDeWe, lively local girls laid aside their school textbooks, wolfed down a sausage supper then tripped off to turn tricks. An erotic guide to 'naughty' Berlin – Curt Moreck's 1931 *Führer durch das 'lasterhafte' Berlin* – mapped out the dark streets, private clubs and chic cafés ripe for sexual adventure.

'All values were changed and Berlin was transformed into the Babylon of the world,' wrote Stefan Zweig, the great chronicler of its 'Golden' Twenties. Like Mann, Brecht and Erich Kästner, he also could not resist the capital. 'Bars, amusement parks, honky-tonks sprang up like mushrooms. Along the Kurfürstendamm sauntered powdered and rouged young men . . . and in the dimly lit bars one might see government officials and men of the world of finance tenderly courting drunken sailors without shame . . . even the Rome of Suetonius had never known such orgies as the balls of Berlin.'

Moral values had collapsed along with the Mark. Berlin was 'a city with no virgins', wrote Spender. 'Not even the puppies and kittens are virgins.'

In Britain Isherwood had first understood the power of myth. His father had been a war hero, or so he was often told, who had vanished into the bloody chaos of battle at Ypres after Fritz Haber's first poison gas attack. Isherwood had been ten years old, and his fond father – with whom he had wrestled and learnt to develop photographs – was elevated into a distant, valorous icon. At boarding school in Repton his teachers used reverence to keep Isherwood in line. Be like your father, they said. Live by his example. He responded by rejecting their authority, 'becoming, in the human jungle, one of those animals who live by escape'. He fled from the callous anonymity of school with – as he wrote – 'the cold, daily, hourly reminder that you are not the unique, the loved, the household's darling, but just one among many'. He ran away from the ordinary.

At Cambridge he befriended the darkly handsome, aspiring novelist Edward Upward, a fellow Old Reptonian. On an evening walk together along Silver Street they happened upon a rusty-hinged door in a high blank wall. Upward ventured that it led to the 'Other Town' and in their imaginations they passed through the secret doorway into a fictional realm. They named it *Mortmere*, or Death Lake, and their creation quickly obsessed them. Over the next two years they peopled it with fantastic characters, capping each other's inventiveness, sharing and linking their surreal and sexual stories. A pair of pornographers named Christopher Starn and Edward Hynd – the authors' first alter egos – emerged as narrators, telling feverish tales of a choirboy-molesting vicar, an experiment to manufacture angels and a brothel devoted to necrophilia. To feed their fantasies the two writers drew on Brontë and Katherine Mansfield, pinched imagery from Poe and the Brothers Grimm. They imagined that ordinary exchanges between Cambridge's residents – shopkeepers shaking hands, drinkers whispering in a pub – linked the parallel worlds. Their obsession led to neglected studies and a failed Tripos but it showed Isherwood that he was a gifted inventor. In *Mortmere* he proved to himself that he could build outrageous fictions from material gathered from life and literature.

Isherwood didn't want to live forever in his head. He wanted to touch, and be touched. He was a sensual boy, hemmed in by an English timidity of physical contact. In London he met W.H. Auden whose attitude to sex, in its simplicity and utter lack of inhibition, took his breath away. The two young men – Auden was nineteen, Isherwood twenty-one – became lovers, then literary collaborators. Auden was determined to be his generation's Poet. He ordained that Isherwood would be its Novelist, even though his first book, *All the Conspirators* – a semi-autobiographical fiction – sold less than 300 copies.

'What I love is this taste of transience on the tongue,' said Max Reinhardt, the Berlin stage and film impresario who would train Marlene Dietrich and manage the Deutsches Theater. 'Every year might be the last year.'

In 1928 tongues and transience drew Auden to Berlin. Isherwood followed him, renting a room on Nollendorfstraße, a shabby, solemn street of monumental houses and bankrupt middle-class families in the west of the city. In his fellow residents the young writer was gifted the characters for a book: Bobby the barman, a modest prostitute with a taste for Japanese clients, and his shapeless, shameless landlady Meta Thurau. 'Fräulein' Thurau had wavy brown hair and fretted about the size of her breasts. She liked to lie with her ear on the floor and eavesdrop on the downstairs neighbours. She called him 'Herr Issyvoo' and – with his fine English manners – considered him to be a cut above her usual lodgers. In his Berlin diary he would immortalise her as Fräulein Schroeder.

Since his early teens Isherwood had been a diligent diarist. Now he put the practice to good use, observing the capital, collecting material, beginning to dream of an epic Berlin novel. He spent his mornings writing in a café on Winterfeldtplatz, lingering for hours over a single coffee, penning stories, snatching snippets of overheard conversation. In the afternoon he taught English and in the evening he ventured to clubs with Auden or to the cinema with Spender to see Louise Brooks in *Diary of a Lost Girl*, Fritz Lang's *M* and Dietrich in *The Blue Angel*. On sultry summer days he rode the S-Bahn to the Strandbad Wannsee and lay on the sand, watching the volleyball players, struggling to read Döblin's *Berlin Alexanderplatz* in German.

Another British resident, William Robson-Scott, thought Isherwood to be 'a very precise sort of man. If you went anywhere with him you saw him watching like a very intelligent bird, picking up everything that there was to be seen and assimilated.' His Berlin novel's working title was *In the Winter*, then *The Lost*, and – as he told his publisher – it would be written in the form of a diary, without any break in the narrative, and be filled with characters and 'news' about the city.

Spender pictured him 'surrounded by the models for his creations, like one of those portraits of a writer by a bad painter, in which the writer is depicted meditating in his chair whilst the characters of his novels radiate round him like a glowing cloud of dirty varnish, not unlike the mote-laden lighting of Fräulein Thurau's apartment'.

In time Isherwood would bring the model for his greatest creation to Nollendorfstraße, letting her stay in his room when she was in need, or in love, or pregnant.

As a girl at home in Egypt, Jean Ross had put on plays for her parents. On a makeshift stage, assembled from golden-threaded Nubian fabrics and dark Victorian furniture, she'd played a ferocious Barbary pirate plundering the African coast and a harem leader deposing a corrupt sheikh. She never cast herself as the victim, never limited herself to submissive female roles. She always radiated a bold independence, which was frowned upon when she and her siblings restaged their shows on the ship back to school in England.

Ross was a clever child, completing her school course work by her sixteenth birthday. But her headmistress decreed that she must remain at school for a final year, repeating her studies, and Ross rebelled by telling another pupil that she was expecting a baby. She was banished to the sanatorium so she could not corrupt the other girls and then, when her lie was exposed, expelled.

Her performance helped her to land a place at RADA. Then after a brief, unhappy flirtation with low-cost Anglo-American 'quota quickie' comedies, she moved to Berlin. She'd heard that there was work for actresses in the Weimar capital. More importantly, her passion for equality – both with workers and between the sexes – had drawn her to embrace Communism. The city's streets were the bloody battleground between two systems of ideas and Ross, a political activist like so many of her generation, wanted to be on the front line.

'That's the man I slept with last night,' Sally Bowles announced triumphantly as she hung up the receiver. 'He makes love marvellously. He's an absolute genius at business and he's terribly rich . . .'

As with *Mortmere* and his first novels, like Konrad von Cölln and Margarete Böhme, Isherwood generated fiction from his life, twisting and tweaking anecdotes and experience for dramatic effect. He chose how much to reveal, and how much to fabricate, slipping on masks and changing identities, augmenting, substituting, mirroring and documenting as he saw fit. 'You cut corners, you invent, you simplify,' he said to explain his creative process. 'You heighten certain lights and deepen certain shadows, as you might in a portrait.'

Jean Ross, like Isherwood's fictional creation Sally Bowles, had arrived in Berlin with a girlfriend. Both archetype and actress sang badly, in a deep husky voice, and spoke poor German. Both had escaped school by faking pregnancy. Both enjoyed sex. Both were nineteen years old. Isherwood believed that Ross was not a tart but someone who had 'listened to what the grown-ups had said about tarts and . . . was trying to copy those things'.

'I'm most terribly tired. I didn't sleep a wink last night. I've got a marvellous new lover,' Sally confessed in *Goodbye to Berlin*. She gave a sidelong glance. 'Do I shock you when I talk like that, Christopher darling?'

'Not in the least,' replied Isherwood's fictional persona; '. . . when you talk like that it's really just nervousness. You're naturally rather shy with strangers, I think: so you've got this trick of trying to bounce them into approving or disapproving of you, violently. I know, because I try it myself, sometimes . . .'

But unlike Ross, Sally's political convictions were only skin-deep. She would not become a journalist during the Spanish Civil War or serve – as is alleged – as an agent of the Comintern, the international Communist organisation determined to create a worldwide Soviet republic.

Isherwood named his character after Paul Bowles, who would later write *The Sheltering Sky*. Together they often lunched with Ross and Spender on the terrace of the Café des Westens, in the same 'corner of a foreign field' – as they called it – where fifteen years earlier a homesick Rupert Brooke had drafted 'The Old Vicarage, Grantchester'.

Like Isherwood himself, Sally Bowles told tall tales. She played at being a jade, fibbed that her mother was French, bragged that she'd performed at the Palladium and the Coliseum. Arthur Norris, the central character in *Mr Norris Changes Trains*, Isherwood's first published Berlin fiction, was an even bigger story-spinner.

Norris's character was based on Gerald Hamilton, a camp, Shanghai-born Edwardian chancer who pretended to have noble blood and spent his life wandering Europe, avoiding creditors and swindling strangers. He hobnobbed with German princes and charmed Rasputin (or so he claimed), implored the Pope to keep Italy out of the First World War and embraced Irish nationalism. He was interned in Brixton prison, either for treason or because of his taste for Arab boys, and wrote three autobiographies which contradict one another. In Berlin he was employed for a time as a sales rep for *The Times*, until the real reason for his attachment to the city came to light. In its energetic S+M clubs, Hamilton was also playing a part.

In the same manner Isherwood transformed his own lover Walter Wolff into working-class Otto Nowak, in whose crowded, cold-water tenement the author lodged for a month. Isherwood entered both the story and building through 'a big stone archway, a bit of old Berlin, daubed with hammers and sickles and Nazi crosses and plastered with tattered bills which advertised auctions or crimes. It was a deep shabby cobbled street, littered with sprawling children in tears.'

In 'The Nowaks', Otto welcomed his lover's fictional persona to the apartment as if they hadn't met in months.

> 'Why . . . it's Christoph!' Otto, as usual, had begun acting at once. His face was slowly illuminated by a sunrise of extreme joy. His cheeks dimpled with smiles. He sprang forward, throwing one arm around my neck, wringing my hand: 'Christoph, you old soul, where have you been hiding all this time?'

Isherwood was veiling reality, teasing the reader with hints of it, while constructing a much more compelling illusion. He even mythologised Stephen Spender's girlfriend, Gisa Soleweitschick, the erudite, chaste, eighteen-year-old daughter of a Lithuanian banker. Gisa – who loved nothing more than long, platonic walks discussing Art – became the fictional Natalia Landauer, aspects of her character being amalgamated with those of Isherwood's wealthy language pupils.

Natalia Landauer 'was a schoolgirl of eighteen', wrote Isherwood. 'She had dark fluffy hair; far too much of it – it made her face, with its sparkling eyes, appear too long and narrow. She reminded me of a young fox.' In the large family sitting room she:

> . . . began talking at once, with terrific animation, in eager stumbling English, showing me gramophone records, pictures, books.

'You like Mozart? Yes? Oh, I also! Vairy much! . . . These picture is in the Kronprinz Palast. You have not seen it? I shall show
you one day, yes? . . . You are fond of Heine? Say quite truthfully,
please?'

Isherwood conceived Natalia Landauer as a foil to Sally Bowles
– a virgin rather than a vamp, innocent instead of libidinous – and
brought the two women together in his story, even though Gisa and
Ross never met in real life.

'I had long meditated the experiment of introducing Natalia
to Sally Bowles,' he quipped, blurring the line between factual
chronicle and fiction. In his story 'The Landauers', Sally arrived
late, announcing that she had been making love 'to a dirty old
Jew producer'. In Bob Fosse's film *Cabaret* – which blended all of
Isherwood's Berlin stories with their Broadway adaptations – the
imagined meeting was made even more daring with a discussion
about syphilis. With prim precision Natalia ventures that the disease can be transmitted by kissing as well as by shared towels and
cups. Sally isn't sure, but she confirms with certainty that it can be
caught by 'screwing'.

With her rudimentary English, Natalia doesn't know the word,
nor any of the string of more graphic synonyms proffered by Sally.
Isherwood's alter ego refuses to help with translation. Then with a
flourish Sally remembers, '*Bumsen*!', the one German word she can
pronounce perfectly.

Through his autobiographical fiction, Isherwood's Berlin became a
literary construct. He transformed ordinary people into extraordinary characters who exuded a new kind of mythical ethos for the
city.

Natalia's fictional cousin Bernhard Landauer was drawn from
Wilfrid B. Israel, an elegant art collector and philanthropist who was
a friend of Einstein and Rathenau. In *Goodbye to Berlin*, after the
Nazis' seizure of power, Bernhard died in their custody, 'a victim
of a heart attack'. In reality Israel was considered by many to be
'the saviour of Berlin', serving as the ambassador of German Jewry

in Britain, helping to arrange the *Kindertransport* mission which rescued 10,000 children from Nazi-controlled territory.

In 1931 a wealthy American named John Blomshield passed through Berlin, indulging Isherwood, Ross and Spender in a week of high-class hedonism. In Isherwood's book Blomshield became Clive, with 'that sad, American air of vagueness which is always attractive, doubly attractive in one who possesses so much money'. Clive flew Sally to Dresden and proposed a globe-hopping *menage à trios*. In *Cabaret* Clive, now a wealthy German baron named Maximilian von Heune, enabled Isherwood's persona finally to come out of the closet. Jealous of the ease with which the rich playboy distorts their friendship, he snaps 'screw' Maximilian. And it's revealed that both he and Sally do.

Berlin meant boys, so Isherwood and Auden claimed. Auden had led the advance to Berlin, drawn by cheap, available partners and sexual freedom. In 'the Passage' he collected teenage hustlers in sailor suits, working-class butcher boys and Eton-cropped youths. He sampled 'rough stuff' at the Hollandais Club and toyed with transvestites at the Eldorado Lounge. Later he and Isherwood – in roll-necked jumper, bell-bottoms and with a perennial freshness – pushed back the heavy leather door curtain and stepped into the Cosy Corner. The scruffy dive on Zossener Straße catered to all tastes, from powdered 'aunties' in pearls to blue-eyed lads with smooth thighs and very short *Lederhosen*. The lavatory had no cubicles. It was a place where things unimagined in their previous fantasies went on, its reality feeding their fictions and vice versa. Isherwood could touch and be touched, stroke and sink into surrender. Homosexuality was illegal in Germany, as was prostitution, yet both hot hunger and cold economic necessity made Berliners flout the law. Auden called the city 'the bugger's daydream'.

But 'Berlin meant boys' was an oversimplification, a soundbite for the 1930s. More broadly the city was both a playground and a laboratory where political radicals battled for the future and lovers coupled as if it didn't exist. Against this backdrop, the true

Isherwood, the gentle Englishman possessed by a romantic view of love, searched for an ideal youth, a partner whom he could cherish in real life.

Before living at Nollendorfstraße, Isherwood had lodged next door to the Institut für Sexualwissenschaft, the world's pioneer institute for sexology. Founded ten years earlier by Magnus Hirschfeld, the opulent Tiergarten mansion housed a busy clinic and research centre. Its library held 20,000 books and over 40,000 confessional and biographical letters. On its panelled wall hung portraits of famous homosexuals, including Frederick the Great. As well as a pre-marital counselling service, the Institute hosted public lectures on all aspects of sexuality.

Hirschfeld's objective was not to 'cure' people but to help them to be at ease with themselves. His work – especially his campaign to decriminalise homosexuality – was supported by Kollwitz, Grosz, Zweig and thousands of other influential Berliners. For five months Isherwood lived in the adjoining house, befriending Hirschfeld and his suave secretary-lover, lunching at the Institute. At its refectory table, where diners often dressed in drag, he began to bring his homosexuality out into the open, no longer hiding it away as a shameful perversion to be indulged only in the dark.

In Isherwood's books the course of heterosexual love rarely ran smooth. Sally – like Jean Ross – became pregnant (Sally by the fictional Klaus Linke, Ross by the charismatic and real Peter van Eyck who'd played the piano at Lady Windermere's). As the Nazis rose to power both men skipped the country, moving to Hollywood where van Eyck later starred in *Wages of Fear* and the Cold War classic *The Spy Who Came in from the Cold*. Like Ross, Sally had an abortion, and Isherwood's publisher tried to cut the incident from the manuscript for fear of upsetting English readers' sensibilities.

To most foreigners Sally became an archetypal Berliner: hustling, sexy, poor and impudent. But as exhilarating as her character remains, Isherwood's books – and their theatrical and cinematic adaptations – endure because of the stage on which he cast his players.

'Here was the seething brew of history in the making,' he wrote later in his semi-fictional autobiography *Christopher and his Kind*, 'a brew which would test the truth of all the political theories, just as actual cooking tests the cookery books. The Berlin brew seethed with unemployment, malnutrition, stock market panic, hatred of the Versailles Treaty and other potent ingredients.'

'I am a camera with its shutter open, quite passive, recording, not thinking. Recording the man shaving at the window opposite and the woman in the kimono washing her hair. Some day, all this will have to be developed, carefully printed, fixed.'

Goodbye to Berlin begins with an illusion of objectivity. But Isherwood was never a mere recorder of surfaces as he once claimed. As a boy he had been given a Box Brownie camera and, through the long summers of childhood, he had taken photographs with his hero father. He had chosen in which direction to point the camera. He had selected, distilled, arranged the action so as to create narrative. In his first book, *The History of My Friends*, handwritten at the age of six or seven, he had developed his childhood companions into characters, tailoring experience into a series of scenes and set pieces, using the techniques of the novel. He had refined his approach through the *Mortmere* saga, and in both his autobiographical fiction and fictional biographies. In part his sexual evasiveness, often disingenuousness on the page, was a source of artistic strength. He created a mercurial, literary persona, substantiated by the illusion of objectivity and authorial detachment, as a fictional synthesis of his true, gay life.

'There is only one protection, one hope for me,' he wrote with apparent intimacy in *Christopher and His Kind*. 'Let me strive and struggle for a certain calm, a certain balance. Let me have courage. Never, never admit one's weakness to one's dearest friend. The only happiness, or indeed sanity, is in a core of detachment. A vital proud core of utter utter indifference, so that one goes one's way. In all humility. But alone.'

Even this 'truth' was also a kind of posturing, another truly elusive illusion.

*

On a late spring evening in 1933 Isherwood watched 25,000
'un-German' books – including Moreck's erotic travel guide and
the Institute of Sexology's complete library – burn beside Unter
den Linden. He heard Goebbels call for jubilant students and Party
thugs 'to commit to the flames the evil spirit of the past'. The Nazi
Propaganda Minister declared, 'The future German man will not
just be a man of books, but a man of character. It is to this end that
we want to educate you.'

Hitler had seized power and willing Germans embraced his bellicose promises, abandoning their Weimar adventure in uncertainty,
beginning their march towards self-destruction. At the entrance
to a Jewish department store Isherwood recognised a youth from
the Cosy Corner, now wearing a storm trooper's uniform. Then he
found himself thinking of Rudi, an enthusiastic Communist who
perhaps, at that very moment, was being tortured to death. Berlin's
pretty boys had become its doomed men.

'I catch sight of my face in the mirror of a shop, and am horrified to see that I am smiling,' he wrote at the end of *Goodbye
to Berlin*. 'You can't help smiling, in such beautiful weather. The
trams are going up and down the Kleiststraße, just as usual. They,
and the people on the pavement, and the tea-cosy dome of the
Nollendorfplatz station have an air of curious familiarity, of striking
resemblance to something one remembers as normal and pleasant
in the past – like a very good photograph.'

'No,' he concluded as if to authenticate his own half-truths.
'Even now I can't altogether believe that any of this really
happened . . .'

The facts of Isherwood's own Berlin days and nights will never all
be known. Around the time of *Goodbye to Berlin*'s publication, in
an act as iconic as his characters themselves, he burnt his original
diaries. He said that he had 'destroyed his real Past' because he
preferred the simplified 'more exciting fictitious Past which he had
created to take its place'. His explanation remains unconvincing
but in truth the diaries would have been only of academic interest.

The work which was distilled from them remains of greater importance than the artist himself.

I am a camera, he wrote, then pressed the shutter and snapped a myth.

CHAPTER 12

*Bertolt Brecht,
Luck and the Epic*

Programme from a production of *The Threepenny Opera* by Bertolt Brecht, 1945. (*Bildarchiv Pisarek/akg-images*)

Theater am Schiffbauerdamm, 1928

Berlin, 1 September 1928

My dear brother

Apologies for not sending word of my arrival sooner. Summer was crazy busy with my graduation, farewells at home and finding my feet here in the Hauptstadt. *Max Reinhardt didn't meet me at the station – as you joked he might – but I have found a theatre job and kissed Marlene Dietrich!*

Let me start at the beginning. Berlin is vast, the size of two dozen Duisburgs, with thirty-five serious playhouses, a gigantic circus, beer halls the size of railroad terminals and wine palaces four storeys high. There are seven U-Bahn lines, a hundred cinemas and a Karstadt department store with fifteen-metre light column which helps to guide aeroplanes into Tempelhof airport. Walk in any direction and you'll happen upon a futurist art exhibition, an international tango competition or a six-day street cycle race. Drop into any cinema and you'll see hundreds of shop

*girls staring at the screen, blotting their eyes in the darkness, their
hearts filled with romance as their spotty-cheeked beau inches his
hand up their thigh. At the Philharmonic Wilhelm Furtwängler is
preparing to conduct his fifth season. Otto Klemperer is running
the Kroll Opera. Richard Strauss, Pablo Casals and Toscanini
are booked for the next Berlin Music Festival. And at this very
moment Fritz Lang and Max Schmeling are probably arguing
about nude revues at the Romanisches Café.*

*I feel that I already know the city, having tramped along
so many of its streets. On my arrival I immediately started
knocking on doors at the Kammerspiele, the Tribüne and the
Berliner Theater. You'd think it'd be easy to find work given that
my* Summernightsdream *was voted 'most innovative' student
production at the Folkwangschule. But not one of the managers
could find my letter, so thanks for the suggestion to bring a
carbon copy. All of them promised to get back to me yet – when I
returned to the Lustspielhaus to retrieve my fedora – I saw that its
manager had filed my application in the bin. I felt so disheartened,
one of the unknown nobodies who will never grasp their dream,
that I almost called by the Hotel Adlon and used father's letter of
introduction.*

*Then on my birthday I spoilt myself with a ticket (restricted
view, in the gods) to* It's in the Air. *The musical review (book
and lyrics by Marcellus Schiffer, music by Mischa Spoliansky) is
the hit of the season. I chose it because of Dietrich, of course, who
sang a duet with Margo Lion about shopping for lingerie,
laughing about the discoveries to be made at a store's 'peekaboo
counter'. Hilarious! Afterwards I waited at the stage door – along
with every other single male in town – and somehow managed
to catch her eye. She autographed my programme and gave me a
peck on the cheek when I said how much I loved her in* Chin Up,
Charly. *Tell that to your boring colleagues at the library, dear
brother!*

*The event did give me a 'chin up' and the very next morning I
tried the Theater am Schiffbauerdamm, which is on the Spree by
old Weidendammer Brücke. As luck would have it rehearsals had*

just begun on a new production and I was hired on the spot as a
backstage assistant! A dream come true!

I was over the moon with the job . . . until I saw the first run-
through. The play is so anarchic that I found myself wishing for a
steady and predictable Lessing or Schiller. I stared slack-jawed at
the arguing actors and foul-mouthed director, too shocked to move,
apart from when they sent me out to replenish their brandy supply.
Where's the emotion? I thought. Where's the catharsis? Theatre was
never like this in Duisburg. If only I could have found a job at the
Komödie with Dietrich (and her legs . . . You've seen the ads for
Etam 'artificial silk' stockings?).

The play is called (at the moment at least, nothing is fixed,
everything keeps changing) The Threepenny Opera *and it's*
written and directed by Bertolt Brecht, whose Man Equals Man
we walked out of two years ago in Düsseldorf (you'll remember his
farcical 'intermission piece' when the protagonist becomes a baby
elephant accused of murdering its mother). The story is promising
enough: crime, immorality and betrayal in Victorian London's
underworld. But Brecht has murdered it with his convoluted
plot and cockeyed theories, the intention of which is to detach the
audience – sorry, the 'observers' – from the 'illusory' narrative
and leave them unmoved by the emotions of the characters.

The production's origins are as warped as its realisation.
Earlier this year Ernst Josef Aufricht – a twenty-nine-year-old
actor who treads the boards here – fancied himself as a producer
and rented the Theater am Schiffbauerdamm (with a loan of
100,000 Goldmarks from his father). But he had no play and
none of the usual suspects – Toller, Feuchtwanger et al – had
anything suitable. By chance Aufricht ran into Brecht at the Café
Schlichter. Never slow at coming forward, Brecht pitched an
idea for a musical based on John Gay's The Beggar's Opera.
According to Kurt Gerron (who plays police chief 'Tiger' Brown
in Threepenny *and has become a bit of a pal), Brecht's erstwhile*
lover Elisabeth Hauptmann had been slogging away at the
translation for months in an attempt to regain her 'maestro's'
attention. Brecht dashed home to Spichernstraße and typed up

*half a dozen scenes from Hauptmann's draft. Aufricht liked them
enough and agreed that composer Kurt Weill could write the music.*

*Rehearsals started at the beginning of August, and disaster
followed disaster. Helene Weigel came down with appendicitis.
Carola Neher – another of Brecht's jam tarts – arrived two
weeks late following her husband's death from tuberculosis. She
worked for a week, swathed in widow's weeds, then quit. In her
place Roma Bahn was recruited only four days before opening
night. Harald Paulsen, cast as the amoral Macheath ('London's
greatest and most notorious criminal'), lost his voice. Erich Ponto
(Peachum) turned up in Aufricht's office with his bags packed,
saying he was going home to Dresden. Naphtali Lehrmann, who
plays the beggar Filch, demanded that his fee be tripled and paid
in cash before the premiere.*

*Brecht's schizophrenic direction seemed to jinx the show. He
ponced about in his proletarian disguise, looking hungry and
old (he's thirty). Every morning he made the actors read the text
afresh, calling the playwright (i.e. himself) a fool, speaking of him
in the third person.*

*'Anyone can be creative; it's rewriting other people's work
that is the challenge,' he declared, rolling his 'r's like a Bavarian
peasant (in fact his father was the managing director of an
Augsburg paper mill).*

*He scribbled a new scene over lunch at the Hotel Bristol. He
admitted to learning (i.e. stealing) 'the essence of the epic' from
Döblin's* Berlin Alexanderplatz. *Time and again he went out
with the actors, ostensibly to discuss his 'alienation effect' but in
truth (I suspect) to drink with the men and to sleep with the women
(or vice versa; one can never tell in Berlin).*

*Above all Brecht 'collaborated', downplaying the importance
of the individual in creative construct (which suits his character
given that he doesn't give a damn about people, unless they are
of use to him). So it was that Feuchtwanger came up with the
title. The Viennese satirist Karl Kraus wrote the second verse of
the* Zankduett. *Weigel, Hauptmann and Neher (before she had
the good sense to get out) looked daggers at each other across*

*the shifting circle. Brecht – in leather jacket, grimy white shirt
and with well-chewed cigar – sat with Weill at the centre of the
conspirators throwing out ideas and general abuse. In this way the
so-called musical was cobbled together from the debris of so many
crises.*

*'The theatre is a debating hall, not a place of illusions,' he
shouted out late one night.*

*He thinks that an audience should watch a play with the
dispassionate detachment of a jury, if you can believe it. He
doesn't want them to be taken out of themselves, to empathise
with a character, or to be lulled into a 'dull, trance-like state'.
Instead he wants them to retain critical detachment. He uses all
manner of trickery to disrupt traditional theatrical illusion:
actors speak of their character's development, or call out their own
stage directions; sudden changes of light interrupt the narrative
flow, banners describe the unfolding action. No surprise that a
character's inner life is not of importance to Brecht.*

*As you know, I like strong, moving stories. I like plays in which
delightful things happen. I like theatre to order the chaos, not to
spew it across the stage. I ask you, what's the good if a red-hot
lump of iron hits you and blots out life and the world?*

*I'm putting this whole period down to 'experience', although
I doubt I'll ever mention it in my curriculum vitae. Mind you,
there has been a single redeeming moment. As I said Brecht likes
to involve any and everyone in his bull sessions. Two days before
the opening – sometime after midnight, while I was collecting
the empties – he dragged me into the circle. At that very moment
Harald Paulsen – in sinister black tailored suit and bowler hat –
threatened to quit if he wasn't given a 'grand' introduction. The
cast threw up their arms in despair. The musicians laid down
their instruments and headed for the nearest bar. No one was in
control.*

*Until then I hadn't been able to open my mouth without
triggering Brecht's sarcasm. But in the confusion I ventured that
he should build on his medieval motif, perhaps beginning with
a* Morität *– or 'deadly deed' ballad – as sung by the minstrels*

who had once frequented London (and Berlin). After all, I knew
– but didn't say – he'd already lifted text for four songs from the
fifteenth-century wandering poet François Villon. Brecht laughed
(he does that when he likes an idea) and by the next morning he
and Weill had won over Paulsen with 'Die Morität von Mackie
Messer', or 'Mack the Knife'. Even I had to admit that the song
wasn't bad.

The final dress rehearsal ended at six o'clock this morning.
Everyone went home to sleep for an hour, apart from Brecht
who stayed up to cut forty-five minutes from the script. The rest
of the day then wasted away organising the lights and failing to
operate a shambolic mechanical horse on which – in a parody of a
happy ending – Queen Victoria's messenger arrives to pardon the
condemned Macheath and grant him a castle and pension. On the
test run the horse jumped its tracks and pitched the rider into the
stalls.

An hour before curtain-up the cleaning ladies arrived with
their brooms and producer Aufricht ordered Brecht, by now
exhausted and frantic, off the stage.

'Never again will I step into this theatre,' he snapped back in
anger.

'Me neither,' added Weill in his tinny voice.

Success seems to be a matter of luck, or fashion, which every
artist must accept, or go mad. Chance can make or break a career,
determining whether talent is thrown into the limelight or left
forgotten in the shadows. The audience sat stony-faced through
the first half, the silence broken only by the backstage roar of
Weill. He'd discovered that his wife Lotte Lenya – who plays the
prostitute Jenny – had been left off the programme. 'This place is
a mess, a pigsty!' he raged at Aufricht. 'I forbid my wife to go back
on stage.'

But Lotte did return after the interval, and soon the audience
started to clap, to shout, then to roar with approval. As they
lost their hearts to this savage critique of the world, a mean
satisfaction came over me. To my mind, Brecht had utterly failed.
His audience were not 'dispassionate jurors'. As they left the

theatre whistling 'Mack the Knife', I knew that despite his best efforts they had been swept away by their emotions. So much for his 'epic' Verfremdungseffekt*!*

On the way home this evening I read the first reviews. In the Berliner Tagesblatt *Alfred Kerr called the play rubbish. The* Kreuzzeitung *dismissed it as 'literary necrophilia'. The* Threepenny Opera *looks certain to close before next weekend.*

Dear brother, I must stop now and try to sleep before the second show, assuming anyone bothers to turn up for it. On Monday I'll see if any jobs have come up at the Komödie. I promise to write to you again but for now it's probably best not to mention to anyone the sort of people I've met here in Berlin (except Dietrich of course).

With fondest regards from your loving brother,
Ernst

CHAPTER 13

*Marlene Dietrich,
on Becoming*

Marlene Dietrich, Anna May Wong and Leni Riefenstahl with an unidentified man at the Berlin Costume Arts Ball, 1928. (*photograph by Alfred Eisenstaedt, Time & Life Pictures/Getty Images*)

Babelsberg, 1929

'Five minutes for light.'

Bodies materialised out of the shadows. Ladders slid into the glare. A ballet of best boys, with clothes pegs in mouths and tools swinging from hips, darted up into the grid. Barn doors scraped and shadows swept across the set. The cameraman spotted the lamps. His gaffer checked for reflections. The boom operator lifted the microphone out of frame. Behind them props flirted with sound. Continuity reset her stopwatch.

At the centre of the cinematic dance, wardrobe trimmed the young woman's spangled black dress with a safety pin. Make-up retouched her lips for the close-up. The assistant director moved through the crew, watching the clock, waiting for the moment.

'Let's do this, people,' he called. '*Ruhe, bitte*. First positions please.'

The technicians dissolved back into the dark. The heavy stage door boomed shut. The studio bell rang and the red light flashed. The director planted himself beside the camera, glaring forward with an intensity as if imagination alone could animate the scene.

'Turn over sound. Mark it.'

Silence fell. Film rolled. In a blaze of light, Marlene Dietrich lifted her eyes to the glinting lens, and stared down time.

The slate covered her face for a moment. When the clapper-loader drew it away, she was in character, laying her smoking cigarette on the edge of the piano, plucking an imaginary shred of tobacco from her tongue. She glanced over her shoulders, flaunting her extravagant beauty and – with a nod to the unseen piano player – started to sing.

'You're the cream in my coffee, you're the salt in my soup . . .'

She sang with charm and calculated resignation, presenting herself as a coy soubrette, until the music faltered and she flashed with professional anger.

'Call that music?' she ad-libbed, insulting the pianist. 'You're not playing a washboard, you know. Play it again.'

Dietrich had been spotted on stage the evening before by the notorious Josef von Sternberg. That morning she had been summoned to Babelsberg for a screen test. She knew that the director was casting *The Blue Angel* but she refused to play the eager pierrette for him. In any case all of Berlin believed that someone else had already been chosen as the film's cabaret singer, except for Leni Riefenstahl who was convinced that the part was hers alone.

In his office, where Sternberg had made her walk up and down like a prize pony, Dietrich had fawned disinterest. She'd told him that she photographed badly and that her nose stuck up like a duck's ass. She claimed that her first three films had failed because of amateur direction (in truth she had already appeared in seventeen movies). She'd shrugged her silver foxes off her shoulders and added that she had seen all his pictures, and realised that he couldn't handle women.

Now in front of his camera, Dietrich dragged again on her cigarette, spat out another fleck of tobacco, and spun a story at the turning point of her life.

'Christ Almighty! Am I meant to sing to that old crap?'

She slammed the piano top with the palm of her hand, stalked out from behind it and swiped at the pianist's head.

'What do you have for brains? I guess you've misplaced your genius.'

She stepped onto the keyboard and hitched up her body-skimming dress. She crossed her long, bare legs and rolled up her stockings, instructing him in German,

'If you screw up again, I'll kick you.'

Then with a flourish she launched into 'Wer wird denn weinen?' 'Why cry when there's another man around the corner?' She leant back on the piano and into her song, her voice throaty and full, her right hand riding on her hip in a kind of private ecstasy. Pleasure seemed to take hold of her like a drug. Her heavy-lidded eyes were at once inviting yet defiant and insolent. The test lasted for only three minutes but her bold, taunting, promising performance was captured for ever.

As the clapper-loader's hand closed over the lens, marking the end of the shot, the actress leant across to her harangued accompanist, dropped her eyes and whispered *'Entschuldigung'*, both apologising for and laughing at her gall.

'Tu was.'

The myth of Dietrich, the singular Berliner who became one of her century's great icons, began with an order. 'Tu was.' Do something, her mother told her. Make something of your life. *Become* someone.

Dietrich all but imagined herself into being. A sensual and sensuous child christened Marie Magdalene, she renamed herself Marlene at the age of three. Her father, a lieutenant in the Imperial Police, vanished when she was six years old. Her mother's second husband, a grenadier officer, also disappeared, fatally wounded on the Russian Front in 1916. Dietrich grew up in a world without men. On summer evenings during the war she balanced on the open metal footbridge over the Anhalter main line near her Leberstraße home, waiting for the puffing troop trains. When they passed beneath, her skirts billowed in the moist steam and she imagined in it the smell of the arms, the leather belts, the warm sweat and breath. She imagined all the fathers and boys gazing up at her.

At home she filled the vacuum by adopting roles which both comforted and challenged her mother. She called herself Paul, a habit which the older woman indulged, playing a part, learning to *become* whomever or whatever was needed. Marlene loved to perform, to stir, to be adored by wandering eyes. She learnt the lute, piano and violin, perfecting fingering and finesse, her discipline giving her the means to express herself.

At eighteen she left Berlin for the Musikhochschule in Weimar, 280 kilometres to the south-west, humbling classmates with her diligence, scandalising them too as she sailed off to private lessons in flimsy chiffon. The power of her budding sexuality now thrilled her, as it did the teacher who became her first lover. She was shaken by the desire that she awoke in him. All that existed was his body, his smell, his hard embrace. His friend, a violin-maker thirty years her senior, became her second conquest. Younger men – including painters and designers from the newly established Bauhaus – waited for her outside Frau Stein's boarding house. When their gaze fell on her, her breath shortened, excitement gripped her chest, and she became their mistress, their whore, their angel.

But by 1921 her mother's eroded pension no longer covered the school fees. It wouldn't even buy a loaf of bread. Dietrich was forced to return to Berlin and into work as an UFA concert mistress. In the dimly lit orchestra pit she played the violin, distracting the other members of the all-male ensemble with her legs. She studied the tempo and tone of the silent films projected above her head, accompanying her screen idol Henny Porten's actions over and over again, learning the hidden grammar of performance and movie-making – until she was fired for ruining the men's concentration.

She laid the violin aside, took off her head-hugging cloche hat and stepped onto the stage. At the Theater des Westens and with Guido Thielscher's high-kicking *Girl-Kabarett*, she felt the erotic frisson which her *becoming* stirred in her audience. She auditioned for Max Reinhardt, the finest impresario in the world, missed her chance by overacting, then wooed her way into his company as a private student. By her twenty-first birthday she had played seven roles in five plays at his Deutsches Theater and Großes Schauspielhaus.

At the same time she began to slip into movies, playing bit parts in a Tolstoy folk tale and comedies like *The Little Napoleon* and *Chin Up, Charly*. Some roles she won through her wiles, wearing a negligée and carrying a puppy to one casting session, but most parts came to her simply because of her presence.

'Many people have their dreams behind them, many before them,' said a fellow Reinhardt actor. 'Marlene carries hers with her, and wears them like a halo.'

War and inflation had made the German film industry. The world's first moving picture had been shown at the Wintergarten on Friedrichstraße in 1895, two months before the Lumière brothers had unveiled their superior system in Paris. Over the next twenty years, Berliners – like audiences around the world – had flocked to the new dream palaces to see Italian comedies, Swedish dramas and above all Hollywood Westerns. But in 1914 the Kaiser banned the enemy's movies. For the next decade foreign producers couldn't – and when the economy collapsed wouldn't – import their pictures. Lillian Gish and Rudolph Valentino were all but unknown in Berlin. German film-makers responded first by churning out patriotic potboilers at the Babelsberg propaganda factory, and then by creating a cinematic culture of their own.

By the mid-1920s Berlin was the fastest city in the world, for the rich and young. Headlamps glittered off wet asphalt, neon flashed on cinema façades, driving away the night, drawing Berliners to screenings of Walter Ruttmann's *Berlin: Die Sinfonie der Großstadt*. In his kinetic, rhythmic celebration of the capital, light bulbs sparked off assembly lines, banks of typists clitter-clattered and newspaper headlines cried out 'Crisis!' then 'Money! Money!' The old, steady values of morality, of ethics, of decency had been lost. On the screen, stage and page Berliners debated how to regain control of their lives, or surrendered themselves to hedonism, materialism and the machine.

Artistic isolation stimulated the production of as many as 600 features a year including the Expressionistic horror *The Cabinet of Dr Caligari* and Murnau's *Nosferatu*. Fritz Lang's *Nibelungen Saga*, an epic set in the mythical past, was succeeded by *Metropolis*, his futuristic masterwork which would bankrupt the studio. German movies were seen as both electric poetry and revolutionary art form, bridging the class divide, acknowledged as Hollywood's only real competitor.

Dietrich swept through the chaotic, creative decade wearing a monocle and boa, or wolf skins and a turban, with laughing yet enchanted strangers following her through the streets. She studied her performances in minor films like *Manon Lescaut* and *The Bogus Baron*, learning to express herself more by doing less. In a self-service photo booth she struck pose after pose in search of her look. She discovered the most flattering light for her face, and found which film stocks darkened her hair and eyes.

She also came out again as a boy, or at least as a *garçonne*, a fast and fearless young woman who behaved like an androgynous young man. In *From Mouth to Mouth*, the lesbian cabaret artiste Claire Waldoff taught her how to put over a song, and much else. She refined her craft and came to personify sex without gender. Both on and off stage she oozed the promise of erotic adventure, ravishing camera and audience alike, as if offering herself to each individual alone, whatever their sex, whatever their preference.

In 1929, when Sternberg first heard Dietrich speak, in both German and English, he knew that he wanted her, and not only for *The Blue Angel*. The ten-week shoot began in November. On the first day Buster Keaton dropped by Stage 5, as did Max Reinhardt, George Grosz and Sergei Eisenstein, the pioneering Soviet director who was in town to promote *Battleship Potemkin* and *October (Ten Days that Shook the World)*. On the afternoon that Riefenstahl – who would later create the Nazis' infamous propaganda films – visited the set, Dietrich sat spread-eagled on a barrel, in silk stockings and white top hat, singing 'Falling in Love Again'. 'You sow, pull up your pants,' barked Sternberg, as she flaunted herself for the visitors. 'Everyone can see your pubic hair.'

The Blue Angel was based on Heinrich Mann's novel *Professor Unrat*, a bitter condemnation of Weimar society in which a stuffy teacher falls in love with a jaded cabaret singer. But the chemistry between Sternberg and Dietrich – as well as the demands of UFA's reactionary boss, Alfred Hugenberg – shifted the focus away from politics and onto the singer. Years were lopped of her character's age as she was transformed into a sultry, unsentimental temptress who simply could not resist falling in love again. Sternberg also changed the character's name from prim Rosa Fröhlich to lusty Lola Lola. The club in which she performed became *der blaue Engel* – 'the intoxicated angel' in German slang.

Babelsberg is the oldest large-scale film studio in the world. A few kilometres south-west of Haber's Dahlem, technicians hurried along its lanes between stages and backlot, prop carts glided from paint shops to production offices. In summer, actors and actresses idled away the hours between shots in deckchairs beneath the birches in the sunny grass courtyard. In winter, extras huddled in the canteen over steaming bowls of *Berliner Bohnensuppe*, counting up their overtime. But behind the studio's vast soundproof doors it is forever spring, or midnight, or a halcyon August evening before the outbreak of war, at least until the scene is shot and the set struck. Women are forever young, leading men heroic and life's turning points clearly defined in cinema's grand narrative structure.

On Stage 5 Dietrich concocted her shocking look – sheer peignoir, threadbare kimono, satin collars and lamé cuffs – from wardrobe left over from her own plays and revues. She plucked the top hat and knickers from a Berlin male prostitute of her acquaintance. 'I dress for the image,' she said, meaning the illusion. 'Not for myself, not for the public, not for fashion, not for men.'

Sternberg also wanted to shock. He wanted to compose seductive, caressing images and – in the early days of the talkies – to capture 'raw, immediate' sound. He wanted to envelop the audience in *Klang*, as he called it, the sound of hard heels on cobble-stones, of barking dogs, of a singing canary, above all of Dietrich's voice.

Sternberg was obsessed with both the woman and the movie. He lavished attention on her cabaret numbers, shooting them in long, uninterrupted takes. He ensured that her smouldering songs slithered into the hearts of the audience, moving them, entrapping them, overwhelming them. The self-important Emil Jannings – a major star who played the part of the teacher – could only watch as the picture was stolen from him. During the filming of the stran-gulation scene his anger flared and he left real bruises on Dietrich's neck.

Only one group failed to be seduced by the picture. The studio executives, including Hitler's future Finance Minister Hugenberg, abhorred it. At the dawn of a new German age, Lola Lola could not be seen to conquer and humiliate a dutiful and obedient estab-lishment figure without consequence. To underline her depravity, and drive home a reactionary message, the end of the movie was changed. But Hugenberg's outrage – and political ambition – blinded him to the qualities of Dietrich's electrifying performance. He cancelled the contract which would have bound her to UFA and Babelsberg.

The Blue Angel became her film, capturing for ever the passion, despair and amorality of – in Döblin's words – 'Sodom on the eve of destruction'. At the Kurfürstendamm premiere, along the red carpet and in a blaze of flash bulbs, Berliners stamped and roared with heady delight. Dietrich, in a long white gown and furs, took half a dozen curtain calls. She clutched a vast bouquet of roses, stepped into her waiting car and left for Hollywood.

Without *The Blue Angel*, Marlene Dietrich might have remained in Germany. She might have focused on her stage work with producer Robert Klein, continued as a musical performer, accepted an in-vitation to meet Adolf Hitler. The rising leader admired her work; not so many years later Riefenstahl found him screening Dietrich's films in private at his Berchtesgaden eyrie. But Dietrich chose to leave, as too did Sternberg, Lang, Peter Lorre, Billy Wilder, Brecht and Weill. Kurt Gerron, who had sung 'Mack the Knife' at the Theater am Schiffbauerdamm and starred in *Diary of a Lost Girl*, stayed behind and was murdered in the camps with so many others.

She made her Hollywood entrance at the Beverly Wilshire Hotel, descending into the ballroom and a Paramount A-list party as if from the heavens; a radiant, mysterious, mortal seductress. Sternberg abandoned his wife to guide and groom his star. He put her on a diet, sent her to a voice coach, supervised a make-up makeover. In California Dietrich became thinner and more beautiful. Her eyes seemed to grow larger, her cheekbones lifted, even her 'duck nose' appeared to straighten when a fine silver line was drawn along it. In his pomposity Sternberg claimed that she was his invention, just another actor who could be 'turned on and off like a spigot'. More kindly Dietrich recalled that 'he was always forcing me to think, to use my brain and learn something when I was working; not merely to do what I was told'. Together they made six more films, including *Blonde Venus* and *The Devil is a Woman*, polishing her screen persona, creating an icon.

In Germany Joseph Goebbels, the diabolical hypnotist, had seized control of the media through men like Hugenberg. He had disrupted showings of Erich Maria Remarque's anti-war film *All Quiet on the Western Front* by letting off stink bombs and releasing white mice in the auditorium. He'd protested against its 'unpatriotic' stance, causing it to be banned as 'a threat to German honour'. He made the film industry subordinate and subservient to the emergent dictatorship, asserting his right 'to supervise the formation of public opinion'. The director Karl Ritter – like thousands of film professionals – responded by 'lifting his ambitions from the depths of superficial entertainment and the pursuit of commercial gain to the level of an artistic and state-political creation'. The directors, producers, performers and technicians who did not – or could not – flee became the Nazis' willing perpetrators, confused collaborators or victims.

Dietrich wanted no part in Goebbels' 'state-political creations'.

She used her Hollywood salary to buy dozens of people passage to America, as well as to donate money to the *Filmkammer's* welfare fund, both to protect her mother who remained in Berlin and because of the Nazis' blackmail tactics. The Propaganda Minister was determined either to seduce the star back to the Reich, or to defame her for ever. As the state press vilified *The Blue Angel* as 'mediocre and corrupting *Kitsch*', Goebbels sent an envoy to meet her. He may have been Rudolf Hess, Hitler's deputy, or Joachim von Ribbentrop, the future Foreign Minister, accounts vary as to his identity; but whoever he was, the envoy clicked his heels and declared, 'The Führer wants you to come home.'

Dietrich responded, 'The only reason he keeps sending his "so important" officers . . . is because he saw me in *The Blue Angel* and wants to get into those lace knickers.'

In the last summer of peace Dietrich became an American citizen. On the French Riviera she danced with a teenage John F. Kennedy and his father, who was American ambassador to Britain, never suspecting that in little more than twenty years JFK would save her beloved Berlin from another enslavement. As her ship sailed west across the Atlantic, towards her twelfth Hollywood picture, she said in a radio interview, 'We Germans wanted a Führer, and we got one, right? We Germans are all like that. We want a Führer. And what happens? The ghastly Hitler comes along and everyone says, "Wonderful, here's a real Führer. Somebody tell us what to do."'

Hitler told them to attack Poland and her countrymen marched towards a holocaust. But Dietrich didn't follow them. Instead she threw herself behind the Allies, promoting the sale of American war bonds and performing for the USO, the military entertainment organisation, bringing morale-boosting shows to the troops, allowing herself to be sawn in half by Orson Welles.

'But Orson, how does this trick work?' she asked once locked in his magic box.

'Just wait, Marlene. This'll kill you,' Wells responded.

As America turned against Hitler's war machine, she pulled together a raucous show with comedian Danny Thomas. She took it to North Africa and then Italy, sweeping on stage in a tailored officer's uniform, slipping into her body-hugging 'nude' gown, singing her hit 'See What the Boys in the Back Room Will Have' and playing a musical saw between her open legs. In Algiers and Naples, on Sardinia and at Anzio she thrilled as many as 20,000 soldiers at a time, standing ankle-deep in mud, huddled under ponchos in the rain, lifting their hearts and courage. She even gave herself to a lucky few.

'Bravery is simple when you're defending your own country,' she said, but the lonely GIs 'fighting on foreign soil . . . had their eyes shot out and their brains, their bodies torn, their flesh burnt. They accepted pain and mutilation as if they fought and fell defending their own soil. That made them the bravest of all.'

Her USO work became her third great passion (after 'music and sex'). But as she cheered for America, she wept for the Germans. She feared for her mother, isolated in Berlin, perhaps killed by the Allied airmen she willed to fight on. During a US Armed Forces Network broadcast she suddenly switched languages, knowing that the radio signal would be carried across the front line.

'Jungs! Opfert euch nicht! Der Krieg ist doch Scheiße, Hitler ist ein Idiot!' 'Boys! Don't sacrifice yourselves! This war is shit, Hitler is an idiot!'

Then she launched into 'Lili Marlene' in German.

She travelled by DC-3 and jeep through Belgium and Holland, slept in the open at the Battle of the Bulge, washed her face and underclothes in snow melted inside her helmet, contracted crabs and pneumonia. George Patton gave her a pearl-handled revolver in case she was captured. In Paris she and friend Ernest Hemingway drafted the guest list for her funeral. Over the border in Aachen she performed in the ruins of a cinema where *The Blue Angel* had once shown. She gave her winter cap to photographer Robert Capa the night before he was killed in the Ardennes. In Bavaria close to Berchtesgaden she wondered, had she accepted Goebbels' invitation and given herself to Hitler as his celluloid Queen of the Reich, 'if I just might have been the one person in the world who could have prevented the war and saved millions of lives'.

In September 1945 Dietrich flew to Berlin wearing her American Army uniform. The Kaiser Wilhelm Memorial Church was a broken-tooth wreck. Beyond it the Tauentzienstraße – where lively schoolgirls had once turned tricks – was in ashes. A downed American bomber had crashed into KaDeWe, gutting the store where she'd bought her silk camisoles and ready-chilled Krug champagne. The rank and dusty *Berliner Luft* rumbled with the sound of thunder, as tottering ruins were dynamited.

Her mother was alive and together the two women went in search of their blitzed family home. They found a building blasted with shell holes, its balcony suspended in space with red geraniums dangling above their heads. Dietrich's mother began to search through the rubble. After a moment she uncovered an undamaged bronze mask of her daughter's face. She clutched it to her chest and wept. One month later she died of a heart attack.

After the war Dietrich went back to Hollywood, leaving her heart behind in Berlin, making *Rancho Notorious* and *Touch of Evil*, until her return to the stage propelled her to greater stardom. At the Sahara Hotel in Las Vegas she launched her solo show and, through the 1950s, became the highest-paid nightclub performer in the world. She toured America and then the world, wearing skin-tight net dresses and little else, thrilling audiences with 'Lili Marlene', 'Falling in Love Again' and – after Burt Bacharach became her musical director – the anti-war anthem 'Where Have all the Flowers Gone?'. Noël Coward introduced her to London. Maurice Chevalier and Jean Cocteau celebrated her in Paris. The Beatles were her support act at a Royal Command Performance. In Poland she laid flowers at the Memorial of the Warsaw Uprising, six years before West German Chancellor Willy Brandt knelt in ignominy at the same spot. In Leningrad – where the Nazi siege had caused the deaths of more than half a million residents – she bowed before the audience and Nobel nominee author Konstantin Paustovsky. 'She *knows* where all the flowers went – buried in the mud of Passchendaele, blasted to ash at Hiroshima, napalmed to a crisp in Vietnam – and she carries the knowledge in her voice,' wrote Kenneth Tynan in *Playbill*.

Dietrich also returned to Germany, her tour preceded by a flood of hate mail and public demonstrations. Patriotic Germans shouted 'Marlene Go Home!', resenting the woman who had risked her life to rebuke them. Vienna and Essen cancelled her shows. Her five appearances in Berlin were reduced to three. On Schlosstraße the Titania Palast handed out free tickets to fill the empty seats. Yet the shows were a critical success. She gave eighteen encores in Berlin and was rewarded with sixty-two curtain calls in Munich. Then in Düsseldorf a twenty-year-old woman caught her sleeve, cried out 'Traitor!' and spat in her face. She finished the tour not with 'Ich hab' noch einen Koffer in Berlin' – 'I still have a suitcase in Berlin' – but with 'Frag nicht warum ich gehe'. 'Don't ask me why I go.'

She never went home again.

Even her last important film was shown for only a single night in Germany. In December 1961 *Judgment at Nuremberg* premiered at the Kongresshalle, a modern, shell-like building which Berliners call 'the pregnant oyster'. In the war crimes courtroom drama Dietrich played a general's widow, a dutiful Prussian who took pride in her discipline and unquestioning obedience. She told judge Spencer Tracy that her mission at the trial was 'to convince you that we're not all monsters'. Yet when the guilty verdict was read aloud, she was unable to comprehend her own culpability.

The Berlin audience reacted with horror, watching themselves portrayed by the actress who had humiliated them in real life. As the tail credits rolled they slipped away into the night, in silence. Germans were not yet ready to confront those years, to face up to a shameful past. They still wanted to believe that the war was – in Thomas Mann's crisp phrase – 'a crime committed against the German people by its leaders'. They wanted to forget.

In her late sixties Dietrich started breaking bones: her shoulder in Wiesbaden, two ribs in Australia, a thumb and numerous toes in Los Angeles. In Washington she fell into the orchestra pit and gashed open her thigh. In 1975 at the age of seventy-three she made her final appearance on stage when she slipped and snapped a femur. She retreated to Paris, becoming a recluse, living in isolation in her apartment on Avenue Montaigne.

Two years later she was asked to appear in the most expensive German film made up until that time. The picture told the story of a young Prussian officer's return to Berlin after the defeat of the First World War. In an attempt to regain his lost honour, the officer joined the ranks of the handsome Eden Hotel gigolos, only to be killed in street fighting between Nazis and Communists. The officer was to be played by then Berlin resident David Bowie.

The producer took six months to convince her to play the part of the gigolo's madame. Every time he telephoned her apartment, a woman breathed into the receiver, 'This is the maid. Madame is lunching at Versailles.'

The maid, of course, was Dietrich.

When they did speak she claimed to be too busy, that she was writing her memoirs and couldn't leave Paris. In truth she was frightened of being incapable of living up to her own legend, frightened of the toll of years. But in the end the chance to sing on screen one of the songs from her Weimar stage days proved too enticing. She agreed, on condition that Berlin came to her: German technicians, two tons of equipment and the complete set of the Eden Hotel.

The seventy-seven-year-old woman who mounted the steps of the suburban Parisian studio brought back few memories of *Shanghai Express*. She wore a tired denim trouser suit and hid by the door. Her lips quivered as the crew were introduced to her. She refused to take off her dark glasses. The make-up artist moved to her side, and spirited her away to the dressing room.

Sixteen years had passed since her last film appearance, fifty years since Sternberg had cast her in *The Blue Angel*. Now, two hours after her arrival, she reappeared, wearing a wide-brim hat and deep veil over her face. In costume she began to find her confidence, the clothes helping to ease her into the role. She walked onto the set without assistance, sat down and let her long skirt – split to the thigh – slip open. As the crew tried not to stare at her still-beautiful, sculpted calves, a smile flitted across her face.

Before the song a few lines of dialogue had to be shot. In the scene Dietrich's character recruited a young David Bowie as a gigolo. But Bowie was not on the set. He wasn't even in France. His part of the scene had already been shot in Berlin. The two actors would come together only in the editing room. Director David Hemmings – who'd played the photographer in Antonioni's *Blow-Up* – stood in for Bowie, feeding Dietrich her cues.

'Do they pay you extra for this crap?' she snapped at him. She was not pleased. Bowie was one of the reasons she had agreed to take the part. 'We learnt this old trick from Mack Sennett.'

The anger swelled her confidence, rather than undermined it. Raymond Bernard, her pianist, helped by filling the pauses between shots with 'Falling in Love Again'. Dietrich stood by the piano and listened, much as she had in that first screen test at Babelsberg. Then with similar irritation she insisted on it being retuned, for the third time that day: 'Otherwise you know what people are,' she said to me. 'They will be sure to think it's me that's out of tune.'

The lights were checked, again. Exposure and focus set, again. As she had only agreed to sing once, the scene was to be photographed with two cameras. I was the director's assistant and asked to operate the second Arriflex. We took our positions, settled ourselves, waited for, 'Quiet please. Turn over. Sound rolling. Mark it. Scene 503 take 1. And action . . .'

I looked through the viewfinder and my eyes deceived me. There was no old woman standing before me. Dietrich's veil and a soft-focus filter had transformed her. The key light caught her eyes and I saw the star of *Blonde Venus* and *Touch of Evil*. She had become again the legendary Dietrich.

The cameras purred. Celluloid glided through the magazine and gate. She sang the song 'Schöner Gigolo, Armer Gigolo':

> There will come a day
> Youth will pass away
> Then what will they say about me?

In all it lasted no more than three minutes but the illusion of intimacy remained. After the cameras had cut and the Nagra recorder
stopped rolling, we remained silent. Then burst into spontaneous
applause. Dietrich smiled once more and offered to sing for us
again – in her own language.

Afterwards the photographer shot stills until he started to shake.
Dietrich then called the crew around her. She asked who were
Berliners. She asked after Ku'damm, Savignyplatz and Unter der
Linden, iconic parts of her city and ours. She talked of her fear of
losing her German, and of returning home. She said, 'There are
many people who imagine I betrayed Germany during the war.
They forget I was never – never – against Germany. I was against
the Nazis. Even the press seems not to comprehend that. You can't
know how it feels. You're going home tomorrow and I can't. I lost
my country. I lost my language. No one who hasn't gone through
that can know what I feel.'

Then she gathered herself and left the set, the last set that she
would ever perform on, the crew standing in a line to the door,
saluting, celebrating, clapping for *die Dietrich*.

The film *Just a Gigolo* flopped because its producer and director
had used Dietrich to authenticate a derivative project. Yet for the
crew – German and foreigners like me who lived and worked in
Berlin – the experience was among the most memorable of our
professional lives. We were moved by the beauty and sheer vital
presence of a star who both was and amplified her own legend; an
artist staring down time, for the last time in her life.

'Tu was.'

In her constant becoming had Dietrich ceased to be herself?
Fritz Lang thought so. He believed Dietrich to be a tragic figure
who could never stop acting. 'Her whole life was built on a grand
illusion,' he wrote. She 'sold the public on her own picture of herself'. But others like Hemingway, who called her 'brave, beautiful,
loyal, kind and generous', understood that she governed herself
with her own rules, 'standards of conduct and decency that were no
less strict than the original ten'. The actress did absorb aspects of

her screen roles into herself, yet such was her means of perfecting herself, of becoming. By her example – and through the myth that grew greater than its frail, mortal shell – the glamorous *Berlinerin* gave Western women a model for a bolder, fuller life and showed all Germans that there is always a choice.

Leni Riefenstahl at the Luitpold Arena in Nuremberg directing the film-ing of *Triumph of the Will* at the Nazi Party Congress, 1934. (*Corbis*)

Kurfürstendamm, 1935

A flash of light. A bugle blare of joy. A mass of young faces gaze in adoration, in hope, in black and white. Eyes and hearts lift in expectation. Arms snap up in salute. Their messiah steps onto the podium. He promises them the world, demands their obedience. 'Here we stand, ready to carry Germany into a new era.' Cut to an eagle clutching a swastika in its talons. Fade in a roll of drums. The massed ranks submit themselves to their new leader, binding their will to his own, falling into step behind him. The camera tracks through the marching men. 'One People, one Reich, one Führer!' Their weapons glint in the sun, catching the wide eyes of the audience.

In the dark hall Leni Riefenstahl saw the tears in those pale blue eyes. She felt his swelling pride. She sensed it spread out from their box, from row to row, through the vast UFA Palast, across Berlin and then the country, wiping away the shame of Versailles. Pride grew also in her own heart, loosening the knot of tension at the base of her spine, igniting a warmth in her groin. She had created a new cinema for the new heroic age. In the next three weeks in

1935 over 100,000 people would be seduced by her work at the Ku'damm's great dream palace. Within a year every man and woman in Germany would have seen it. She no longer needed to feel like a victim. Instead she felt elated, empowered, and later bowed for form alone when her patron presented her with an enormous bouquet of lilacs on the cinema stage. Adolf Hitler praised her film's 'incomparable glorification of the power and beauty of our Movement'. Now Riefenstahl knew that his will would carry her – like Germany itself – to triumph.

Where did her journey to fame, and infamy, begin? In her childhood obsession with fairy tales? As a vivacious, headstrong Berlin teenager who seduced a Jewish banker to finance her dance debut? As a slender, topless servant girl in her first movie, *Ways to Strength and Beauty*? Or as a grasping, ambitious film star reading *Mein Kampf*?

Hitler's egocentric and racist tome had exhilarated her. In 1931 she read it from cover to cover on a single train journey, and again on the set, by the mountain streams and forest locations of her latest movie. She called it beautiful. His proposals to tackle social problems – six million Germans were unemployed at the time – impressed her. She sensed that Hitler could 'save' the country and a 1932 Nazi rally confirmed her intuition. At Berlin's Sportpalast his performance and presence struck her 'like lightning'. He radiated 'a kind of hypnotic effect' and to Riefenstahl 'it seemed as if the earth's surface were spreading out in front of me like a hemisphere that suddenly splits apart in the middle, spewing out an enormous jet of water, so powerful that it touched the sky and shook the earth. I felt quite paralysed'.

But not paralysed enough to prevent her picking up a pen and writing to Hitler. She wanted to meet the man who she calculated was destined for greatness. She wanted a part of that power for herself. She was invited to spend the afternoon with him near Wilhelmshaven. The actress and the politician strolled along the beach, chatting about movies. She was thirty years old, beautiful and flirtatious, with big dark eyes, cascading hair and a full, vivacious mouth. He was forty-three and eight months away from seizing control of Germany. In private he struck her as a modest person, 'natural, straightforward, honest and friendly'. She turned on her charms. He had seen all her film performances, he said, as well as her first picture as director, *The Blue Light*. He especially admired her dance by the sea in *The Holy Mountain*. Her screen persona intrigued him, he told her. In her movies Riefenstahl tended to play an alpine heroine, a visionary beyond the reach of the masses. Hitler understood the power of myth and the moving image. He recognised that the clever, persistent use of propaganda could make a people see heaven as hell, and vice versa. He knew that the public needed an idol. Both he and Riefenstahl were captivated by the public projection of themselves. At the end of the afternoon he told her, 'Once we come to power, you must make my films.'

All her life Riefenstahl had wanted to be famous. At school in Neukölln and Schöneberg she was sporty, not academic, excelling at swimming, skating and gymnastics. Her father, a busy Berlin plumber and entrepreneur, forbade her to go to parties or the cinema and because of him she learnt obstinacy and deception. Her striking good looks invited her into the excitement of the adult world, and she schemed to free herself from her family. She left school in the last year of the First World War and, as gunfire echoed along the Kurfürstendamm, signed up in secret for the Grimm-Reiter School of Dance. In its studio she pushed herself, training until her feet bled, once standing in at a recital for Anita Berber – the wild, uninhibited dancer who had stood in the Marienkirche, been painted by Dix and starred in the sequel to *Diary of a Lost Girl*.

Riefenstahl was no layabout, lounging in bed until nine, yawning, 'Ah was, quatsch, früh aufstehen.' Why bother getting up early? Instead she used every moment and every attribute to get ahead. After graduation she persuaded an infatuated admirer to bankroll her first professional appearance. In Munich's Tonhalle – only one kilometre and two weeks away from the Bürgerbräukeller where Hitler staged his 'beer hall putsch' – she performed the *Three*

Dances of Eros in a scandalously brief tunic. Appearances followed in Dresden, Frankfurt and half a dozen other cities. Critics were enticed to attend and their reviews were quoted in her press book with words like 'problematic' and 'sentimentality' removed. A general remark in the *Berliner Tagesblatt* – 'the glory of the dancer who appears once every thousand years with consummate grace and unique beauty' – was cited as if it referred to her. The paper's conclusion that Riefenstahl's 'superficial perfection is not blessed with the grace of an inner gift, with the grandeur of genius, or with the flame of the demonic' was cut from her publicity material. She also chose to overlook the comments of the capital's most discerning dance critic, John Schikowski, who wrote: 'All in all, a very strong artistic nature, that within its own territory is perfectly adequate. But that territory is severely limited and lacks the highest, most important quality: that of the soul.'

A lack of soul only helped her in advancing herself, although a knee injury ended her dancing career. On stage in Prague she fell and, after a last few hobbled performances, never danced professionally again. She cast around for a new outlet for her intense ambition until – in a story often repeated – her eyes settled on an ad for the film *Mountain of Destiny*. Beneath the tea-cosy dome of Isherwood's Nollendorfplatz U-Bahn station she stared at the poster as if hypnotised, missing both her train and a doctor's appointment. She walked across the road to the Neues Schauspielhaus and – in the building where Goebbels would soon ferment protests against *All Quiet on the Western Front* and where in 1980 David Bowie would perform with Iggy Pop – sat down with purpose to watch the movie which set the course of her life.

Mountains are to Germany as Hollywood's Wild West is to America. The high, pure peaks are a place of heroic destiny, where myths and folklore were reinvented by Goethe, Schinkel and Caspar David Friedrich. Climbers ascend through a sublime yet dangerous realm towards the ultimate goal.

The first German to carry a hand-cranked film camera into the Alps was Arnold Fanck, a geological engineer and high-altitude skier. Fanck was a pioneer, scaling out of the studios to fill the screen with billowing clouds, howling blizzards and swooping chains of fire lit by night skiers holding magnesium flares. His first documentaries, edited on his mother's kitchen table, lost money. The unpredictable alpine weather prevented him from keeping to schedule and raising production finance. Fanck distributed his films himself, renting theatres like the Neues Schauspielhaus to show them, bringing himself to the edge of bankruptcy.

Riefenstahl had only seen mountains on postcards until *Mountain of Destiny* cast its spell over her. With impetuous calculation, she asked her lover and banker – whom she had separated from four months earlier – to take her to the Dolomites. She hoped to meet Fanck there, although kept her intentions to herself. But no sooner had she arrived than she learnt that Fanck was in Berlin. She returned to the capital to meet him, giving him her doctored press book. She told him that she intended to be his star. In less than a week – according to her – Fanck presented her with a script on which he had written, '*The Holy Mountain* – written in three days and nights for Leni Riefenstahl'. He told her that he would make her 'the most famous woman in Germany'. In her autobiography Riefenstahl failed to mention that the banker had agreed to co-finance the project.

Almost two years in production, the vertiginous melodrama was plagued by affairs and accidents. Riefenstahl slept with its director, its cinematographer and its leading man. She suffered frostbite and broke her foot. The cameraman injured his spine and their skiing instructor shattered his thigh. But the finished film triumphed at the box office, premiering at UFA's Palast am Zoo, where Riefenstahl appeared on stage before every showing during its five-week run.

The Holy Mountain typecast Riefenstahl. In her next seven pictures she would build on her role as the eager and aloof heroine, bounding fawn-like into a mythical Romantic landscape, swooning over battling lovers and fluttering her frozen eyelashes. She claimed later that F.W. Murnau wanted her in his *Faust*, and that Sternberg

nearly cast her as Lola Lola in *The Blue Angel* – assertions which
were never substantiated by any other source – but again and again
she chose to return to mountains. The simple truth is that she knew
that none of her screen rivals – Dietrich, Garbo, Louise Brooks and
Lilian Harvey – would dare to climb the Alps without a rope. The
mountains were her world. Among them she shaped her identity.
She *was* a fearless climber. But she used her physical courage to
disguise her moral cowardice.

The mountain films stirred a foggy sentimentality in the German
soul and in 1930 she penned a script – its story plagiarised from a
Swiss novel – which she called *The Blue Light*. Her 'legend of the
Dolomites' was a soft-focus fairy tale in which a beautiful mountain girl – played by herself – guarded the secret of a mysterious
alpine light. In a self-mythologising metaphor, the simple, swarthy-
skinned lowlanders misjudged her, looted her sacred grotto and
sent her plunging to her death.

To produce the project Riefenstahl again charmed and seduced
the industries' top professionals. *The Blue Angel*'s cameraman (and
her former lover) Hans Schneeberger became her cinematographer.
The Jewish writer and critic Béla Balázs – whom she would later
denounce to the Nazis – reworked the script and co-directed the
picture. Finance was arranged through her besotted banker (after
the studios had rejected it as a vanity project). Even the now-jilted
Arnold Fanck was persuaded to overcome his bitterness to make
the final cut, teaching her to edit.

For Riefenstahl *The Blue Light* – shot over three summer months
in South Tyrol – was 'symbolic of the ideal one always dreams of
but never attains'. But despite her manic energy and perfectionism,
its 1932 Berlin premiere – again at the UFA Palast – brought as
before a mixed critical response. The right-wing press celebrated
the picture, none more so than the *Westfälische Volkszeitung*, which
heralded it in bold capitals, 'THIS WAY, GERMAN FILM,
TO THE HOLY MOUNTAIN OF YOUR REBIRTH AND
THAT OF THE GERMAN PEOPLE!' In contrast, liberal
papers like the *Berliner Morgenpost* and *Berliner Tagesblatt*, owned
by the Jewish Ullstein brothers, branded the film as 'inwardly sick'.

When it died at the box office Riefenstahl needed a scapegoat. 'As long as the Jews are film critics, I'll never have a success,' she complained in a radio interview, recalling the anti-Semitism of *Mein Kampf.* 'But watch out, when Hitler takes the rudder everything will change.'

In early 1933 the Nazis began to ease Jews out of the media. Contracts were terminated, agreements dishonoured. Even foreign film companies were instructed to dismiss 'all representatives, rental agents and branch managers of Jewish extraction immediately'. When Warner Bros refused to comply, their Berlin rep Joe Kaufman was murdered by the brownshirts. Within a year some 2,000 film professionals left the country.

Goebbels was enthralled by the power of the cinema, and its ability to manipulate the masses. He took control of UFA, the great Berlin dream factory with its dozen Babelsberg sound stages, 5,000 employees and 120 cinemas. He poured money into production, overseeing during his years in power a staggering 1,097 features. His genius was not only to make overt propaganda films but also to 'co-ordinate' popular entertainment. 'We do not expect everyone to play the same instrument,' he told industry leaders in the banquet hall of the Hotel Kaiserhof, 'only that people play according to the plan.'

Through his ministry of illusion and the Reich Dramaturgy Office, he approved romantic musicals, epic war films, sham historical dramas and the two greatest films made by a woman in the twentieth century.

Riefenstahl 'is the only one of the stars who understands us', he wrote in his diary. As Germany slipped into collective madness, she met with him and Hitler. Magda Goebbels invited her to sit under the birches in their garden overlooking Wannsee. Hitler dropped by her Hindenburgstraße apartment. At film premieres and the opera, beneath sweeping spotlights, she hobnobbed with the Party elite, charming her way into the heart of the Third Reich. She stayed in touch even when she was away from Berlin. During the shooting of *SOS Iceberg* in Greenland, she rephotographed large portraits of Hitler – which she had brought with her – against icebergs and fjords. On the night that he became Chancellor, and ranks of torch-bearing supporters marched through the Brandenburg Gate, Hermann Göring – the future head of the Luftwaffe – telephoned her on location in Switzerland with the news. She greeted it with fierce delight, standing stark naked outside a hotel sauna. In a full-length mirror she caught sight of her reflection and turned towards it, lifting her hands high into the air, stretching out her long, strong body.

Goebbels wanted Riefenstahl to make a 'Hitler film' and over the summer of 1933 she discussed it with him more than a dozen times. She also discussed the project with Hitler at the Chancellery, in his residence and during a private picnic excursion to the Baltic. As her Jewish friends fled the country and opposition politicians vanished from their homes, she expressed her gratitude by giving him a leather-bound, eight-volume set of the writings of Johann Gottlieb Fichte – the eighteenth-century philosopher who had linked German Romanticism and nationalism – with the inscription 'To my dear Führer, with deepest devotion'. The books, marked with hundreds of marginal strikes, exclamation marks and comments, remained in Hitler's personal library until the end of the war.

Riefenstahl was an actress, with only a melodramatic fairy tale to her credit as a director, but she understood that Germany's new sorcerers needed to spin their own fable. Those sorcerers knew that the heroic idealism of the alpine films was akin to the Nazi spirit. They admired the photographic effects of *The Blue Light*. They sensed that a determined artist might help them to sanctify their idol. In her cold ambition Riefenstahl, unrestrained by moral concerns, willingly gave them her gifts. By the end of August, she was in Nuremberg making her first, cinematic 'documentary' for the Reich.

The result, *Victory of Faith*, was no masterpiece. The pre-production period was too short. She had less than three months to edit the film. But during the shoot she befriended Albert Speer, the rally's stage manager and later Hitler's architect and wartime

Minister of Armaments. Speer had transformed the Nuremberg parade ground into a ceremonial sanctuary with vast banners, lofty speaker's podium and stylised wooden eagle. He and Riefenstahl collaborated on the film's staging, on lighting and camera positions as well as – later, in Berlin – on the construction of sets for the many re-enactment shots. The finished film – which Goebbels' propaganda sheet *Der Angriff* (*The Attack*) trumpeted as 'a contemporary document of inestimable value' – portrayed a unified nation free of dissent and discord. In grateful thanks Hitler gave Riefenstahl a Mercedes convertible.

Yet *Victory of Faith* was only the warm-up act. In May 1934 Riefenstahl began the movie that would finally convince Germans of their invincibility. Her new work would not simply glorify Hitler, it would deify him.

To make *Triumph of the Will* she was given unlimited resources: 100,000 soldiers, the city of Nuremberg, two aircraft for aerial photography and a production staff of 200 including fifty cameramen. She had unrestricted access to Hitler, and – as before – traded on their relationship to secure top collaborators such as Walter Ruttmann, director of *Berlin: Symphony of a Great City*. Riefenstahl also demanded absolute creative control, as well as the guarantee that her production company would own the copyright. No other documentary film would ever have greater support.

Riefenstahl's shooting schedule was as meticulously choreographed as the rally itself. Her camera teams – dressed in light grey uniforms to blend in with the troops – glided through the assembled ranks on roller skates. Her photographers tracked around Hitler as he spoke, shooting him from below, exaggerating his height. Speer built a small elevator into one of the vast flagpoles to give her a soaring overview. In her distinctive white greatcoat she moved beneath the towering swastika banners, between her crews and the storm troopers, actors in a new kind of political drama. Often she was the only woman on the parade ground, demanding, flirting, weeping when necessary, and revealing an intuitive genius for innovation. When the rally finished, Riefenstahl returned to Berlin.

Untroubled by her inability to distinguish between fact and fiction, she restaged dozens of shots – heroic *Reichsarbeitsdienst* volunteers, marching boots, fanatical speeches recorded with direct sound – and then began a gruelling six-month, sixteen-hour-day edit.

The March 1935 premiere at the UFA Palast – its façade dressed with defiant Nazi eagle and banners by Speer – was attended by the nation's new elite. In the dark cinema drums rolled, trumpets blared and on screen an aircraft nosed through majestic clouds accompanied by a hymn-like rendition of the Horst Wessel song. In bold Gothic script the introductory titles proclaimed:

Twenty years after the outbreak of the World War,
Sixteen years after the beginning of Germany's suffering,
Nineteen months after the beginning of the rebirth of Germany,
Adolf Hitler flew to Nuremberg to review his faithful followers.

The three-engined Dornier dropped through towers of cumulus clouds, its shadow sweeping over medieval rooftops and cathedral spires. The Führer descended from the sky like a god, his arrival on earth cheered by shouting, ecstatic crowds. Eager women and children near to tears raised their arms in fervent salute. His motorcade swept by innumerable, stone-faced soldiers, into the city, to celebratory parades and martial music.

A new dawn broke over Germany. Leaded windows opened onto the perfect day. Flowers raised their heads towards the bright sun. At the Hitler Youth camp, across a vast plain of bell tents, the nation's youth awoke, washed and laughed in preparation for the rally. At the Luitpold Arena, beneath the proclamation *Alles für Deutschland*, Rudolf Hess opened the Congress, remembering Hindenburg and 'our fallen comrades' of the First World War, subsuming every German's individuality by declaring to Hitler, 'You are Germany! When you act, the nation acts. When you judge, the nation judges.' At the same podium, to the same cameras, Goebbels called, 'May the bright flame of our enthusiasm never be extinguished. It alone gives light and warmth to the creative art of modern political propaganda.'

In her execution of that art Riefenstahl cut to Hitler on the parade ground as he urged thousands of young men and women to harden themselves and to prepare for sacrifice. 'We want you, German boys and German girls, to absorb everything that we wish for Germany,' instructed the leader. In the stadium and on film, they gave themselves to him without reservation.

In the climax of both rally and film, the anointed leader walked along a wide avenue formed by dense, closely formed blocks of troops. One hundred thousand men stood to attention as Hitler laid a wreath at the First World War memorial. Wagner's *Götter-dämmerung* – which ironically would be the Berlin Philharmonic's last performance before their evacuation from the capital in 1945 – swelled on the soundtrack as Hitler's disciples answered his summons, reaffirming their loyalty, and awaiting his orders while declaring that they knew 'only to obey'.

'The Party is Hitler! Hitler is Germany as Germany is Hitler!' proclaimed Hess, and on screen a giant swastika dissolved into lines of marching men.

Hitler had seen and approved the seductive masterpiece before the Berlin premiere. His Propaganda Minister lavished it with praise, declaring, 'Whoever has seen and experienced the face of the Führer in *Triumph of the Will* will never forget it. It will haunt him through days and dreams and will, like a quiet flame, burn itself into his soul.'

As an advocate for her patron's ambitions, Riefenstahl manip-ulated the viewers' emotions and swept away lingering notions of doubt. Her lie, different from her first publicity scrapbook only in scale, was that Germans were already united. By amplifying the Führer's message, she helped to convince disciples and doubters alike to merge their wills with Hitler's own. In sharp focus, and on thirty cameras, she blurred the distinction between the Party, the state and the people.

In truth her documentary was a drama, a tale told using feature film techniques to glamorise raw power and legitimise a barbaric, murderous regime. Her potent images and coercive editing created an aesthetic devoid of ethics. She perpetuated Nazi iconography, binding it to Berlin and Germany.

Triumph of the Will was not a work of genius but of relentless hard graft. Its success meant that Riefenstahl could choose her next project and, never short of ambition, she chose the Olympics. The 1936 games had been awarded to Berlin before Hitler had come to power and, realising their propaganda potential, he had ordered the building of the world's largest sport complex. Its stadium would seat 100,000 spectators. Its Olympic Village would house 5,000 athletes. It would become – after his conquest of Europe – the home of the Games for the next thousand years. 'Who else but you should make a film of the Olympics?' he said to Riefenstahl.

In preparation the capital was sanitised for visitors. Vagrants and ethnic minorities were moved to the suburbs. Anti-Semitic posters – like those depicting long-nosed rapists defiling innocent Aryan maidens – were stashed out of sight. Riefenstahl looked in the other direction, as she had when the first Jewish shops were closed, and travelled to ancient Olympia in Greece to shoot the opening sequence. She filmed classical statues which would dissolve into naked German athletes and dancers. Once again the symbolic and the mythical entranced her, as did the perfect forms of the competitors in Berlin. Her lens appeared to stroke the young, muscular bodies. She mounted cameras in underwater housings, hung them around marathon runners' necks, sent them aloft in dirigibles and balloons.

For Berlin the Olympics was a political enterprise to show the world 'the grandeur, the permanency and respectability of the new regime', wrote the American-born British diarist and MP Henry 'Chips' Channon, who attended the Games as a guest of the Reich. 'Whenever there was a win, the entire stadium stood up and, with right arm uplifted, sang the National Anthem, as best they could, of the victorious country. German wins were frequent and then, not only "Deutschland über alles" was bellowed, but also the Horst Wessel song, the Nazi anthem, which I thought had rather a good lilt.'

No film-maker had before attempted to record the whole of the Games, and – dressed in grey flannel trousers and a jockey's cap – Riefenstahl rose to the challenge like the athlete she herself had been, storming across the field, complaining about referees' interference, capturing mass callisthenic displays reminiscent of *Triumph of the Will.*

Riefenstahl had no natural gift for storytelling – that is, the humanity of narrative – because of her lack of empathy. But she could join together dynamic images with intoxicating effect, creating mood and evoking emotion through juxtaposition and cutting pace. Her intuitive working method depended on both an artificial timeline – for example, the schedule of a Party rally or the Games – and a mountain of material. She exposed almost half a million metres of film – a staggering 240 hours – for *Olympia.* Over seven months twenty co-editors helped her to shape it. Almost all its sounds were created in the studio. The score was performed by the Berlin Philharmonic with a chorus of 340 voices. Again, money was no object. The film was financed by the Propaganda Ministry, although in secret, to give the illusion of political independence.

The April 1938 premiere, held on Hitler's forty-ninth birthday, was even grander than that of *Triumph of the Will.* Once more the façade of the UFA Palast am Zoo was redesigned, this time with entwined sharp-edged swastika and five-ringed Olympics banners. Inside the cinema the confident Nazi nobility now mingled with diplomats and industrialists from three dozen nations. Gestapo chief Reinhard Heydrich shook hands with the Greek envoy. The Italian ambassador chatted to Goebbels as he plotted *Kristallnacht.* The Czech film star Lída Baarová, fresh from the set of her picture *The Gambler's Story,* flirted with the new directors of Rathenau's AEG. Albert Speer took his seat beside Heinz Riefenstahl, Leni's brother and inheritor of their father's sanitation business. Soon he would be awarded the contract to install plumbing in a dozen prisoner-of-war camps. General Keitel – chief of the Armed Forces – saluted Hitler, with whom he was already planning the invasion of Czechoslovakia. The lights dimmed, the curtain opened and in the dark auditorium, as later at a dozen gala showings

across Europe, Riefenstahl proffered her dazzling spectacle to
the world.

'Years ago the Führer said, if artists knew what great tasks were
reserved for them in a more beautiful Germany, they would join
the movement with greater enthusiasm. Today every artist realises,
as does every German, that reality yields more than any artist could
have imagined,' she wrote in *Film-Kurier*. 'Greater Germany has
become a reality' and artists are obeying 'the call to fall in with the
troops of millions to declare their allegiance to the Führer and his
deeds for Germany's freedom, honour and greatness'.

Stalin himself – who was about to enter into a non-aggression
pact with Hitler – handwrote a letter of admiration to her, well
aware of the power of the movies to deceive.

Eighteen months later the Wehrmacht invaded Poland and Riefenstahl went with them, wearing a tailored Luftwaffe uniform.
She filmed Hitler's victory parade in Warsaw and, when France
fell, she telegraphed him 'with indescribable joy, deeply moved
and filled with burning gratitude, we share with you, my Führer,
your and Germany's greatest victory, the entry of German troops
into Paris'.

But her heroic camera angles could not disguise or transcend
the truth of the atrocities. Tens of thousands of civilians died in
the first weeks of the war. At Końskie, the pretty Polish town with
a Gothic church and Egyptian orangery, she witnessed one small
atrocity in the vast, unfolding slaughter. A Wehrmacht soldier in
town on the same day happened to have a small still camera. He
photographed her arrival with her film crew, and her watching the
execution of a dozen Jews in the central square. Yet Riefenstahl
would forever deny having seen the killings or mass grave, claiming in her memoirs that 'in Poland, I never saw a corpse, not of a
soldier, not of a civilian'.

After Końskie she asked to be excused from the war. The
'Special Riefenstahl Film Unit' with its handpicked cameramen
and Mercedes sedans was disbanded and for the next five years
she concentrated on making *Lowlands*, a multi-million-Mark

star vehicle with many of its Sinti and Roma extras pressed into performing on their way to Auschwitz. The first casting call was organised for Riefenstahl beneath the watchtowers at the Maxglan 'collection camp'. Her grotesque picture was financed in person by Hitler.

As Coventry and London burned, she ordered the construction of a vast, flower-strewn, alpine film set. She danced the flamenco for her cameras while the Wehrmacht bled and froze to death in Stalingrad. She edited and dubbed her kitschy melodrama as the Red Army stormed East Prussia and American bombs rocked her Berlin home. Her gargantuan ego drove her to finish the film even as the great, proud capital was pounded to dust. She developed a twitch, an involuntary shiver of her upper lip, which she managed to disguise until it was caught inadvertently on camera and she exploded in apoplectic fury. Finally when she could work no longer, she ran south to her fairy-tale Alps, carrying *Tiefland*'s negative with her. Over its production period some sixty million Europeans had been killed, the war's prime perpetrators roused to battle – in part – by the infectious energy and dreadful certainty of her two great films. On 30 April 1945, when Hitler committed suicide in Berlin, the Third Reich's great myth-maker, hiding miles away in Bavaria, was seized by a chaos of emotions. She fell to the ground and wept.

In the following months Riefenstahl began to construct her last self-serving fiction. She told her American interrogators that she could not grasp how people who had 'shared Hitler's political ideas have the courage to continue living'. She claimed never to have 'received an invitation from any Party man, and if I had I would have rejected every one of them'. She maintained that she had been coerced into making *Triumph of the Will* and that it was an unadorned documentary which had faithfully photographed reality. She asserted that *Olympia* had no political agenda. She denied any involvement in the making of *Victory of Faith*, an ode to bellicosity complete with glinting bayonets and fighter aircraft flying in swastika formation, until a print of the lost film turned up in a British archive. She swore both that Goebbels hated her and that she knew nothing about concentration camps, then claimed that she did what he asked so as not to be sent to Buchenwald. Above all she declared that she was an artist, answering a higher calling, and so unable to think politically. 'That's true of practically every artist in the past who produced great works; be it Michelangelo, Rodin, Rubens or the Impressionists,' she said. 'None of these people had any time or feeling for politics.'

She continued to defend her cowardly lie to the grave, long after many far less culpable Germans had found the moral courage to confess to wrongs as a condition of their own and their nation's healing.

'Just imagine what would happen if, a thousand years from now, people could see what we have experienced in this era,' Hitler had told Riefenstahl in 1942. Across the world's silver screens she had perpetuated his messianic vision, glorifying his murderous regime, deceiving and dancing on the broken bodies of millions. Perhaps she really was naive. Perhaps she was reaching only for beauty and truth, as she claimed. Or perhaps the dictator's celluloid muse was so wilful and greedy that she simply sold her soul.

Her work endures, its impressive images attracting the admiration of modern myth-makers like George Lucas, Mick Jagger and Andy Warhol. Her persuasive techniques – startling camera angles, tracking shots, emotive juxtapositions – have influenced generations of advertisers, enabling them to perfect marketing and ad campaigns that manipulate our everyday lives. Even modern political candidates are promoted utilising methods which she initiated. Yet Leni Riefenstahl herself, the most technically talented filmmaker of her age, must remain a pariah. She was the only woman to play a significant role in the rise of National Socialism, and she never showed remorse, convinced – in her make-believe, fairytale world – that she had no reason to do so. In all modern history there are few more powerful, few more shocking examples of moral compromise.

For the last decades of her life, in the dimly lit dusk *entre chien et loup* when the light is too dim to distinguish 'between dog and wolf', the haunted Berliner was surrounded by ghosts. She denied them of course, as she had always denied knowledge of anything which might tarnish her terrible, glittering reputation. But alone in her basement viewing room she threaded *The Blue Light*, *Triumph of the Will* and *Olympia* onto the Steenbeck editing table, reaching back to her glory days, watching with visible pride the movies which had mesmerised the nation.

CHAPTER 15

*Albert Speer,
and Germania*

Albert Speer's New Reich Chancellery, 1937. (*Roger-Viollet/Getty Images*)

Lindenallee, 1938

'Imagine a city,' Speer told the assembled architects, designers and modellers. 'Imagine a capital greater than Paris and Rome, a metropolis that will eclipse Babylon and Karnak,' he said walking among them, meeting their eyes, challenging them to succeed where kings and kaisers had failed. In his voice was a whisper of wonder. In the light and open workshop rose an air of historical opportunity. Among the desktops and drafting boards Speer – tall and startlingly handsome, with tie askew – told his staff that they had the chance to carve a new identity on the city, to rid it for ever of old neighbourhoods which lacked order and beauty, the unwanted places that had evolved without plan. He put his hand on young Schönecker's shoulder and willed them all to 'imagine a new Berlin'.

For as long as he remembered, Stefan Schönecker could imagine space. As a child, he'd tingled on realising that the rooms of his world – his bedroom, the apartment's central *Berliner Zimmer*, his father's architectural office – were no more than spaces prescribed by brick, cement and plaster cornices. He'd stand in a room and sense the emptiness around him, feeling it, inhabiting it, until the air itself seemed to glow.

At home in comfortable Westend, once a sandy, wooded plateau where Napoleon had a military camp, then an affluent suburb of villas and shady circles, he'd made a model of their building from cardboard and hobby clay, matching floor plan to elevation, learning how the different dwellings were contained in it. He measured foundations in footsteps and windows with a ruler. He spotted wasted cavities and aberrant corners and – in cherry wood – began to change the model to fill the nothingness, creating a more efficient structure. A cabinet-maker who worked in a cellar workshop took him under his wing, letting him handle walnut and maple, nurturing his feeling for the texture and grain. Schönecker loved to sit on the steps in the summer sunshine, gulping in the scent of lime blossoms, shaving and shaping and bringing life to wood. At the Gymnasium zum Grauen Kloster he focused on physics and mathematics, graduating top of his class, and decided to become an architect.

In 1938 *Generalbauinspektor* Speer had plucked him out of his first year at the Technische Universität, along with ten other promising students, and the dream of his youth, that heady insanity, seemed to become reality. Speer told them that he was 'wild to accomplish things', that artists and technicians had to rise to meet the promise of the future. He also assured them that – with their skills – there were other ways to serve the Reich than as soldiers.

Like all his TU classmates, Schönecker had followed Albert Speer's meteoric rise, from private practitioner to 'Inspector General of Buildings for the Renovation of the Federal Capital' at the age of thirty-two. He'd seen Speer's renovation of the Party's first Berlin headquarters and the handsome Schinkel building (a shared hero) which he'd rebuilt for Goebbels. He knew that he'd dressed and staged every Party rally since 1933; suspending above the Tempelhof Field three mighty swastika banners, each of them taller than a ten-storey building; raising a cathedral of light above Nuremberg's Zeppelinfeld with 130 anti-aircraft searchlights; helping Riefenstahl

to capture the audacious vision on celluloid. But nothing had prepared him for the excitement of the New Chancellery.

In Schönecker's first week at the Lindenallee workshop, Speer
had signed off Hitler's palace. He had been given the whole of
Vossstraße and less than twelve months to create it. On the
sixteen-hectare site behind Potsdamer Platz, 4,500 men had worked
in two shifts a day to build the fabulous, forty-two-room mansion
which stretched from Wilhelmplatz to the Tiergarten. Into it Speer
had incorporated the whole Palais Borsig, built a century earlier by
the great industrialist's son on the site of the old Marschall Palace,
once the finest building in the Great Elector's Friedrichstadt.

On the night before its official opening, Schönecker and the *Büro*
staff had followed Hitler through the bronze gates into the court
of honour. They stepped past Arno Breker's giant, proud-chested
bronze athletes, ascended a grand flight of stairs and passed through
six-metre-high double doors into the sky-lit mosaic hall. Electric
lights glinted off its mirror-polished, blood-red Saalburger marble.
Two hundred vases of cut flowers lined the gallery beyond, which
was twice as long as Versailles' Hall of Mirrors. In the extraordinary
structure, in the joy of the moment, Schönecker had taken secretary Annemarie Kempf's hand without thinking, overwhelmed by
emotion.

The man who was changing their future, who was rebuilding
Germany, stopped in the imposing, gilded reception hall and they
gathered near him as if in the presence of the Master of the World.
In his delight Hitler called the Chancellery 'the first architectural
creation of the new, great German Reich'. Schönecker noticed that
Speer's design had no curves, only rows of horizontal lines to re-
inforce the idea of order. Like so many young Germans, he felt
there was nothing that couldn't be achieved – including the creation of a new Berlin.

At the workshop Schönecker's job was to model the 'millennial'
metropolis. In preparation for its new role, the western city's heart
was to be ripped out, destroying 50,000 existing apartments, and
the emptiness filled with structures the like of which – according

to Hitler – 'haven't been built for 4,000 years'. Two magnificent, intersecting boulevards were to be laid across the sandy earth. The North–South Axis – dominated by clean-lined ministries, neoclassical theatres, soaring hotels and the headquarters of all the major German corporations – was to celebrate the Reich's ambitions and achievements. At its southern end, near Tempelhof airport, a new Südbahnhof would open onto the world's largest public square. Five kilometres to the north would rise the colossal Great Hall. Its hulking dome would be sixteen times larger than St Peter's. Within its body 180,000 faithful spectators could stand to listen to the Führer's speeches. Its forecourt would be flanked by his vast residence, a new Parliament and the High Command of the Armed Forces clad in granite, marble and bronze.

Germania – as Berlin was to be renamed – would be the capital of all Germans, impressing them with their own power, bonding them into a single unity with one spirit. The Victory Column would be moved to punctuate the East–West Axis and a tambour added to increase its height. A seaplane airport would be built to the south of Berlin at Rangsdorf. Around the city vast pine forests would be replanted with deciduous trees, completing a project initiated by Frederick the Great two centuries earlier. Germania's towers, obelisks and ordered majesty would take people's breath away, said Hitler.

Schönecker let go of his ambition to be an independent architect so as to serve the best. He joined the model-making team, working at a feverish pace, shaping the fantastic metropolis in wood, plaster and 1:200 scale. As neighbourhoods were levelled to make way for the axis boulevards, he immersed himself in a world of plans. He imagined himself into the *Große Halle*, making the model's brass frame, using cherry wood for volume work and sorbus for detail. He coloured dozens of birch dowel columns to look like pink Swedish granite, then topped them with miniature bronze capitals. In plaster he shaped the *Soldatenhalle* – the Soldiers' Hall – wetting his palette knife, describing its high arched ceiling and low, sombre crypt. He balanced mass and void, heavy porticos and simplified colonnades, noting that classical proportions increased the feeling of grandeur. In separate glass pots he collected maple, lime and oak sawdust to mix with glue to fill any imperfections.

The project was so ambitious that designs had to be farmed out to dozens of architects. As well as Speer's plans, Schönecker worked up Paul Bonatz's drawings for the Naval High Command building, Bestelmeyer's ideas for the new City Hall and Peter Behrens' sketches of AEG's new headquarters. When each model section was finished, it was sprayed white and moved from the Lindenallee to Pariserplatz. In the private galleries of the Academy of Arts, where Else Hirsch had met Friedrich Drake, the great model grew to be over thirty metres long. On display around it, individual buildings were fashioned in tyrannical 1:50 scale and mounted on chest-height stands. Spotlights were positioned to imitate the illumination of the setting sun. Hitler ordered a covered passageway to be built between the Chancellery and the Academy. Most nights after supper he went to the Modellhallen to stare at the shape of his dreams.

'Das g'fallt mir,' he confessed to Speer in the true, heavy Austrian accent which he never used on formal occasions. 'I like it.'

In *Mein Kampf* Hitler had described himself as a potential architect who had sacrificed his career for politics and his 'patriotic duty'. He had an ability to recall precise details of the height of rooms and the volume of tunnels. He could spot minor alterations to cornice decoration and in building schedules. He kept architectural books beside his bed. He wanted Germania to be 'a stone witness to history' that would survive for 1,000 years. It had to be big so as 'to restore to each individual German his self-respect' and to emphasise the idea of a racial community. Its vast halls, virile nudes and huge amphitheatres were to be triumphant declarations of both his and Aryan power.

At least once every week Speer returned late to the Lindenallee workshop after dinner at the Chancellery, at what Hitler called the 'Merry Chancellor's Restaurant'. No matter what the hour, Schönecker would still be in the workshop. The boy liked order in his life and routine at work and never cared much for interruptions such as a free evening or Sunday. At those times Speer would sit beside him at the lathe or easel to talk about a new design or the Führer's after-dinner movie screenings (Hitler watched two films every night, preferring light entertainment pictures, avoiding stories with a tragic plot). He'd speak about *Versammlungsarchitektur*, buildings that brought people together for 'mass experiences', or Schinkel during 'the last golden age of architectural creativity'. One evening he talked about Italy – he'd just returned from Sicily and the ruins in Syracuse and Selinus – and his wish to travel the world after their work was done in Berlin. He wanted to visit Moscow and America, he said. Schönecker replied that he hoped to see the Pantheon in Rome, which had inspired both Schinkel's Altes Museum rotunda and Speer's Great Hall.

One of those nights Schönecker was putting the final touches to a massive, three-metre-high model of the triumphal arch. Speer leant forward to touch its minute plaster panels. He stroked the tiny sorbus friezes and examined the precise sculptures by Breker and Thorak. When built, the Berlin arch would be vast enough to contain nine Parisian Arc de Triomphes, sublime enough to honour the names of Germany's 1,800,000 First World War dead, monumental enough to stand at the centre of the new capital of Europe.

Speer looked from the model to its maker. Schönecker's prototype had made the idea work. The boy had understood the building. He had *felt* its architecture.

'That's it,' Speer said, breaking the charged silence. 'That truly is it.'

In the quiet, darkened studio, the exchange engendered an unexpected intimacy between them.

On the eve of Hitler's fiftieth birthday, Speer stood with city dignitaries at the Brandenburg Gate. Behind them huge crowds massed on the pavements. Ahead of them the now-completed East–West Axis stretched to the Siegessäule and beyond. Along it ranks of solid, spot-lit white columns were crowned with bowls of flame. Three dozen swastika flags fanned around the four-horse Quadriga chariot. Distant cheers swelled into a roar as the motorcade approached. The open-top, dark blue Mercedes 770K swept to a stop in front of Speer, and Hitler stepped out to shake his hand.

'*Mein Führer*, I herewith report the completion of the East–West Axis. May the work speak for itself!' called Speer into the microphone.

Along his boulevard – and around the Victory Column – marched, rolled and thundered the largest military parade ever then seen in Europe. As many as 100,000 troops – including twelve companies of the Army, Navy, Luftwaffe and SS – took four and a half hours to pass the grandstand and its 20,000 official guests. Two hundred warplanes flashed overhead. Artillery, motorised units and dozens of tanks processed past their leader, drowning out all conversation, shaking the ground, to a final rendition of 'Deutschland über alles'. A wedge of hundreds of swans, disturbed by the roaring procession, rose up from the Tiergarten as if on cue. In the birthday broadcast, Goebbels declared, 'The Reich stands in the shadow of the German sword. Trade and industry, and cultural and national life flourish under the guarantee of the military forces . . . Imagination and realism are harmoniously combined in the Führer.'

Away from the astonishing celebration, Schönecker helped to load onto a flatbed truck the model of the arch, delivering it into a side salon of the New Chancellery. Beside it in the Cabinet Room were assembled the ostentatious presents from *Reichleiter* and *Gauleiter*: white marble nudes, bronze casts, cushions embroidered with 'Heil mein Führer', a Titian oil painting and a whole table laden with Meissen porcelain.

At midnight the assembled birthday guests offered their congratulations to Hitler. Glasses were lifted above an earthy field of blond, tan and black, by Wehrmacht officers in grey and green, by SA brownshirts and *Politische Leiter* in golden brown, by pure League of German Girls in pristine white and their mothers in glittering evening gowns.

After the toast Speer leant forward and whispered to Hitler of the special gift awaiting him. Immediately the Führer left the party and hurried past the Cabinet Room to the salon. He stood for a long time contemplating the vision of his youth, the massive mock-up having been created from his own twenty-year-old sketch. The model was perhaps the most hopeful gift ever given, a triumphal arch not to celebrate victories already won but those yet to come. With visible emotion and without a word, Hitler gave his hand to Speer.

With the start of the war Schönecker saw less and less of Speer. He stayed at the studio during the balmy summer of 1940, as more than 100,000 people – including 30,000 prisoners-of-war – were set to work building Germania. At the Mauthausen concentration camp complex, known by the nickname *Knochenmühle* or the bone-grinder, forced labourers died in their thousands cutting the stone for the Soldiers' Hall, carrying it by hand up the infamous 'stairs of death'. At the Flossenbürg quarry-camp, political prisoners pre-pared acres of white-flecked granite for the façade of the Führer's residence. Sachsenhausen's inmates were dragooned into a nearby brickworks, which was set to be the largest in the world. But as he cycled along Berlin's wide new streets, and paused in the sunlight by the canal to watch the silent work gangs, Schönecker questioned not where the men and materials came from, as if not asking was the same as not knowing. Later at Lindenallee he asked no ques-tions when ordered to make models of *Typenbunker* air raid shelters.

When in 1942 Speer became Minister of Armaments – in an or-ganisational role not unlike that which Rathenau had performed in 1914 – work stopped on the gargantuan capital, and the folly's 1950 completion date was put on hold. *Büro* Speer was closed and Schö-necker cycled home along bicycle paths made bumpy by the roots of trees and the bombing. The next morning he answered the call for patriots to do their duty on the battlefield. He fought at Monte Cassino, saw the Pantheon, and survived.

In the last days of the war he heard that the undamaged parts of his models had been taken into – and were hence lost with – Hitler's bunker. He listened to Speer's final radio broadcast, which com-pared the destruction inflicted on Germany to that of the Thirty Years' War. Speer had then escaped the besieged city, taking off along his East–West Axis which had been converted to a runway lined with red lanterns. The shadow of the Victory Column, lit by the fires of the burning dream, had rushed by the right side of his Dornier.

Speer had seized the chance to build without limits, with a melodrama which violated human scale, and Schönecker had helped him. Yet in the end not one of Speer's buildings remained standing in Berlin. Hitler's vast Chancellery was razed and its marble used to clad the Soviet War Memorial and an underground station. After all the hope, all the graft, all the deaths, all that was left of his work was a double row of lamp posts along the East–West Axis, later called the Straße des 17. Juni.

In 1946, at the Nuremberg War Trials, Hitler's architect did not shirk responsibility for his actions, directing guilt away from ordinary Germans towards the Nazi leaders. As a result he was not condemned to the gallows but sentenced to twenty years' imprisonment. At Spandau prison, 'Prisoner No. 5' read, wrote, gardened and set out to travel around the world. He measured the length of his daily walk around the prison yard, then calculated the distance from Berlin to Heidelberg. Once he had reached it, he extended the idea of his journey, visualising the places through which he travelled, measuring every step. He had smuggled into Spandau guidebooks to picture more clearly the unseen cities and seas which he reached, and soon he passed through Moscow and Asia, crossed the Bering Strait and turned south to walk down the length of America. His journey – and sentence – ended in an imagined Mexico.

On the September night that Speer was released, Schönecker – now fifty years old and an urban planner's clerk – stood unrecognised in the crowd outside the prison. The streets were black with people and huge TV spotlights illuminated the gates. At one minute past midnight Speer stepped through them and into a waiting black Mercedes, pausing only to wave to someone in the crowd. Schönecker didn't speak, didn't try to respond, even though there was a question he wanted to ask Speer, one which had haunted him for so many years.

On one of their last evenings together, Speer had asked the boy to alter a small detail on the Great Hall model. At the time it had seemed to be a minor matter, another task to add to his never-ending to-do list. But over time its importance had grown in his mind. Above the podium in the Great Hall there was to hang a vast gilded eagle, a swastika clutched in its talons. In the Lindenallee workshop, Speer had asked Schönecker to replace the swastika with a globe. For more than two decades he had wanted to ask from whom the idea had come. Had it been Hitler's suggestion? Or Goebbels'? Or Speer's? Who in fact was the master builder of the German capital, of the Third Reich?

The boy knew the answer of course, as did every German. He – another vital, anonymous player in history's grand drama – could sense it, feel it, in the terrible emptiness of those heady, mad and poisoned years.

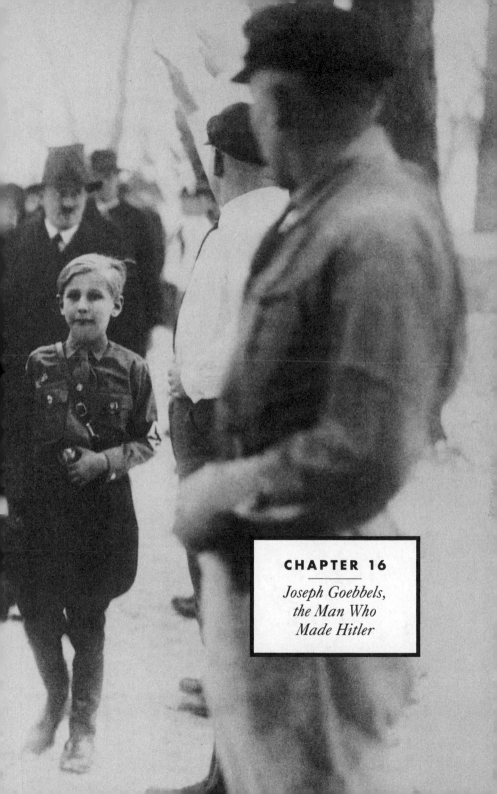

CHAPTER 16

*Joseph Goebbels,
the Man Who
Made Hitler*

Magda Quandt and Joseph Goebbels at their wedding, with Hitler (seen behind them) as their witness, 19 December 1931. (*Gamma-Keystone/Getty Images*)

Vossstraße, 1945

When I first knew Berlin in the 1970s, Prenzlauer Berg in the old Soviet sector was a gritty, grey neighbourhood of crumbling apartment blocks and stifled memories. Coal smoke dimmed the light and muffled every noise until the entire eastern half of the city seemed submerged in dark, haunted silence. I don't recall ever hearing a clear sound there, or seeing sunshine, even when children played on its cobbled streets. Perhaps I only ever visited after dusk, or simply remember my last visit alone.

In those days I used to go to a bar called the Wörther Eck around the corner from Käthe Kollwitz's old home. I'd sit in a quiet corner nursing a Pils, watching the drinkers. No one spoke out loud, at least when I was there, and almost all the customers went home to supper at seven o'clock. The few who stayed were either offered *Bauernfrühstück* – a greasy scramble of egg, fried potatoes and a chunk of inedible fat – or left with their thoughts.

To me the bar was a place of acute poverty. Its acid air reeked of sadness and decay. Yet something kept drawing me back to its lonely drunks and cheap vinyl-topped tables.

One night, on my fourth or fifth visit, an old man sat beside me. I'd seen him before and noticed that the other drinkers tended to avoid him, as they did me. I'd read somewhere that words had greater impact in Eastern Europe because they were rationed, so when he began to speak to me quickly, quietly, I listened.

The man wore his despair like an overcoat. His face seemed to have crumpled in on itself as if drink – or tears – had doused his last spark of life. Yet at the same time his gestures were so sharp and urgent that he seemed about to break into a run. Over the beers he dipped his head to tell me that he had escaped to Moscow before the war and returned with other 'Red' Germans in 1945. I didn't believe him of course. In those days few East Berliners risked telling their life stories to strangers. Nevertheless his apparent frankness disarmed me and – in one of those rare moments of unexpected affinity – we took to each other. He told me that his name was Felix. I noticed that his teeth were short and neat, like little pearls. He said that he had tried to find work – he'd trained as an optician and could recognise a lens prescription without instruments – but that he had to give up in the end because of ghosts.

'Ghosts?' I said.

'Around the corner,' he whispered. 'I will show you.'

'When?'

'Now.'

On that evening – the last one I ever spent at the Wörther Eck – the old man led me in silence to nearby Schönhauser Allee. Beyond a wall I caught a glimpse of thousands of graves through the Star of David motifs. Once every European Jew had been eliminated, this old Jewish burial ground was to have become part of the Nazis' planned 'Museum to a Lost People'.

'This way,' whispered Felix.

He knew a secret way into the cemetery. I ducked in behind him and squeezed through the high brick wall. We followed a broad cobbled path, flanked by oaks and chestnuts, easing aside the ivy to read the headstones. A white marble obelisk seemed luminous in the moonlight. I noted the solid German names – Wolff, Volger, Familie Rosenberg – and the concentration of dates: 1937, 1939,

1940, 1941, 1942 . . . One child-size stone read simply '*Warum?*' Why.

On the five-hectare site lay lawyers, parliamentarians, Bismarck's banker, artists like the painter Max Liebermann and publisher Leopold Ullstein. I recalled that at the start of the twentieth century one third of the hundred richest Prussians had been Jews. Back then Berlin had been among the largest Jewish cities in the world.

Suddenly Felix thrust his arm in front of me.

'There,' he hissed, dropping to his knees.

Beneath the high, dark trees he seemed to have spotted movement. I followed his gaze uneasily but saw only shivering leaves.

'What do you see?' I asked him.

'Men,' he replied, his voice not rising above a whisper. 'Dead men.'

In his mind's eye a tight cluster of exhausted, unknown men, dressed in dirty striped pyjamas and with heads bowed, moved between the worn tombstones. They circled the graveyard and in their midst Felix – with a cry – pointed at a single, infamous figure: drawn, skeletal, limping on his twisted club foot.

'He must walk here for ever,' my mad guide told me.

Like his victims, the ghost was tired, tortured, suspended between life and death. Unlike them, he would never be permitted to rest. Felix told me that he was doomed to shuffle around and around the silent cemetery without end.

'Berlin, Berlin, great city of misery,' wrote Heinrich Heine, the nineteenth-century Jewish poet and German patriot, whose words seemed to rise out of the broken stones. 'In you there is nothing to find but anguish and martyrdom.'

Suddenly the old man leapt to his feet and began shouting at the top of his lungs into the empty darkness, beating on a wall with his fists.

'Get away!' he howled with rage. 'Get away, *um Gottes Willen.*'

In his madness Felix tore the vines away from the stones, tossing them above his head, throwing them wildly about him. Then he collapsed onto the ground and the coal smoke descended upon us, muffling his whimpers, submerging us and the dark, divided, broken city into silence once again.

This desert of stones. This cesspool of sin. This 'repulsive accumulation of pirates, pederasts, gangsters and their like'. Berlin 'must disappear from German soil', scrawled Goebbels in his diary by the wan gaslight that seeped through the dirty window. 'I do not want to kneel in its filth.'

On that cold November morning in 1926 he had limped off a train at the Anhalter Bahnhof. His heart had sunk on meeting the disorganised, disheartened 'body of the discontented' in the Nazis' dingy cellar office. He'd despaired away the afternoon alone in a Kurfürstenstraße café. All evening he wandered aimlessly through the 'sordid' streets, past Nollendorfstraße's gay bars and posters for Dietrich's latest, risqué revue *From Mouth to Mouth*. At Winterfeldtplatz the door of a nightclub had sprung open in front of him, spilling onto the pavement a dozen penguin-suited ponces and half-naked girls, still dancing and laughing, their bodies smelling warm, rich and lucky. Goebbels shuddered with revulsion, and envy.

The Party had offered him the post of the capital's chief *Gauleiter*, as if some sick joke. At the time Berlin was the largest Communist city in the world after Moscow. The Reds boasted a quarter of a million members, twenty-five newspapers and 4,000 active political cells. In contrast the Nazis were banned after a failed march and had fewer than 200 signed-up supporters.

But Hitler – an Austrian surrounded by Bavarians in Munich – considered the 'capture' of Berlin to be one of his highest priorities. He had given Goebbels the job of seizing it.

'History gives peoples the greatest men in the greatest times of need,' Goebbels wrote the next morning on the way to Potsdam. At Sanssouci he stood at Frederick the Great's tomb. The sight of Old Fritz's portrait had inspired him. He decided to stage his arrival as one of the great moments of his life. To elevate himself in his idol's eyes, he had to change his own attitude. He paused like a theatre director setting a scene and then wrote in his journal, Berlin 'really is the centre for us – a world city'.

*

Paul Joseph Goebbels was born in 1897 into a poor, devout family in parochial Rheydt. He was a child of the 'superfluous generation', weaned on bombastic Prussian history, fired by euphoric patriotism, yet too young to vent his militant zeal in the First World War. Defeat in 1918, and the deaths of his elder brother in the trenches and a sister to tuberculosis, shattered his Catholic world view. He lost his faith, felt anger rise in him and tried to channel it with writing and further education. He penned three plays and a novel. He was unable to sell them or to find work after university. He retreated home in raw disappointment to read and dream of redemption through sacrifice, for himself and Germany.

'I can't bear the agony any longer,' he declared at the age of twenty-five, twisted over his childhood desk. 'I have to write the bitterness out of my heart.'

He had no money, rarely went out, lived too much in his imagination. His terrible frustration bred resentment and then hatred. His first notebook diary cost 1,000,000,000 Marks. Well-to-do neighbours, whose life savings had been wiped out by inflation, burnt their furniture to keep warm through the winter then, with the arrival of spring, drowned themselves in their ornamental pond. Tuberculosis killed 100 children every month in nearby Cologne. As Weimar Germany collapsed around him he searched for an explanation for its misfortune.

'I think so often about the Jewish question,' he wrote, a lone wolf picking a scapegoat, drawing on old Christian prejudices as well as new racial theories. 'The problem of race is indeed the deepest, and most secretive which must be grasped in public life today.'

Goebbels started to define 'the Jews' as the enemies of 'the Volk'. He developed a story from the half-baked hypotheses of Alfred Rosenberg and Oswald Spengler. He convinced himself that the 'true Germans' were creators and guardians of Western civilisation. In contrast he saw Jews as parasites, exploiting the creativity and productivity of others, bent on a systematic plan to take control of the world. He – like many others – linked them to Bolshevism, to exploitative stock exchange capitalism, even to the loss of the First World War.

'I stand on the *völkische* side – I hate the Jew from instinct and from understanding,' he asserted. 'I hate him from the depths of my soul.'

Goebbels dreamt of a new German revolution, of driving out remorseless enemies, of a *Volksgemeinschaft* – or people's community – that would join all classes in a common national purpose. His diaries – which he'd keep for the next twenty-nine years – read like epic poems in which he cast himself as romantic narrator. He fantasised playing a part in the nation's rebirth. But he could not bear 'this awful waiting'. 'My time will come! I believe and I hope!'

In *völkisch* ideology a leader rises out of the masses as if by the force of nature. He is a divine visionary who binds individuals into a people, making them capable of deeds which they could not otherwise achieve. He offers them an ideal, and to grasp it they surrender themselves to him.

'I read Hitler's book in a single sitting,' enthused Goebbels on finishing *Mein Kampf.* 'Who is this man? Half plebeian, half God. Is he Christ, or only John? This man has everything to be king.'

Goebbels had an intuition about Hitler. He yearned for him, or a leader like him, and that yearning mirrored the nation's need. He joined the local Nazi Party in the Ruhr and became its speaker. He spoke out in public against Judaism and Marxism, called for 'real' German freedom, meaning 'the freedom of belonging'.

'A young man sat in the front row and I noticed during my speech how his eyes started to glow,' he said after a rally in Mönchengladbach, thrilled to find an outlet for his 'talents', amazed at his ability to stir an audience. 'His inner passion came back to me and created a deep inner connection between us two unknown people, which bonded us, as if in our souls, at that moment.'

His speeches were at once eloquent and evangelical, entertaining and inflammatory, winning over converts and critics alike. He revelled in demolishing hecklers, and in joining the fist fights which often broke out at the end of the evening. He began to travel beyond the Rhineland, talking at workers' clubs and town halls, sleeping on late trains and Party members' floors, or riding home in the back of an open lorry with singing supporters. He started to write for the upstart *Völkische Beobachter*, the main Nazi newspaper. He penned *Das kleine abc des Nationalsozialisten* (*The Little ABC of the National Socialist*), a handy catechism for the growing membership. He declared in his diary, 'I have a voice! I suffocate no longer in my thoughts!'

His empty hours were now packed with zealous journalism, speech-writing and frenetic political activism. The vacuum left by his loss of Catholicism was filled by political faith, and a new messiah. 'What a voice! What gestures! What passion! Exactly what I wanted from him. I can scarcely contain myself. My heart stands still. I hang on every word,' he wrote on first hearing Hitler speak. 'Now I know that he, who leads, is born to be Führer. I am ready to sacrifice everything for this man.'

As a young man Hitler had no special qualities which predestined him for leadership. He had fought bravely in the First World War, like so many others, had been injured, like so many others, and had cried with bitterness on defeat, like so many others. He had been drawn into politics as he had few other prospects. Both his 1923 Munich beer hall *Putsch* and the 'March on Red Berlin' had failed. He had been imprisoned. But rage had forged him into a cunning political animal. He possessed a mesmerising gift as a public speaker. Now Goebbels' fierce devotion would set him apart.

'He jumps to his feet. Shakes my hand. Like an old friend. And those big blue eyes. Like stars,' Goebbels recorded in his diary after their first meeting in Braunschweig in 1925. 'A born people's tribune. The coming dictator.'

Hitler recognised the depth of the young radical's infatuation. He promised him friendship. In return Goebbels harnessed the expectations of his followers, determined to win Berlin for him, then Prussia and finally the Reich.

*

'If we believe in a new Germany we must first get out of this hole of a cellar.'

In his new office on Berlin's Lützowstraße, across the road from Else Hirsch's 'preacher's prison' and near to where her biographer Margarete Böhme had watched prostitutes, Goebbels set about shaping the Nazis' public image. First, he organised a series of talks in taverns and youth clubs, the fervour of his speeches winning new members. Then, with the Party's Sturmabteilung fighting unit of unemployed bully boys and racists (enticed by offers of free beer and a smart uniform), he launched the fight for the capital. He staged brawls and beatings, casting the Nazis as innocent victims. He marched 400 SA men to KaDeWe's Wittenbergplatz, instructing them to beat Communists and Jews along the way, then manipulated the press by lying, 'We came into Berlin with peaceful intentions. The Red Front Combatants League has compelled us to spill our blood. No longer will we let ourselves be treated like second-class citizens.'

Across the city in working-class Steglitz and Wedding, Goebbels armed his thugs with revolvers and iron flagpoles, taunted the Reds into battle then portrayed the Nazi dead as martyrs for the cause. He spun their stories in *Der Angriff*, his slanderous smearsheet that focused hatred on Communists, Jews and the Weimar Republic. He recruited the illustrator Hans Schweitzer to design crude posters of noble Aryan fighters, fat capitalist bankers and lecherous Jewish profiteers. 'Propaganda . . . has only one goal, and in politics this goal is always the conquest of the masses,' he wrote. His audacious campaign caught the public's attention and won converts: by the tens, by the hundreds, by the thousands.

The 1928 election disappointed him, with less than two per cent of voters choosing the Nazis, but the Wall Street Crash transformed the Party's prospects. More than half a million Berliners lost their jobs. Men sat on the kerbsides or in desolate tent camps, staring into space in despair. Women collapsed of hunger on street corners. Goebbels moved quickly to exploit the city's misery.

He latched on to the idea of a Third Reich, linking the upstart Nazis to a mythical past, propagating an idealistic vision of the future. He told Germans that they had the chance to create a new nation, united by race, compelled by history to build on the legacy of the 'first' great Holy Roman and the 'second' Hohenzollern empires. He offered hope to the needy, the vulnerable and the hungry. He coined the slogan 'Freedom and Bread'. He cast himself as Hitler's instrument of 'divine will'.

Above all he focused on the Führer's image, elevating the demagogue into a demigod, charging him with near-mystical qualities. Postcards were printed showing him in heroic poses, in SA uniform, with his hand raised in a fist. Marching songs celebrated his leadership. His hate-filled diatribe *Mein Kampf* was reissued in larger and larger reprints as Party membership swelled. At the first great Berlin rally, Goebbels packed the gigantic Sportpalast arena with 100,000 supporters. He kept them waiting for two hours to heighten the suspense. Spotters then whipped the faithful into a frenzy, calling from outside the hall, 'Er kommt! Er kommt!' 'He's coming!' Hitler, a consummate actor, stepped onto the stage and his disciples responded with frenzied applause.

'Fellow Germans!' he roared. 'Join forces with the brown front marching at the head of an awakening Germany!'

By instinct, and from mass manipulation theorists like Gustave Le Bon and Edward Bernays, Hitler and Goebbels knew how to play the crowd, to tap their frustrations and fears, to direct ferocious, primal passions. Their delirium demanded victims and Goebbels' 'brave lads' pulled Jews off buses, beat them to the ground with chains and chair legs, legitimising a shocking brutality in German youth. Hatred exploded suddenly on street corners, in cinemas, in the middle of the afternoon. Knives flashed in the sunlight. Jewish shops were attacked along Ku'damm. In the Grunewald woods a Czech diplomat observed three young cyclists singing together, 'When the hour of vengeance comes, we will be ready for mass murder'. In a Nollendorfplatz café, Isherwood overheard a young Nazi discussing the future with his girlfriend.

'Oh, I know we shall win, all right,' he exclaimed, thumping the table with his fist. 'But that's not enough! Blood must flow!'

The girl stroked his arm reassuringly. She was trying to get him to come home.

'But, of course, it's going to flow, darling,' she cooed, 'the Leader's promised that in our programme.'

In the 1930 election the Nazis won six million votes. Their 107 deputies took their Reichstag seats in uniform. Eighteen months later Goebbels orchestrated the 'Hitler over Germany' campaign, for the first time using aircraft to fly a leader to political events. In one month alone Goebbels' agitators whipped up over 400 street battles in Berlin, pushing the city to the brink of civil war, beating, burning and murdering opponents. He delivered speech after speech in his rich and sonorous baritone voice. He was always in a hurry, leaping – rather than stepping – through life. Together in the Lustgarten, facing Frederick's palace with tears streaming down their faces, he and Hitler fooled 200,000 supporters into believing that they alone could save Germany from Bolshevist anarchy.

'The greater and more towering I make God, the greater and more towering I am myself,' Goebbels crowed in his diary.

The Nazis' 1933 electoral victory sucked Berliners – even those who had voted against them – into compliant lunacy. On the evening Hitler was made Chancellor, and the singing, torch-bearing marchers paraded through the Brandenburg Gate, Goebbels spoke live on the radio of his pride in how 'a whole people' had risen up, workers, farmers, students, soldiers and the middle classes, 'a great *Volksgemeinschaft* in which one never asks, whether one is bourgeois or proletarian, Catholic or Protestant, in which one only asks, "What are you, what are you part of, and do you declare your support for your country?"'

Now their proud 'revolution' was made fast with lies and systematic violence. In the first weeks after the election, 50,000 opponents of the regime were arrested and held in 'wild' concentration camps: locked barracks and basements where hundreds literally were starved to death. Lawyers and journalists had their jaws and noses broken with rifle butts, then were shot 'while attempting to escape'.

Beating stations were set up near 'the Passage' in Friedrichstraße and on Kastanienallee. At the infamous Columbia-Haus prison near Tempelhof, loud music was played to cover the screams of the victims. Civil liberties ceased to exist when the 'Law for the Protection of the People and the State' suspended the constitution.

Yet most Berliners chose to ignore the facts and look the other way, returning to old Hohenzollern habits, welcoming the end of uncertainty. They fell silent, stopped gossiping at work, and let both stability and malice enter their lives. Thousands joined the Party as Hitler began to print money, buying the people's allegiance, investing in gigantic building projects. Within a year 200,000 Germans were employed creating his huge Autobahn network. Beer consumption and the birth rate soared. In return for betraying their trade unions, loyal workers were awarded subsidised holidays on the Baltic through the *Kraft durch Freude*, 'Strength through Joy', programme. Germany was no place for dissent.

'This morning, as I was walking down the Bülowstraße, the Nazis were raiding the house of a small liberal pacifist publisher,' wrote Isherwood at the end of his Berlin days:

> They had brought a lorry and were piling it with the publisher's books. The driver of the lorry mockingly read out titles of the books to the crowd.
>
> 'Nie wieder Krieg!' he shouted, holding up one of them by the corner of the cover, disgustedly, as though it were a nasty kind of reptile. Everybody roared with laughter.
>
> 'No More War!' echoed a fat, well-dressed woman, with a scornful, savage laugh. 'What an idea!'
>
> By the end of the decade Germany would be Europe's most powerful nation, and Berlin its largest armaments producer.

As Minister for National Enlightenment and Propaganda, Goebbels' role was to shape public opinion. He refuted the notion that propaganda was something of inferior value, declaring in an arrogant speech to radio executives, 'We would not be here in ministerial seats if we had not become the great artists of propaganda.'

Its purpose was to be 'so cleverly and virtuously concealed that he who is to be imbued with this purpose is unaware of it'.

To direct hearts and minds he used spectacle, repetition and saturation. Torch-lit parades were ordered to be held in every city and town. Swastika flags were hung from every window. The Volk were to be imbued with doctrine and dogma by constant repetition, forever told the same message in forever-changing forms. No other Nazi spoke more often or wrote so much. The 'Popular Enlightener' took control of every newspaper and magazine, instructing that street-corner loudspeakers and even restaurant radios relay all his speeches. Radio wardens enforced this legal requirement. Every day he chaired two or three press conferences to dictate what could and could not be said. Through the Reich Chamber of Culture he suffocated the arts, replacing satire with sentimentality, freedom of expression with bigotry.

'Now the public itself functions as critic, and through its participation or non-participation it pronounces clear judgement on its poets, painters, composers and actors,' he lied. Yet it was Goebbels alone who decided who could write, paint, compose and act in the new Germany.

Goebbels believed that he was purifying society, ridding it of the corrupting influences of Freud and Mann, skimming away the 'degenerate art' of painters like Kollwitz, Klee and Grosz. He learnt from Bernays – who coincidentally was Freud's nephew – how to manipulate irrational emotions, channelling inner desires to bind people together and to an idea. He coerced the public into accepting his version of events as their own. In his sanctification of Nazism, he created a surrogate religion, with its own liturgy, replacing the tenets of Christianity with faith in the Volk.

In 1936, during the celebration to mark Goebbels' ten years as Berlin's *Gauleiter*, Hitler saluted his loyal co-conspirator, raising his arm and calling out, 'Unser Doktor Goebbels, Heil!' 'Hail, our Dr Goebbels.'

Under National Socialism, the task of a woman was to bear children for the nation. She had to 'recognise that war is the father of all things' decreed Goebbels, at once embracing and perverting motherhood. 'She bears her child in battle and protects it. It remains in combat throughout its life until death.'

In newsreels and picture magazines, Goebbels and his wife Magda – an ambitious divorcee who'd also caught Hitler's eye – played the role of exemplary first family, especially as Hitler remained a bachelor. At the Schwanenwerder villa bought for them by the Führer, husband and wife were shown raising their children, celebrating birthdays, enjoying the duties and pleasures of parenthood. In their garden overlooking the Wannsee, not far from Frederick the Great's Sanssouci, the children paused from picking daisies to gather around a gramophone and sing 'Mein Papa ist mein bester Kamerad'. My father is my best companion.

Their wedding had been simple and picturesque, witnessed by Hitler and Franz Epp, the Freikorps general who had used secret army funds to buy the *Völkische Beobachter* for the Party. 'I am quite blissful,' Goebbels had written in his diary. 'Hitler takes me emotionally in his arms. Magda gives him a kiss. Tears are in his eyes.' But soon Magda was having an affair with her husband's State Secretary Karl Hanke. At the same time Goebbels fell for the Czech actress Lída Baarová. Another kind of madness possessed him and he gave up ambition, children, wife and work to be with her. His strict, tailored control dropped away. He explored her, kissed her, lost himself in her. He'd had other affairs, of course; power was a gratifying aphrodisiac. But when she danced for him by the lake, wearing only her smile, filling the night with laughter, he yielded to her beauty.

He began to live a double life, escaping from the ministry to a secluded cabin on the Bogensee. He rarely went home. As rumours of the double infidelity began to spread through the Reich, Magda met Baarová and offered to share him. 'He's a genius you know,' she told the younger woman. 'We need to be there for him, both of us.'

But Goebbels wanted only his 'Liduschka', announcing he would become a tie salesman in Japan rather than renounce her. Magda lost her patience and, as public gossip began to undermine official cant, she turned to Hitler. Their Führer ordered a reconciliation,

demanding that Goebbels end the affair. The Propaganda Minister gave up the woman to follow the man. He could not stomach
the loss of Hitler's favour. Husband, wife and beloved leader – the
true participants of the love triangle – were photographed with the
children at Berchtesgaden. In one haunting image Goebbels' eyes
appeared hollow, his chin weak, his long skeletal fingers cradling
his son's hand. His daughters posed and pirouetted around him in
beribboned white dresses. His twisted club foot was not visible in
the photograph.

Goebbels plunged into bitter depression, fell back into profound
loneliness, recording in his diary, 'And now begins a new life; hard,
cruel and dutiful to obedience alone. Youth is over.'

His melancholy deepened and his speeches – though still
greeted with wild enthusiasm – began to sound too strident, as if
now devoid of any real feeling.

'Whatever the Führer orders, I will do,' he cried, a prisoner of his
iniquitous success and his desperate need for Hitler's love, tied to
him by crime and in blood, his soul banished to a flinty wilderness.

Goebbels suffered no doubts over his racism. He needed no en-
couragement to attack the Jews, time and again egging Hitler on
towards the dreadful genocide. His first speech as Minister had
been a savage attack against them. 'You cannot talk on the stage, in
films or in newspapers on behalf of the German people. You have
no right to represent the German nation.' In 1933 he had led the
nationwide boycott of all Jewish shops, calling it 'a great moral victory', and in 1938 he 'unleashed the anger of the Volk' on *Kristallnacht*.
On the Night of Broken Glass, state police were ordered not to
'hamper spontaneous public demonstrations'. By dawn a quarter of
all Jewish males in Germany had been arrested. In Berlin dozens
of Jewish-owned department stores and restaurants – including
Wertheim, Café Dobrin and Café Wien – were vandalised by roaring, applauding crowds. 'Das hat gesessen,' Goebbels congratulated
himself in his diary. 'That hits the nail on the head.'

Goebbels wanted the country to be emptied of Jews. He advoc-
ated that they should wear a yellow star in public. All were forced

to adopt the name 'Israel' or 'Sarah'. In time he would commission rabid, anti-Semitic movies like *The Eternal Jew*, with sinister scenes of starvation, gluttony and sexual depravity staged in Polish ghettos, and the notorious, inflammatory costume drama *Jud Süß*, in which a villainous Jew raped a naive Aryan virgin who then drowned herself in shame. Over 20,000,000 people saw the film in the three years after its release, making it one of the Nazis' great box office successes. Himmler made it compulsory viewing for the SS and the police. After many screenings bands of youths would take to the streets to attack Jews.

At every step of his malevolent journey, Goebbels drew the German people with him, making them fellow travellers. Illustrated essays on Dachau and Oranienburg appeared in popular periodicals like *Deutsche Zeitung* and *Bayerischer Heimgarten*. Hundreds of roadside signs declared 'Juden sind in unserem Ort nicht erwünscht'. 'Jews are not desired in our town.' In every city Jewish property was openly seized and looted, loyal Party members moving into vacated apartments, government trucks carrying away crates of paintings and furniture. Rival bureaucrats and bureaucracies began to compete with one another to be more radical, more racist, and so win favour with the Party bosses.

'The future of our Volk lies in the solution of the Jewish problem,' declared Goebbels. In the Reichstag Hitler announced that any war would lead to 'the destruction of the Jewish race in Europe'.

No one was ignorant of the direction in which the Nazi state was travelling.

When Hitler unleashed mechanised fury on Europe, Goebbels redoubled his propaganda offensive. The public were fed the old lie that Germany was acting in self-defence. Six corpses from Sachsenhausen concentration camp were dressed in Polish uniforms and dumped at the border as proof of a Polish attack. Photographs of ethnic Germans with severed noses and amputated arms further inflamed Berliners' anger, no one suspecting that the mutilations had been performed by Propaganda Ministry officers. In response Germany invaded Poland with sixty Wehrmacht divisions, 2,750 tanks and 2,315 aircraft. Five weeks later 66,000 Polish soldiers were dead. A hundred thousand civilians were deported and 'ancient German lands made ready for German resettlement'. Teutonic Marienburg and Krakow were German again. In Warsaw Riefenstahl filmed Hitler's victory parade and in cinemas around the nation jubilant Germans celebrated the annihilation of Poland.

The weekly *Wochenschau* became Goebbels' greatest weapon. In time, 1,000 camera teams would provide regular film reports to every cinema in the Reich. The newsreels – all of which were edited, narrated and scored under his supervision – made Germans feel that they were fighting alongside their sons, brothers and husbands.

'Before us lies the Maginot Line,' declared the rousing, rat-a-tat narration, sweeping audiences forward with the advancing grenadiers, implicating them in the violence. 'Before us is Verdun . . . Now Strasbourg, the old German city, is back in German hands and freed from French servitude . . . In Metz immortal German works of art have been reclaimed by German soldiers.'

The *Wochenschau* also intimidated foreign audiences. The shocking images of Hitler's unstoppable war machine, scored with the stomp of martial music, overawed the Dutch and Belgians. In the Ardennes tens of thousands of French soldiers threw away their weapons and surrendered without a fight. When Dunkirk fell, and the British Expeditionary Force was driven into the Channel, Berlin's church bells rang for three days.

Goebbels' cameramen recorded the French surrender in Compiègne, aboard the same railway carriage that had been used for the signing of the hated Armistice in 1918. They filmed Hitler standing at the Eiffel Tower with Speer and by Napoleon's tomb. They showed the new Caesar reading the old Kaiser's congratulatory telegram. 'Gentlemen, it is pretty much certain that the war is over,' Goebbels told friends in July 1940.

To the iron-heeled Nazi leadership the British reaction to the initial Blitzkrieg seemed timid. In a move to legitimise his gains, Hitler announced that he could see 'no compelling reason which could force the continuation of the war'. Germany had settled old scores, consolidated the Reich and seized *Lebensraum* – living space. Now he and Goebbels hoped that Churchill would let Germany keep its spoils, for the sake of peace. When he refused, Hitler launched an aerial onslaught on Britain's airfields and then its cities. Many Germans, fed on Goebbels' propaganda, did not understand how Britain could object to its 'defensive' war. Goebbels wrote that England would be liquidated by the Luftwaffe, noting in his diary the daily tonnage of bombs unloaded over London, Liverpool, Bristol and Portsmouth. Ten days after the start of the German bombing campaign, the British responded with the first RAF sortie over Berlin.

In retrospect Hitler made two errors which cost him the war. First, he suspended his attack on the UK in late 1940, which preserved the island as a base for a future Allied assault on the Continent. Second, he decided to turn on Russia. But the decisions seemed sensible at the time. A swift, preventive campaign against the Soviets would secure the oil and economic wealth needed for a longer war against Britain and America.

'If the blow succeeds, and it will succeed, then we are for the first time secure. Afterwards what plausible goal will England have to fight on?' Goebbels asked himself.

Over the years his black art had dehumanised both Jews and Slavs. The Reich's enemies were seen as animals. Their lives were cheap. Within two weeks of the start of Operation Barbarossa, Russia suffered half a million casualties. The Red Army fell back, surrendering in unimaginable numbers. In Minsk 750,000 Russians were taken prisoner, ninety per cent of whom were then starved to death in barbed-wire compounds. Half the Soviet soldiers sent to German forced labour camps died. In Berlin alone 150,000 perished slaving in arms factories. The Wehrmacht pillaged and murdered as it advanced deep into Russia, burning villages, massacring civilians, abandoning any pretence of an honourable code of behaviour. Hitler called the Soviet campaign 'a war of extermination', instructing soldiers to close their hearts to pity and act brutally. 'The two-faced Jewish Bolshevist rulers in the

Kremlin' were 'lengthening the war', scowled Goebbels; they had to be 'eliminated at any cost'.

By autumn the German Army had reached the tramlines on the outskirts of Moscow. Leningrad was surrounded and starved over an 872-day siege. In Alexanderplatz and along Ku'damm, military successes were trumpeted over the loudspeaker network. The fall of Kiev and Odessa was greeted with applause and spontaneous sidewalk renditions of 'Deutschland über alles', as in 1914. Goebbels' mass-circulation Sunday newspaper, *Das Reich*, anticipated imminent victory. 'The Great Hour Has Struck!' screamed its headline. Then the snows came, the Soviets regrouped and the ghost of Napoleon's Grande Armée appeared in the blizzards.

Of the 3,250,000 Germans who died in the Russian campaign, 100,000 literally froze to death. 'The cold pushes us to the edge of insanity,' wrote one soldier. 'Everything is frozen. If we want bread we must chop it up with a hacksaw and then put the pieces in our trouser pockets to thaw. To combat the lice, we make fires from brushwood and then take off our clothes and hold them over the smoke. What that feels like, in temperatures far below freezing, is hard to describe.'

In November 1941, with the mercury at minus 40 degrees, the Red Army inflicted the first defeat on the overstretched Wehrmacht. Forty new Siberian divisions in white winter uniforms and a thousand T-34 tanks pushed back the German juggernaut, scattering panic-stricken soldiers in its wake. The following year Hitler's proud Sixth Army – with a quarter of a million men – was trapped in Stalingrad. A mere 5,000 of them survived the battle and Stalin's gulags. Yet Goebbels' deceitful press release celebrated 'the great, heroic sacrifice which the troops encircled at Stalingrad offered the German nation'. The men had 'fought shoulder to shoulder until the last shot, dying so that Germany might live'. In truth the Wehrmacht would never recover from the shocking defeat. The retreat began and – as Germany was bled of its youth – the Hitler myth began to lose its potency.

In a desperate response Goebbels whipped the German people into suicidal hysteria. At the Sportpalast in February 1943 he demanded, 'Do you want war that is more total and radical than we can even imagine today?'

His speech had been rehearsed two dozen times. Every word and gesture had been planned in advance. His top twelve cameramen filmed the spectacular, and the roars of the Party faithful as they answered his key questions.

Will the people join the Holy War to protect Europe from the Bolshevik Asiatic beast?

'Ja!'

Will they fight to preserve Germany from anarchy?

'Ja!'

Will they support the 'complete and radical extermination – elimination of Jewry'?

'Ja!'

Do they want Total War?

'Ja!'

'German men to the rifle! German women to work!' bellowed the seething, stomping mass.

'Nun Volk steh auf und Sturm brich los!' Goebbels called out, his resonant voice quivering with calculated emotion. 'Now People stand up and unleash the storm!' It was the greatest performance of his career, and he condemned a million more Germans to throw themselves to their deaths.

Berliners embraced the call for Total War in part because the majority were complicit in (or acquiescent to) the Reich's atrocities: typing the orders to shoot fleeing civilians, delivering the memos which classified gypsy children as 'negative human material', making no complaint when Jews were forbidden to buy eggs (22.6.1942) or books (9.10.1942), enjoying their *Kaffee und Kuchen* as the columns were herded to Grunewald S-Bahn station, driving the trains to Auschwitz, melting down gold teeth in the Prussian State Mint. At his desk in Schöneberg a policeman penned a note to a woman, whose husband had been arrested for owning a canary after the ban on Jews keeping household pets, instructing her to pay a three Mark fee when collecting his ashes. In the comfort of their offices on Mehringdamm and Fehrbelliner Platz, in a million guilty or intimidated acts, Berliners had spread the empire of death across Europe. They had every reason to fight to the end.

Goebbels could not turn back either, even if he knew the battle was lost. The Total War speech marked his descent to diabolism. While Hitler – his greatest creation – withdrew into seclusion, Goebbels refashioned himself as the 'guardian of morale on the home front'. He adopted the role of compassionate 'defender of Berlin', driving through the blitzed streets after air raids, listening to residents' concerns and complaints, deepening their devotion to him. Over 15,000 buildings were obliterated by British and American bombers during the last two years of the war. Two million people were left homeless. One mild autumn night when the air was unseasonably warm, and before the all-clear sounded, he stood on the roof of his ministry, watching a flaming river of phosphorous sear along Wilhelmstraße, past Bismarck's blitzed old residence and around the burning New Chancellery. The tempest swept people along like withered leaves, tearing their clothes from their bodies. His eyes followed a running woman, clutching a bundle to her breast, a child perhaps. Her hair and clothes were on fire and he found himself thinking of his Liduschka and her long, tanned legs, summer-brown except for the white scoop at the back of her knee.

Goebbels did not flinch in his resolve, and at the same time he remained the vile scourge of the Jews, deporting the last of them from the capital only weeks before the arrival of the Red Army. 'These Jews must be killed off like rats, when one has the power to do this,' he wrote in his diary in March 1945. 'In Germany, thank God, we have already honestly taken care of this.'

After D-Day and the liberation of Paris, his Saturday newsreels had become brutal and explicit, flashing upon the remaining cinema screens shots of enemy dead, unshaven defenders and Jews being beaten with rifle butts as 'retribution' for their crimes. In his last New Year's Eve broadcast he warned millions of listeners

– if the Allies triumphed – of 'drunken niggers' and 'garrulous Anglo-American agitators' enslaving the nation and reducing Germans to medieval serfdom.

As the Soviets captured East Prussia, he marched tens of thousands of teenage boys and tired old men into the flames. Injured soldiers were dragged from their beds and returned to the front as *Himmelfahrtskommandos*. In the capital's rubble-strewn streets his shameful *Werwölfe* – or Werewolf squads – executed deserters and 'defeatists' who were unwilling to fight to the bitter end. 'I once conquered Red Berlin, and I will defend Berlin against the Reds to the last breath,' he said.

In the last hours of the war, during street battles when the Russians were briefly pushed back, diehard Nazis entered the houses which had hung out white bed sheets, dragged the residents onto the pavement and executed them.

Goebbels created the iconography which empowered and sustained Nazism. He preached a fanatical *völkisch* doctrine of racial superiority. He cultivated the mass hysteria which was channelled into the Third Reich's most horrible acts. He nourished Hitler's obscene genocide and terrorised a continent.

In the grim *Führerbunker*, both he and Hitler gazed at Frederick the Great's portrait. Goebbels then read aloud from Thomas Carlyle's biography about the miracle that had saved the king in 1762: '. . . the great king himself no longer saw any way out of his difficulties, no longer had any plan; how all his generals and ministers were convinced that his downfall was at hand; how the enemy was already counting Prussia as destroyed; how the future hung dark before him . . . Brave king!' wrote Carlyle, read Goebbels. 'Wait ye a little while, and the days of your good fortune stand behind the clouds, and soon will rise upon you.'

When the Tsarina died, and her successor ordered the Russian troops to change sides, this Miracle of the House of Brandenburg had saved Prussia.

After the reading 'tears stood in the Führer's eyes' and – a few days later, when news came of the death of US President Franklin

D. Roosevelt – the Reich's leaders entombed beneath Vossstraße 'felt the wings of the Angel of History rustle through the room'.

But there was to be no change of fortune, no miracle of the House of Adolf Hitler. In his final radio broadcast the haggard Propaganda Minister spoke of satanic powers destroying the most beautiful culture that the earth has ever seen. 'Never will history be able to say of this time that a people deserted its leader, or a leader his people,' he called into the dark, his face ashen, his poison phial in his tunic pocket. 'That is victory.'

Above them the capital was a desert of stones. The defender of Berlin had destroyed Berlin. Hitler killed himself. Goebbels and his wife, who had brought their six children down into the concrete tomb, fed them hot chocolate laced with sleeping potion and slipped glass cyanide capsules into their mouths. One by one Magda cracked them open between their teeth. Goebbels – who had become Reich Chancellor – then killed her and himself, expecting every loyal German to do as he and his Führer had done at the end of their hateful, faithful, demonic play.

CHAPTER 17

Dieter Werner,
Wall Builder

Russian propaganda poster, 'Let's hoist the Victory Banner on Berlin!', designed by Viktor Semenovich Ivanov, 1945. (*Archives Charmet/Bridgeman*)

Bernauerstraße, 1961

War wasted Berlin. Europe's bellicose giant was beaten into submission, then violated and vandalised. In April 1945 two and a half million Red Army soldiers encircled the city, then throttled its 500,000 defenders.

The Soviet 5th Shock Army attacked from the south-east, breaching the S-Bahn defensive ring at the Teltow Canal. The 8th Guards and the 1st Guards Tank armies fought through the southern suburbs and seized Tempelhof airport. The 3rd Shock Army came from the north, preceded by a relentless barrage of artillery. In the final two-week campaign the Soviets fired as many shells on Berlin as British and American bombers had dropped over the previous four years.

Civilians cowered in their shelters, or ran into the streets, screaming, gasping, crazed by the roar of explosions and the cries of the wounded. German 'tank hunters' hid in shell holes and, after Soviet armour rolled over their heads, attacked them from behind with *Panzerfaust* grenade launchers. In a day or two the

Russian drivers learnt to spin their tanks over craters, grinding the defenders – usually boys – to pulp.

The Germans were forced back by the five converging armies, taking up defensive positions around Hermannplatz, the Tiergarten and Alexanderplatz. When those were overwhelmed they fell back to the Havel bridges and government quarter. The Soviets pushed on through blackened neighbourhoods, working in tight combat teams of fifty men. Around Wilhelmstraße and the Chancellery, the enemies fell into hand-to-hand combat, the Russians bent on exacting a terrible revenge for Nazi atrocities. Ninety heavy guns opened fire on the Reichstag, the struggle for it alone claiming 5,000 lives. Almost 100,000 civilians died in the shelters and on the streets. As many as a million German men were marched off to Siberian gulags. The Battle of Berlin was among the bloodiest confrontations in history.

At its end ninety per cent of the city centre was ruins. Streets were choked with seventy million cubic metres of rubble. The mangled dead lay crushed under collapsed walls, blanketed in pulverised brick dust, blasted through doorways, tossed like dolls into trees, washed together five bodies deep in flooded U-Bahn tunnels, locked in each other's arms after a macabre orgy in the dank Bahnhof Zoo bunker. Bloated flies fed on pools of black blood. A widow and her daughter huddled in a burrow beneath their smashed apartment. Above them rose a blasted staircase and twisted mess of bricks open to the sky. Corpses of German deserters hung from lamp posts. There was no electricity, no clean water, little food. Skeletal refugees ate horse cadavers and grass. Tanks and trams stood spent and smoking between the shattered buildings.

In defeat Berlin became part of the Soviet empire. Its clocks were changed to Moscow time. Its survivors were put to work dismantling the Reich. In a month both country and capital would be divided into four sectors but at first the trusting Western Allied armies waited at the Elbe, some 150 kilometres to the west. Until the arrival of American, British and French troops, the Russians stripped all the city's workshops, laboratories and factories. Every working machine at Rathenau's AEG, as well as those at Siemens and Borsig, was removed and shipped to the USSR. The IG Farben Seewerk facility, which produced the poison gas Sarin, was dismantled. The archives of Goebbels' ministry, Haber's institute and the whole German rocket industry were loaded onto a thirty-wagon train, after which the track itself was pulled up and dispatched to Russia.

As well as military and industrial goods, 'Trophy Brigades' looted the ancient Pergamon Altar, hundreds of classical sculptures, thousands of paintings and seven million books, including a precious, late-medieval parchment that would never be seen again. Some 2,389 kilos of gold – much of it stolen by the Nazis themselves – was taken from the Reichsbank vaults and shipped to the Kremlin.

Soviet soldiers claimed another spoil. Berlin's daughters, mothers and grandmothers were raped in stairwells, in burnt-out bedrooms, at gunpoint. Sons who tried to defend them were shot. Husbands – emasculated by defeat, hiding in cupboards – could only watch. Gang rape became so widespread that thousands of women gave themselves to Soviet officers in exchange for protection. Stalin laughed off the violations with the words, 'Can't you understand it if a soldier who has crossed thousands of kilometres through blood and fire has fun with a woman or takes a trifle?' About 100,000 *Berlinerinnen* were violated in the weeks following defeat, many of whom later died from internal bleeding or untreated venereal disease. Some of those who fell pregnant killed themselves. One anonymous diarist recalled the soldier who, in the moment after raping her, spat into her open mouth.

In the occupied city red Communist flags replaced the Nazi banners. Once again Berliners began to adjust themselves to a new regime, like animals – as Isherwood had written in *Goodbye to Berlin* – which change their coats for the winter. 'Thousands of people like Frl. Schroeder are acclimatising themselves. After all, whatever government is in power, they are doomed to live in this town.'

*

Dieter Werner's first memory was of sounds: the clip-clop of wooden-soled feet, the rattle of handcarts, the faint breath of fine rain against shards of glass. His mother's low whispers brushed warm against his ear, blocking out the cries of other women. He remembered her in tight headscarf and hunger, working alongside his grandmother as a *Trümmerfrau*. The bent lines of 'rubble women' zigzagged over the mountains of masonry, clearing away broken buildings, stacking the bricks in tidy rows, ten by ten by ten, a thousand bricks to every pile. As they worked he heard the sharp chip-chip of their hammers, the metallic clink of their buckets, their clipped voices. In the ruins his mother found horrible things: unexploded shells, cast-off SS uniforms, the corpses of crushed children. The British had dropped 123 types of bomb, with ninety-eight different kinds of fuses, he'd been told, and when they exploded, sometimes taking a bomb disposal man with them, the old, smoke-blackened walls collapsed with a terrible roar. His mother wept, again and again, and Dieter's grandmother sent him away to gather nettles or to queue for their ration of bread. As he grew older he wanted to stay, to protect her from all that frightened her, but his grandmother was determined to shield them both.

Dieter had been born in a cellar at the height of an air raid. He had slipped from one darkness into another, from the heartbeat warmth of the womb to the wild thump of high explosives above his head. Bombing often induced early labour and the first face he had seen in the gloom was his grandmother's, lit by candlelight as she guided him into the shrill and cold world. His father was over a thousand kilometres away, besieged or dead in Stalingrad. No one knew his fate for Hitler, in order to substantiate the lie that every Wehrmacht soldier had fallen in the battle, had ordered the men's last letters home to be burnt in secret. His mother in turn kept truths from Dieter, shutting him in the dark, shielding him from both flames and shame.

Dieter lived through Total War and utter defeat, without shoes or breakfast. In the hushed ruins he scavenged for scrap metal, collected glinting crystal tears from shattered chandeliers and avoided the sleep-walking refugees who milled about the neighbourhood in search of lost relatives. Once he found three cigarettes which his grandmother traded for needles and wool. Another time she exchanged six lumps of coal for a cabbage. On Christmas morning 1945 his mother laid an extra place at the table and held Dieter in her arms while singing the softest, strangest Christmas carol – until his grandmother returned from the water pump and hissed her into silence, sweeping the extra plate and spoon from the table.

His neighbourhood was a place of unspoken fears and resourceful women. At the end of the war over 15,000,000 German men had gone missing from the Reich, either lost in battle or locked in gulags. But Dieter did not venture into the wide world beyond broad Bernauerstraße, noisy with the gear-clash of Red Army lorries. He knew nothing of the strident division of the city, of Stalin's blockade of the Western Allies, of the distant drone of the Airlift. He could not know that the Soviet occupiers had reopened Buchenwald and Sachsenhausen, filling the camps with thousands of Berliners who opposed Communism. He did not see KGB snatch squads pluck opponents off the street, or shoot dead a couple outside a cinema in broad daylight. He would not understand that the war had ended without ending. He knew only that Russian men wore smart uniforms and stood tall and rode in vehicles. They dished out soup and protected loyal citizens from bad men called spies and terrorists, or so he was told at his crèche.

In the first decade of his life he only once left Prenzlauer Berg. On a balmy August morning in 1950 he and 60,000 other East Berlin children marched towards West Berlin. The wall was not yet built and the 'crusade' was a half-baked notion to seize the city's western half. The children were to swarm across the border, occupy key buildings and then call on the *Volkspolizei* to protect them.

Dieter walked alongside teenagers carrying bold red banners, banging drums, calling 'Für Frieden und Sozialismus seid bereit – immer bereit.' Be ready, ever ready for peace and socialism. He wore a Pioneer necktie. Older boys blew trumpets. He loved the fighting workers' songs, the idea of belonging to something bigger than himself. He felt safe in the crowd.

But at Potsdamer Platz the *Volkspolizei* stopped the rally, pulling its FDJ – Free German Youth – organisers aside, telling the children to return home. Americans troops had been put on alert and the Soviets were alarmed by the possibility that the crusade could provoke military confrontation.

In the confusion Dieter's group advanced over the boundary, in part because they had not heard the order above the noise of the drums. Fifteen minutes later they found themselves on Kurfürstenstraße, slated for demolition only ten years earlier to make way for Speer's Germania. Saturday shoppers stared as the rank of chanting children broke step to gaze at the full shop windows. Voices faltered as a dozen marchers slipped into Woolworths. A street vendor spontaneously began to hand out sausages. Grocers gave away liquorice and jellied Gummi Bear sweets. Dieter walked ahead with the ever-shrinking procession, passing gawking Freie Universität students on the steps of the café where Margarete Böhme and Goebbels had each passed an afternoon, looking left and right at the neon lights and new buildings, until he reached Wittenbergplatz. There he and two other boys stumbled into KaDeWe. The blitzed department store – the first two floors of which had reopened only one month earlier – was filled with unimagined luxuries: shiny leather shoes, French perfumes, washing machines. The crusade's last three marchers finally came to a stop in front of a brightly lit hot chocolate fountain. A security guard took them in hand and gave them glasses of Coca-Cola. No one remembered to call the *Vopos* for protection.

As East Germany began to fail, with more food shortages and harsher restrictions, thousands of its citizens followed the children over the open border, registering as refugees and joining the West German *Wirtschaftswunder*. Young Dieter and his family were not among them. He had been pleased to return to quiet Arkonaplatz, even if his contentment had paled when his grandmother pulled the sticky sweets from his pocket and, warning him that they might be poisoned, threw them into the fire. His mother wouldn't leave Prenzlauer Berg, fearing that her husband would never find her if they went away. His grandmother, who believed that her son-in-law was dead, was also unwilling to stray; she had already lived through enough change. For his part Dieter felt only that his father had abandoned and betrayed them. If he was alive then he was in prison or already in the revanchist West, along with all the other Nazis. He told himself – and his teachers – that his father meant nothing to him.

At the age of twelve he and the other boys made weapons for their own wars: pistols of wooden clothes pegs, bows and arrows from the skeletons of umbrellas, blow pipes from hollowed-out elder canes. At school he had learnt that Nazism was a form of capitalism. Hitler had been a puppet, propelled to power by AEG, Siemens and the Dresdner Bank. These 'Western' firms – alongside British monopoly capitalists – had initiated the war to feed their voracious hunger for raw materials and new markets. From the earliest days East Germans had fought to destroy the Nazi dictatorship, Dieter was told. Communist cells had operated in every neighbourhood and factory. German Communists had called on German soldiers to halt their meaningless fight and surrender to their true comrades, the Soviet Army. Stalingrad had been a great victory for freedom-loving socialists. In his new, cloth-bound history book there was no mention of D-Day, Arctic convoys, Lend-Lease or the Marshall Plan. Instead Dieter learnt that the Western Allies had abandoned Stalin and that the Red Army had liberated Eastern Europe. Patriotic East Germans had stood alongside the Soviets against the fascists and traitorous capitalists. The children of the poor, grey nation embraced the new lies for they freed them from their parents' guilt.

Dieter embellished the falsehoods with fantasy. In civics class he wrote an essay on Marx and Lenin's surprise visit to Bernauer-straße. With pride he led the fathers of Communism through his neighbourhood, assuring them that their ideas had become reality in the German Democratic Republic: free childcare, universal health care, stable food prices. He told them that there were no capitalists in East Germany, and that all the Nazis had been deported, imprisoned or eliminated. At the kitchen table, over a hearty meal of sausage and bread, Marx and Lenin reminisced about their own days in Berlin (Marx had attended its university from 1837 to 1841, Lenin passed through in 1895 and 1917). They talked about the achievements of the intervening years, and how much work remained to be done. Marx put his hand on Dieter's shoulder and promised him – with scientific certainty – that Communism is inevitable.

The story was published in *Der junge Pionier*. Two years later at his *Jugendweihe* coming of age ceremony, a local Party leader asked, 'Are you prepared to use all your strength, to fight for peace with all those who love it, and to defend it to the last breath?'

'Yes, we pledge!' replied Dieter and a dozen other dutiful fourteen-year-old boys, each wearing a new white shirt and waistcoat.

'Are you prepared to use all your strength, to fight together with all patriots for a united, peace-loving, democratic and independent Germany?'

'Yes, we pledge!' cried the Young Pioneers in charged voice, pronouncing each word with earnest deliberation, echoing the form of an earlier, equally sinister induction.

As he received his identity papers, Dieter's mother fussed with his hair. His grandmother addressed him with the formal *Sie* for the first time in his life. The Party man clasped his hand and asked what he hoped to do on graduation.

'I want to protect socialism,' he replied.

The man nodded with approval. 'Too many young men want to be radio journalists. You must consider the army.'

That autumn Dieter was appointed class rep, or Chairman of the Collective Council. In his first lecture to the school he blamed milk shortages on the hoarding of empty bottles. In his second talk he warned about American spies importing potato bugs to ruin the harvest. In the summer he went to a Pioneer camp in Saxony where – while playing war games and building bunkers brick by brick in neat alignment – he pledged to eradicate militarism. On his eighteenth birthday he joined the Party because it was right, not because it was useful. He believed that the individual's life belonged to the collective. He stood shoulder to shoulder with workers, farmers and *apparatchiks*, singing 'Die Partei, die Partei, die hat immer recht.' 'The Party, the Party is always right.' He ran home in high spirits, determined to play his part in building Stalin's Germany. By the time he reached Schönhauser Allee he had decided to volunteer for the newly formed *Volksarmee*, sprinting up the dark stairwell to tell his mother, and coming face to face with a ghost.

All his life Dieter had been haunted by his father: through his mother's reminiscences, in the small studio portrait with the oak-leaf lapels of his uniform scissorred away, in his grandmother's refusal ever to mention his name. He was both a presence and an absence in the home, a spectre of what once had been, and might have endured in Germany. Now he sat at their kitchen table, a gaunt, skeletal stranger who was more bone than flesh, and into whose open palm his mother was weeping. His other hand patted her hair in short, absent strokes. His cheeks were flushed by a lattice of broken blood vessels. Two of his front teeth were missing. He had not removed his musty, threadbare greatcoat.

Eighteen years had passed since the proud young officer had marched east to rid the world of Bolshevism. In 1958 he returned as if from the dead, a broken old man carrying a cardboard suitcase.

Dieter's mother lifted her head and told her son, 'Your father has come home.'

In East Germany the imprisonment of fathers, brothers and sons was like a shameful family secret. In the years after the war hundreds of thousands of German POWs had died in Soviet forced labour camps. Dieter's father was among the last 85,000 *Kriegsverurteilte* – war criminals – to be released from the gulags. It took him eighteen months to walk home from Siberia. Along the way he had been rearrested, branded an 'undesirable element' and sent to work in the Wismut mines in the Erzgebirge mountains, not far from his son's Pioneer summer camp. For a year he had laboured knee-deep in radioactive slime, toiling alongside inmates dying of tuberculosis and leukaemia, hacking out the raw ore to be refined into weapons-grade uranium for Soviet bombs. When he was finally released, and reached Berlin, he felt no love for Dieter's socialist paradise.

Dieter sat beside his mother and she took the hands of both her men. He felt her tears on his cheek. His father was sparing with both words and affection. Dieter felt drawn to him, as if a magnetic force tugged at his heart, yet at the same time he resisted and resented the disruption to their little world. That night his grandmother – who had not spoken since the stranger's return – moved into Dieter's room. In the dark they listened to the muffled sounds of argument, sobbing and, later, bedsprings.

In the morning he took his father into the neighbourhood. Together they walked along grey Dimitroffstraße as far as Leninallee, searching for the words that might bind them together. But every sentence faltered into empty silence, not unlike the vacant lots which time and again stopped Dieter's father in his tracks. The barracks where he had sworn his oath of allegiance were gone, as was the furniture factory where his own father had worked. The changed street names also disorientated him. In his day Leninallee had been Altlandsberger Chaussee. On Wilhelm-Pieck-Straße, once called Elsässerstraße, they paused to watch a workman chisel away a last swastika from the talons of a stone eagle. Dieter's father remembered the building had been the headquarters of the Hitler Youth. Now it was a Communist Party office.

'I miss the trees,' he said to his son. In the first, hard post-war winters every tree in the city had been hacked down for firewood. In East Berlin they were yet to be replaced. 'I often dreamt of the smell of lime blossoms.'

'There were never any trees on Leninallee,' replied Dieter coldly.

In renamed Marx-Engels-Platz, where for centuries the Berliner Schloss had stood until dynamited as a symbol of Prussian fascism, they paused to eat a sausage. The older man's hands shook as he raised it to his mouth. Tears flowed down his cheeks. 'I didn't think I would ever return home,' he confessed to his son.

For twenty minutes they sat side by side in silence on the weedy cobbles. Then Dieter's father revealed that he and his own father had once heard Hitler speak in the square. He took him to the spot where they had stood, on the steps of the Altes Museum.

'*Opa* lifted me onto his shoulders,' he said, suddenly talking as if in a fever, his words in a jumble. He spoke of the excitement of the crowd, of the intoxication of common purpose, then – calming himself – he added, 'You never met your *Opa*.'

In all Dieter's life no one had ever admitted to attending a Hitler rally. Since 1945 the dictator had been portrayed as evil incarnate, a distant and satanic vassal of capitalist forces. 'That was the war, but this is the peace' was the current, cryptic catchphrase, meaning that most Berliners felt no responsibility for those years. To hear that his father had gazed at Hitler and – as was obvious from his lack of condemnation – been moved by the occasion both shook and horrified Dieter.

The historical lie of a wartime anti-fascist resistance had been constructed to enable returning prisoners to claim to have been closet Communists. They could deny any enthusiasm for Nazism, maintaining that its defeat had enabled them to reveal their true passion for socialism. Dieter's father however was unwilling to accept the fiction.

On the museum steps Dieter asked if his father had heard Walter Ulbricht – a German Communist leader who'd lived in the Soviet Union during the war – call on Wehrmacht troops to surrender at Stalingrad. A photograph of him in a trench shouting through a loudspeaker was printed in every East German schoolbook.

His father only laughed in bitter reply.

That night, after a quiet *Abendbrot* supper of bread and *Mettwurst*, his parents argued again. At the dinner table they seemed to speak a different language. Common expressions like *Hitlerfaschismus* and 'Soviet liberators' made the old man flinch. Without a word he plucked off the wall his mother's cheap Kollwitz lithograph *Memorial Sheet to Karl Liebknecht*.

Later another point of contention arose between them. Through the bedroom wall Dieter caught the occasional word: shameless, whore, traitor.

In the confusion of Dieter's heart and mind, his father again became an enemy. The Nazis had been villains, hence his father – with his lack of repentance – could not be absolved of war crimes. Their militarism linked them to Bismarck, to Prussian aggression, to Frederick the Great. The new beginning – the brave new world – that Dieter craved could not be with his father in the family. He was a liability, an unwelcome refugee from whom his mother needed protection.

As he tossed and turned in the narrow bed, his grandmother did nothing to calm his whirlwind emotions. She knew that Dieter had been the result of a brief liaison. Her daughter's lover had always frightened her. She too wanted him out of their lives.

Two days later Dieter's father vanished. As suddenly and unexpectedly as he had appeared, he was gone. Dieter told himself that he had simply crossed to the West, even though he had left behind his cardboard suitcase. In his heart – and in his mother's tears – he may have sensed a different truth, but he asked no questions.

His mother begged him to try to find his father, to go to the Marienfelde refugee centre for information, but Dieter would not risk another visit to revanchist West Berlin. Many of his friends had caught the U-Bahn two stops to freedom, never to return, and he could have asked for their help, but he refused to communicate with such traitors. His refusal silenced his mother. Their mute, grey life had been restored and he preferred its quiet continuity.

One week later Dieter joined the Volksarmee. He trained near Dresden, fought war games alongside Warsaw Pact allies and vowed to protect peace and socialism. He marched in the May Day Parade wearing the red-trimmed epaulettes of an NVA captain. His company goose-stepped past Party leaders whose right fists were raised in salute. His stone-grey uniform with dark, high-necked collar and tall boots was not unlike that which his father had worn twenty years earlier.

Summer spread out over the city, the dry air thick with the dust kicked up by runaways. In its first decade almost three million East

Germans – about eighteen per cent of the population – had slipped away to the West. At first the refugees were professionals: 4,000 doctors and nurses, 2,000 scientists and the entire Law Faculty of the University of Leipzig. The Party denounced their flight from the Republic and – to drive home the point – its newspaper *Neues Deutschland* feigned that polio was endemic in the 'capitalist zone'. But in July 1961 alone another 30,415 East Germans from all walks of life streamed into West Berlin. In the first week of August 20,000 more citizens followed them. Dieter's promised paradise was being abandoned by its people.

At midnight on Saturday, 12 August Dieter was asleep in the Tucholsky barracks. Sunday was to be his free day and he planned to go home for the afternoon. But his dreams were interrupted by the arrival of urgent orders. As he blinked himself awake, Dieter scanned the document. In a lengthy preamble he read that the 'Ultras' – as the 'extremist' leaders of West Germany were called – wanted to revoke the results of the war and attempt again to impose German imperialism across Europe. To achieve the goal NATO – with its 'infamous' DECO II war plan – was preparing at that moment to attack democratic East Germany. As a result, Dieter and his fellow officers were to build a wall to protect their half of the city and country.

Within an hour in the surprise 'defensive' operation, 40,000 *Kampfgruppen* troops encircled West Berlin. East German workmen tore up flagstones and unrolled coils of barbed wire. Dieter stood in the rain at the western end of Bernauerstraße alongside Combat Groups of the Working Class, directing the erection of the fences. He helped to steady the wooden stakes which the men hammered into the earth. He insisted on the neat alignment of bricks. He directed the sealing of the doors of the Nordbahnhof. No S-Bahn train would stop at the station for the next twenty-nine years. In the shadows behind him were the Stasi and Volksarmee. On the radio an announcer read from a prepared script, explaining the need to safeguard East Germany from NATO, foreign intelligence agencies and rapacious West German business elites.

At dawn thousands of would-be refugees – alongside workers en route to weekend jobs in the Western sectors – were turned back at the new 'Anti-Fascist Protection Wall'. At Bergstraße a woman begged Dieter to let her join her husband and child standing three metres away on the other side of the divide. Dieter recognised her from Markthalle VI – his mother bought cabbages from her stall – but he had his orders. At the same moment on Potsdamer Platz, the busiest East–West crossing point, as well as at Invalidenstraße and Friedrichstraße station, hundreds of other men and women – clutching small valises and their children's hands – broke down and wept, their means of escape closed for a generation.

In the first weeks there were fears that the Americans and British militarists might retaliate over the brazen division of the city. Dieter expected them to drive over the barrier with their jeeps. But the lack of Western response emboldened the regime and by the autumn the wire was replaced by stones and then cement blocks, creating one of the largest structures ever built to keep people apart. Hundreds of lookout posts rose above kilometres of electrified fences. As one side of Bernauerstraße belonged to West Berlin, and the other to East Berlin, the buildings themselves were turned into border fortifications. Dieter oversaw the bricking-up of their doors and windows. He didn't like the lines of mortar to look careless.

In Communist propaganda Berlin (West) became Westberlin. Berlin (East) became Berlin, *Hauptstadt der DDR* – capital of Democratic Germany. Underground trains crawled through sealed 'ghost stations'. Armed *Vopos* blocked the few crossing points. Billboard-sized blinds were erected to prevent relatives from waving to each other. Dozens of escapees were killed trying to breach the barrier: eighteen-year-old Peter Fechter bled to death at the base of the barricade after being gunned down by East German border guards, a tailor named Günter Litfin was shot as he swam across the Spree, the elderly spinster Ida Siekmann died when she jumped from her third-floor window. Yet on official maps the encircled enclave ceased to exist, appearing as a blank no man's land at the heart of the Republic.

*

On the first Christmas Eve in the divided capital Dieter was on duty. Along the far side of the Wall the fascists had lined 1,000 Christmas trees. Fifty thousand fairy lights twinkled above the barbed wire. A few nights earlier their mayor, Willy Brandt, had called out that East Berliners 'are not forgotten by us who live in freedom'. His speech was vile provocation which spat venom at the border soldiers and proved that the 'Ultras' and their agents could not accept the defeat of NATO's invasion plans. The East German authorities responded by blaring martial music through loudspeakers, drowning out the Western Christmas carols.

Dieter stamped his feet to keep out the cold, a shivering silhouette in boots and baggy trousers. He couldn't think for the noise. He didn't hear the sound of the footsteps behind him. When he felt the touch on his shoulder he almost yelped in surprise.

His mother stood beside him in the shadows. Her face seemed to radiate an unearthly whiteness, caught for a moment in the chalky glow of the arc lights. Her now-bony frame was draped in a thick winter coat. In her arms she clutched his father's cheap suitcase. She said, 'Help me'.

Without a glance behind him, he pushed his mother into a neo-Gothic doorway. He fumbled for his pass key, turned it in the old lock then pushed open the wooden door. The strident music masked the groan of the hinges. In the darkness of the deconsecrated church, the woman told her son that she had to find her husband, that she could no longer live apart from him.

The shock of hearing her voice, and the clamour from the speakers, unnerved Dieter. The carols also affected him in a way that he could not explain. He took her hand and led her up the dim aisle, around the remaining pews to the far end of the chapel. In the days before its demolition, the Church of Reconciliation straddled no man's land. Its tower was used as an observation post. As a boy Dieter had played in its graveyard.

He flicked on his torch for a second, guiding his mother into an alcove. Again he fumbled for a key, felt the keyhole and snapped open the second lock. In the darkness she touched his cheek. 'I will write when I find him,' she whispered.

The escape lasted less than a minute. Dieter did not watch his mother slip into the West Berlin night. Instead he hurried to close the door, seeing only his swift breath rise in the cold air. In the gloom, he gathered the muffled silence around him like a blanket, wondering for a moment if he was dreaming. He picked his way back across the nave. Without a sound he slipped through the old doorway. On Bernauerstraße the *Grenzpolizei* were waiting for him.

On that Christmas long ago the frightened man who had helped to build the Wall was arrested and imprisoned. He was stripped of rank then cast out of both the Party and Berlin. He was exiled to the Wismut mines, though as a manual labourer rather than a slave. Times were changing even in East Germany. His grandmother had disowned him but nevertheless she lost the family apartment.

In the 1970s Dieter's mother finally wrote from West Germany, although the letter took over two years to reach him. In it he learnt that she had not found his father. She would never find him, or see her son again.

'She died too young,' Dieter Werner told me decades later, shaking his head. 'My family – and my country – were like a Greek tragedy. All these years I've wondered, why did she and they do it to us? To her own daughter? To me?' he sighed in wretched sadness. 'In the end you have to ask, did she ever really love us? Or just pretend all her life?'

At the height of its power the Stasi – 'the shield and sword' of the East German Communist Party and trained by the KGB – employed hundreds of thousands of informers. Its huge, fortified central compound occupied an entire city block in Berlin-Lichtenberg, 10365, with barracks, arms depot, spy school, remand cells, even exclusive gyms and an employees' hospital. Its thirty-eight buildings and 15,000 officers were linked by a private telephone network and the remit to know everything about everyone. On its shelves stretched 160 kilometres of documents on its 17,000,000 captive citizens: stolen love letters, transcripts of canteen conversations, denunciations by 'unofficial collaborators', certificates denying university education, instructions for the 'Operational Control of Persons' and detailed plans for the invasion of West Berlin. With a million manila folders, filled with the minutiae of other, ordinary lives, it terrorised and cowed a generation of East Germans.

To many, the Second World War didn't end in 1945. Nor had the First World War lasted for only four years. The Great Twentieth-Century War, which began in 1914, shattered empires and killed one hundred millions souls, severing Germany and heralding decades of repression. No other city suffered for as many of its seventy-five years than Berlin, until 1989 and the final fall of its Wall.

CHAPTER 18

*Bill Harvey, and
the Tunnel*

East Berlin children on newly divided Waldemarstraße, Berlin-Kreuzberg, 13 August 1961 (*Archive of Modern Conflict*)

Rudow, 1955

B eyond the window the world was black. Darkness spread to the far horizon. No lights burned in the distance. Without reference points to link it to the ground, the DC-4 appeared to be cut adrift, perched between departure and destination, earth and sky, yesterday and today. Its engines whined, air rushed along the fuselage, but the passengers seemed locked in limbo, poised above a dark and unchanging place. The man in seat 1A pushed his forehead against the cool Perspex pane, craned his thick neck and gazed into the night.

'Would you like to come up now?' asked the stewardess. He put down his drink and followed her dark blue jacket and pencil skirt to the cockpit. The door was unlocked.

'Make yourself at home,' said the captain in a no-frills Midwestern voice. He wore dollar-sign braces and gestured at the fold-down jump seat. In Frankfurt the passenger had asked to ride up front during the flight. In the 1950s it wasn't an unusual request.

'First visit to the island?' the pilot asked, turning to face him, looking forward to conversation.

The shapeless passenger seemed more shadow than substance, despite his bulky size. He growled a monosyllabic reply. At the start of any journey he liked to keep quiet, to let silence draw out the other party.

'Business trip?' probed the pilot after a moment. 'Or military?'

'Greetings cards,' said the passenger with a weary air. 'I sell greetings cards.'

In 1952 the United States and Soviet Union were at war.

After 'Little Boy', the atomic bomb dropped seven years earlier on Hiroshima, had come Russia's 'First Lightning'. America had responded with Minuteman missiles and the Soviets came back with the RDS-3 plutonium nuke. In the escalating arms race, tens of thousands of ballistic missiles, long-range bombers and submarine-launched SLBMs were to be built and targeted on European, American and Asian cities. Every single fission warhead was at least a dozen times more powerful than the bombs which had devastated Japan.

MAD, or mutual assured destruction, was becoming the pyrrhic military strategy – and suicidal deterrent – that guaranteed any nuclear attack doomed both the aggressor and the defender. At the touch of a button all life on earth would be extinguished. Fearful governments in the East and West were desperate for the intelligence which could secure the possibility of their survival. Berlin was the epicentre of their espionage efforts. It was an unlikely place to sell greeting cards.

'We get a lot of military men up here,' said the pilot, not buying the passenger's story. When there was no response he went on, 'You know, sometimes when I fly this route at night, I imagine what it might look like if the balloon went up: Soviet Tupolevs massing on the horizon, vapour trails of Superfortresses and Honest Johns criss-crossing the heavens, a mushroom cloud rising above West Berlin.' He shook his head. 'It'll be quite a show.'

'Civilisation's last, greatest fireworks display,' said his co-pilot. 'With no greetings cards at the end of it.'

The passenger stroked his pencil-thin moustache and grunted, 'Not a pretty thought.'

For five minutes they cruised on in silence, in the dark, as if making no progress. Then far ahead across the bleak Prussian plain the sky began to lighten. A bright island of light glimmered on the horizon. The pilot – who hailed from Michigan – eased the Pan Am DC-4 along the narrow air corridor, descended from 10,000 feet and banked into his approach.

The passenger returned to his seat as East Germany's fields fell behind them. Beyond his window glittered Ku'damm's theatres and cafés. A thousand new street lights illuminated Kantstraße. Beneath the aircraft the encircled outpost of Western democracy – gaudy, brash and free – shimmered in a dark Communist sea.

Two and a half years later, in spring 1955, a pair of US Army Leitz binoculars flashed in the sunlight. In a concealed lookout post at the edge of the American sector a soldier blinked and said, 'Nuts!'

Five hundred metres away across the border a Red Army convoy rumbled along sleepy, rural Schönefelder Chaussee.

The lookout man turned his swivel chair and punched the panic button. He lifted the handset of his field telephone and barked, 'Check. Russians. Right to left. Three trucks, one jeep, two T-34s. Tanks, man. Goddamn tanks.'

Beneath him a secret, steel-lined tunnel stretched half a kilometre under the frontier into the Soviet Zone. Along its length two dozen US Army Engineers bagged the sandy soil. A noiseless, electric forklift truck hauled equipment forward on wooden tracks. At its head, at the top of a vertical shaft less than a metre below the surface, British sappers probed the loose earth with long screwdrivers. The two Allied teams had been digging for eighteen weeks and were now within inches of their target.

Suddenly the tunnel lights flashed from white to red. In their earphones the Brits heard the lookout's warning. He was their eyes and ears, alerting them to intrusions into the 'silence bracket'.

'Get out,' he hissed to them. 'Can you get out?'

The sappers were balanced on wooden beams, their heads pressed against the top of the vertical shaft. They were directly under the road, perched high above the tunnel floor, deep in Soviet territory. They couldn't retreat. They couldn't move forward. Discovery meant arrest, death, maybe even war. At the most vulnerable moment of the operation, they could only wait – and hope – in silence.

John Wyke, the team leader, was the first to hear the lick of the lorries' tyres. He braced himself against the Mole as the walls started to shake. The vibrations began to release showers of earth and sand. In their earphones the lookout narrated the convoy's approach. 'First truck . . . Second truck . . . First tank . . .' The diesel roar of the vehicles echoed around the tiny chamber. The treads of the T-34s seemed to tear at the pavement over their heads. A working light broke free from its anchor and swung wildly in the confined space. The earth seemed to groan under the weight.

As the vehicles passed overhead the air filled with dust. Below in the main tunnel men choked and coughed, then – breaking the rule for absolute quiet – called up to the tap chamber, 'Are you alright, sir?'

The Royal Engineers wiped the grit from their faces. The tunnel hadn't collapsed. Above their heads, hanging from the crumbled workface, were three thick, military communications cables. The underground wires connected the sprawling Wünsdorf Red Army headquarters to central Berlin and Moscow. The tanks had shaken free the remaining earth to reveal the tunnellers' target.

'You beautiful, horrible, dirty bunch of voices,' whispered Wyke, reaching up to stroke their black, secret prize. 'We've done it. We've bloody well done it.'

Since the end of the Second World War, Stalin's intention had been to bind Berlin – and then the whole of Germany – into the Communist orbit. 'All of Germany must be ours, that is, Soviet, Communist,' he'd instructed the Politburo.

To achieve that end he had needed to have the atomic bomb. He'd known from his spies that the Russian programme lagged far behind America's Manhattan Project, which had produced the first atomic bomb. He had known also that at the Kaiser Wilhelm Institute, in laboratories once used by Haber and Einstein, German radiochemists had unravelled the mystery of nuclear fission.

On his order, KGB squads had stripped Berlin's atomic research establishments in 1945. The stolen uranium had been used to fuel the first Russian nuclear reactor. Dozens of top German scientists had been deported to Moscow and with their help, as well as key espionage successes, Moscow had managed to build and detonate its own bomb by 1949.

Stalin's belligerence, and Communist coups in Poland, Czechoslovakia and Hungary, had convinced America that a surprise attack was inevitable. Their fear of nuclear war was real, and surviving the apocalypse relied on intelligence. When would the Reds' missiles be launched? What were their targets? Where would their armour break into West Germany?

'I don't care what the CIA does; all I want is twenty-four hours' notice of Soviet attack,' said George Marshall, Chief of Staff of the US Army and then Secretary of State. The Central Intelligence Agency had been formed to provide early warning of enemy action. But with Soviet borders sealed, satellite surveillance not yet invented and most Western agents betrayed by Philby, Burgess and Maclean, members of the infamous Cambridge spy ring, a new way had to be found to forewarn of the start of World War Three.

In late 1952 the taciturn, shapeless American had emerged from the DC-4 at Berlin Tempelhof. At the top of the steps he grasped the handrail and lit a cigarette. Under his gabardine jacket he holstered a pearl-handled revolver. A second gun was jammed in his belt.

'Big Bill' Harvey was no greetings cards salesman. He was the CIA's new Berlin station chief. His swelling bulk and duck-like walk – part-waddle, part-swagger – made him an unlikely man of the shadows. He was wily, gruff and profane with something animal in his narrow brown eyes. In Washington he'd seemed to live on martinis alone. Yet at the same time he had an uncanny ability to blend into his surroundings, to pass by unnoticed – except to his CIA bosses. His intuition and flick-knife memory had made him the Agency's leading expert on Soviet espionage. He was a zealous, canny, two-hundred-pound missionary, thrust to the Cold War's front line to run agents, to recruit informers and – above all – to tap enemy communications.

Since 1949 British intelligence had been burrowing makeshift spy tunnels under Vienna, which at the time was divided and occupied like Berlin. In four different locations Russian-speaking officers had eavesdropped on Soviet military telephone calls, recording important conversations on dated Edison wax cylinders and – as the value of the information became apparent – new BTR reel-to-reel machines. When the CIA learnt of the Viennese tunnels they wanted to be part of them, and to extend the operation to Berlin.

On his arrival Harvey – aged thirty-six – leased two acres of land in Rudow, a sparsely populated, outlying neighbourhood of *Schrebergarten* allotments and shanty shacks built from rubble scavenged by refugees. He contracted a German builder to erect three large warehouses near the boundary of the Soviet Zone. The buildings were described as 'emergency equipment storage units' and had oversized cellars. On the roof he installed a sophisticated antennae cluster to give the look of a clandestine radar listening station. East German *Vopos* patrolling the border lifted their eyes and telephoto lenses towards the impressive AN/APR9 aerial which pointed at nearby Schönefeld – later BER – airport. It didn't occur to them to look down at their feet.

Operation Gold's success depended on absolute secrecy. A security leak would not only endanger the lives of its tunnellers and inflame political tensions, it could enable the Soviets to mislead the Allies with disinformation. At two meetings in London the partners agreed to divide both responsibilities and spoils. The Americans volunteered to dig the long, horizontal tunnel. British sappers – with their experience in Vienna – would burrow upward from the head and make the tap. A forward listening team would be stationed in the tunnel itself, to relay warning of any imminent

Soviet attack. Voice and data tapes would be flown to the UK and US every week.

In a meeting room overlooking St James's Park, Harvey – suspicious of more British double agents – voiced aloud his hope that no Philbys were present in the building (in 1954 Philby was widely suspected but not yet exposed as the 'Third Man'). To reassure him Scotsman George Young, an SIS controller who later became deputy director of MI6, shook his head and joked, 'We don't want to be caught with our kilts up again.'

The London discussions were confidential, convivial and productive, and were minuted by a trusted Section Y officer named George Blake. As instructed Blake typed up his copious notes, distributing carbons to Harvey, Young and the other key players. But he made one extra copy. A week later he left the office as usual, wandered through Soho, dawdled over a cup of tea on Oxford Street, caught a Northern Line train to Belsize Park and then – certain he was not being followed – climbed onto a bus. On its all but deserted upper deck he slipped the complete plans for the tunnel into his KGB controller's hand.

The digging of Harvey's Hole began in September 1954. A team of forty US Army Engineers – dressed in Signal Corps uniforms – first sank a vertical shaft beneath the basement floor of the warehouse. To calculate the tunnel's precise angle and length, an object of known size had to be placed at the target point. A softball game was organised, the engineers' best batsman slugging the ball across the border onto Schönefelder Chaussee. But before the distance could be measured with a hidden theodolite, the *Vopos* lobbed it back to the players. Harvey then sent a vehicle into East Berlin, arranging for it to break down above the Soviet cables. The driver placed a small reflector on the road as he changed the tyre. The horizontal tunnel had to measure exactly 1,476 feet long.

The Americans worked ten men to a shift, twenty-four hours a day in a secret underworld beneath the flashpoint of the world. No alcohol or women were allowed on the site. Underground conversation had to be kept to a whisper. A cylindrical shield six feet in diameter moled forward into the soil, the engineers standing inside its rim, digging between removable vertical plates. Every three inches the earth was cleared from within the shield, the unit was jacked forward and a steel ring bolted into place behind it. Grout was pumped around the liner to fill any gaps. The spoil was bagged and sent back to be stacked in the warehouse's oversized cellar. Once the team hit a perched water table, which flooded the tunnel and threatened to drown them all, and soon afterwards they burrowed through an old cesspit, which almost gassed them to death. At least a dozen times a day the red warning lights flashed, the diggers reached for the earphones and listened to the lookout describe a *Vopo* foot patrol or curious Russian officer, standing only three metres above their heads.

As the Americans pushed into East German territory, taking an alignment check every few yards, British sappers at Aldershot perfected the technique to make the vertical shaft. John Wyke – who had worked on the Viennese operation – designed the Mole, a bottomless steel box with Venetian blind top. Its slats could be opened and closed one at a time, enabling the Royal Engineers to tease out the soil overhead, then claw upward inch by inch without causing a collapse. Five months after excavation had begun the British team was flown to Gatow, issued with American uniforms, given GI haircuts and delivered to the site. Like the US engineers, they were confined to the warehouse, fed on protein-rich steak dinners and banned from visiting the city.

That winter was especially long and cold. Early in March 1955 Wyke's small No. 1 Specialist Team RE took over from the Americans. One misty morning, after they'd begun the upward thrust, the warmth of the tunnel – from the sappers' body heat – melted the surface frost. A distinct line ran under the perimeter fence and across the border to Schönefelder Chaussee. A *Vopo* foot patrol happened to pass and pause, stamping their feet on the pavement to keep warm. But neither they, nor a Soviet sentry, looked down at the ground. Only the low-lying mist, and the pumping of freezing air down the ventilation ducts, saved the operation from exposure.

*

Bill Harvey had a morbid fascination with the underground; places that were hidden and – in a Christian sense – related to death. As a child in small-town Indiana he'd dug a secret den in the woods behind the family home, burying his dead pets in the ground around it. In Berlin he'd spied the entrance to Hitler's blasted bunker off Vossstraße. He'd descended into the vast subterranean halls beneath Tempelhof where Messerschmitt fighters had once been assembled. He'd crouched in the clammy, claustrophobic bomb shelter beneath Gesundbrunnen U-Bahn station. Now he was driven to the tunnel every other night, changing vehicles to shake off any tails, arriving in a closed truck so as not to raise the suspicion of enemy observers. He liked the feeling of dropping down the ladder into the cold embrace of the earth. He also liked the sense that he was doing a job that none of his stuck-up Ivy League peers would undertake, going out on a limb, getting his hands dirty.

In Washington he had badgered the chiefs, stripping away their objections, convincing them to go with Gold. CIA director Allen Dulles had approved the six-million-dollar budget (about $55,000,000 today) on the condition that as little as possible be put in writing. He had added, 'Be sure nobody gets hurt, Bill.'

On the nights when he didn't visit the tunnel Harvey stayed at his Föhrenweg office in the American sector, battling to sustain the East Zone network, forming shadowing teams, handing out the stacks of twenty-dollar bills to keep informants sweet, often putting in twenty-hour days. Afterwards he might take in a cocktail or square-dancing party where, no matter how warm it became, he never removed his jacket. 'Can't take it off,' he'd whisper to his host, revealing the revolvers strapped under his sweaty armpits.

From time to time he dawdled at the ruins of an abandoned mansion off broad Clayallee, its upper floor blasted away, and gazed at an old oak immured in its small walled garden. In the high enclosure he saw the tree shed its autumn leaves, then bud virgin green, feeling himself strangely moved. All the other trees in Berlin were so young.

He even went home to his wife, CG. Clara Grace was the Berlin base's mother hen, a bright, likeable teetotaller and the first female major in the US military. At their rambling house on Milinowski-straße (near to the curious Onkel Toms Hütte, named after either the American novel or a pub landlord who'd installed cabins in his beer garden), 'Big Bill' mixed Gilbey's gin with a whisper of Noilly Prat. To lubricate loquaciousness he encouraged his guests – embassy men, States-side business people, soldiers who believed in risking their lives for an ideal – to gulp down the first martini. He liked them to linger over the second round, so as to engender reflection, allowing the layers of reserve to melt away. The third drink tended to bring on intimacy, even confession and Harvey would observe, listen, say little. After that, as the sozzled Americans carefully set their empty bird-bath glasses on the coffee table and staggered away to bed, he usually returned to the office.

The Berlin staff were his family, even after he and CG adopted a baby who had been left on the doorstep of another CIA officer.

'Look what the Lord has sent us!' CG told Harvey, blessed with the child they'd been unable to conceive themselves. The birth mother had been an East German who – according to her note – wanted the child to grow up in the free world. 'It's a strange feeling to become a mother overnight without knowing it.'

'This city is seldom dull,' grunted Harvey, downplaying the media attention.

Later his staff asked, 'Is the kid wired?', joking that the Harveys' little girl was the ultimate Soviet penetration agent.

The British sappers took four weeks to reach the three black, rubber-sheathed cables. After the vibrations from the Soviet convoy had exposed the target, the Mole was cemented around them. Two dozen chromium steel tubes were driven into the earth to make a solid ceiling. With a hydraulic jack the cables were stretched down into the chamber. Two 'jointers' from the British Post Office's Special Investigations Unit – both of whom had worked on the SIS Vienna operations – were flown in from London. In the cramped space beneath Schönefelder Chaussee they made the final tap in a single four-hour night shift.

On 11 May 1955 the system went live. The Soviets' 1,200 communications channels were fed down a lead-away cable to the Forward Operations Chamber, a subterranean room with a dozen racks of sophisticated British electronics. Here the weak signals were amplified for transmission along the tunnel to the principal transcription point. Special equipment also readjusted the lowered impedance of the tapped lines so that the infringement could not be detected. To protect both tap and equipment from humidity, the relay chamber was sealed behind a vapour barrier. As the operation was always known to be finite, Harvey ordered a sign to be fastened to an anti-personnel door warning in both Russian and German, 'Entry is forbidden by order of the Commanding General.'

'The Reds are like Pavlov's dogs. Rebellion has been slaughtered out of them,' Harvey told Wyke in his deep, rumbling voice. He believed that Communists would lie down under tanks if ordered to do it. 'The sign will hold them back for an hour or two if necessary.'

In the cover station the reels of 150 new Ampex tape recorders began to turn. Half a dozen British linguists slipped on their headphones to monitor the key military lines. The atmosphere in the warehouse was contemplative, with minds focused and voices subdued. In the first day alone a mile of recording tape was produced. That evening all the voice and teletype reels were packaged in camouflaged boxes, driven to rendezvous points and flown on special flights to London and Washington.

The tap produced a bonanza of intelligence. In London's Chester Terrace, SIS employed 300 translators and transcribers to handle the 1,000 tapes delivered every week. Across the Atlantic, 350 Russian and German linguists worked – in shifts of fifty at a time – on the teletype traffic in a windowless, steel-clad building on the Washington Mall. Over the lifetime of the operation, 50,000 reels of magnetic tape were recorded, 430,000 conversations translated and 1,750 intelligence reports distributed to President, Prime Minister and throughout the Western intelligence community. None of the scoops were headline-grabbing sensations. The tunnel provided insight into Khrushchev's denunciation of Stalin, the Soviet plutonium bomb and secret atomic weapon research sites as well as the doubling of Tupolev bombers around Berlin. But the ordinariness of the information reassured the Allies that a Soviet attack was not imminent.

On the day that the tunnel went live, George Blake – who more than a year before had betrayed the operation to the KGB – was in Berlin, and beside himself with anger and fear. He did not understand why the Soviets had not acted. Spies were not priests, saints or martyrs. As novelist John le Carré would later write, perhaps thinking of the Dutch-born Blake (Alec Leamas, the anti-hero of *The Spy Who Came in from the Cold*, was also linked to Holland), spies were vain fools, traitors, 'pansies, sadists and drunkards, people who play cowboys and Indians to brighten their rotten lives'.

Five years earlier during the Korean War, Blake had been captured and – to survive the horror of imprisonment in Manchuria – had converted to Communism. On his release he had been welcomed back to the UK as a hero. The national papers had celebrated his return, printing a photograph of a lean, bearded man in thick-spun overcoat in their first editions. SIS had rewarded him with sympathy, holidays and promotion, then entrusted him with its most sensitive projects. In response Blake gave away the names of dozens of British agents who were then murdered by the Russians.

In April 1955 he had been posted to West Berlin, settling into a top-floor apartment on Platanenallee, around the corner from Speer's old Lindenallee workshop. He enjoyed the ten-minute walk to his office near the Olympic Stadium. Ironically his new role was to recruit KGB men as double agents, the names of whom he fed back to Moscow. To keep him above suspicion in British eyes, the KGB gave him the identities of a few minor Soviet operatives in the UK. Blake's continuing duplicity succeeded in all but destroying MI6's operations in Eastern Europe.

Berlin also made it easy to meet his controller. Instead of a furtive rendezvous in a men's lavatory in Regent's Park or secret trips to Holland, he bought a small sailing boat to run up and down the Havel. On Pfaueninsel, the island close to the border and to where

Goebbels had had his villa, Blake demanded an explanation for the lack of Soviet action on the tunnel. 'I have seen it with my own eyes,' he hissed, fearing for his skin. 'Nothing has been done. Nothing.'

Blake looked like he'd had the hell posted out of him, as was said then in the espionage world. He was terrified that his code name might be revealed on the tapped lines. His controller reassured him that Moscow had decided not to expose the tunnel so as to protect him, their most valuable agent. Its betrayer had become its guardian. But the explanation was only half the truth.

Above Berlin the sky grew dark, sank lower and split open under the weight of rain. The sodden spring soured Harvey's mood. As the torrents lashed against his office window he toyed with the lid of his Zippo lighter, flicking it open and shut, open and shut. Spooks came and went in Berlin, assuming an identity, doing a job, living by their wits and subterfuge. On Harvey's desk was a file on Yevgeny Pitovranov, his counterpart in East Berlin. Much had been gleaned on the KGB *Rezident* from the intercepted telephone conversations: he was a fighter, a professional, the hardened 'fixer' who on his arrival from Moscow had built the Stasi intelligence service. Like Harvey he loved guns, although the Russian preferred hunting wild boar at night using rifles with infra-red sights. If any Soviet knew about the tunnel it was Pitovranov, and Harvey followed his conversations and movements with fanatical attention.

In early April the ice-cold rains swamped Rudow's lanes. The Rudower Fließ and Meskengraben overflowed their banks. Telephone cables began to short-circuit all over the city. In Wünsdorf, Red Army engineers set about bypassing defective lines. Harvey was called to the station. As the downpour drummed on the roof, he was told that the Russians had ordered the East German Post Office to help to fix the faults. Their repair vehicles were rolling along Schönefelder Chaussee.

Harvey dropped down into the tunnel, waddling his distinctive bulk towards its head. He wanted to reassure himself that the floods were not being used as an excuse to expose the operation.

The line faults were too extensive to raise suspicions, yet he had an inkling that all was not well. As was his habit, he spun the cylinder of his revolver. Everything seemed in place in the tap chamber. He locked the door behind him and returned to the West.

On 22 April 1956, eleven months and eleven days after the reels of the Ampex recorders had started to turn, the East Germans began to dig up Schönefelder Chaussee. A hidden microphone picked up the sound of probing shovels, falling debris and muffled voices.

'The box opens onto a shaft,' said a surprised telephone engineer as he uncovered the Mole.

Across the border Harvey – having ordered the evacuation of the tunnel – sat with the translators listening on headphones. Neither the Germans nor their Russian guards seemed to realise what they had uncovered.

'A cable runs under the street,' reported a Soviet soldier.

Harvey heard heavy breathing as the men dropped down into the pre-amplification chamber. Then there was a moment of silence.

'Donnerwetter!' gasped an engineer in *Berlinerisch* dialect, ''s ist ja fantastisch. It's not a capsule, it's a complete installation. A telephone exchange.'

'Menschenskind!' said another workman, marvelling at the equipment. 'Man alive, this must have cost something.'

'It's so neat and tidy,' remarked the first German.

'Hallo? Hallo?' they called into the darkness.

In the warehouse Harvey asked for permission to blow the tunnel. As the explosion could have killed Russian soldiers, the US commander in Berlin refused him with the words, 'I don't want to start World War Three.' Instead Harvey ordered sandbags and barbed wire to be placed under the sector boundary. On a sheet of cardboard he wrote, 'You are now entering the American sector.' A few metres behind the sign he himself set up a .30 calibre heavy machine-gun. When he heard footsteps approaching he pulled back the bolt. The clack of gunmetal echoed down the steel tube. The footsteps stopped, then slowly retreated back into East German territory.

The machine-gun had not been loaded.

Twenty minutes later the cable tap was cut and the microphone went dead. The last words caught on tape were those of an American linguist telling a colleague, 'It's gone, John.'

Once again West Berlin became a dangerous place. The Red Army reinforced its positions around the capitalist island. No one knew the Soviets' intentions any longer, and no resident felt safe. Searchlights, white and brilliant, swept the edges of the enclave and people began to work out their escape routes. Harvey attached a thermite bomb to his office safe, ready for detonation in the event of invasion. The old Dietrich song 'Ich hab' noch einen Koffer in Berlin' took on a double meaning: the Allies kept Berlin in their hearts and West Berliners tucked a packed bag under the bed, ready to run. But where can you hide when the world is about to end?

In 1961 Khrushchev bullied the new American president, John F. Kennedy, at their Vienna summit. The Soviet leader – who perpetrated Stalin's offensive and opportunistic foreign policy – was determined to belittle the newcomer. He called Berlin 'the testicles of the West', boasting later that 'every time I want to make the West scream, I squeeze Berlin'.

Khrushchev demanded that American troops leave the city, threatening to sign a 'peace treaty' with East Germany which would block Western access. When Kennedy refused to capitulate, the Russian told him, 'Force will be met by force. If the US wants war, that's its problem . . . The decision to sign a peace treaty is firm and irrevocable.'

'Then, Mr Chairman, there will be a war,' replied Kennedy. 'It will be a cold, long winter.'

As tens of thousands of East Germans (including Dieter Werner's classmates) fled to the West, an irate and disheartened Kennedy began to prepare for nuclear war. He added billions to the defence budget. He reiterated that an attack on West Berlin would be an attack on the US. The construction of the Wall brought him a moment of relief. As the president perceived it, Khrushchev had found a way to solve his refugee crisis and preserve East Germany without violating Allied rights. The face-saving, heinous compromise reduced the risk of global conflict.

'It's not a very nice solution but a wall is a hell of a lot better than a war,' he told his aides.

But the Western press saw the Communists' action as a defeat. Kennedy was accused of appeasement. One million free people in a cage, screamed the headlines. West Berliners took to the streets carrying placards which read 'Where are the Americans?' and 'Munich 1938 – Berlin 1961'. University students posted Kennedy a black umbrella similar to the one which Chamberlain had carried when meeting Hitler in Munich. West Berlin mayor Willy Brandt, breaking all rules of protocol, wrote to the White House warning of a severe 'crisis of confidence' if the Western powers remained 'inert and strictly on the defensive'.

To show that its half of the city would not be sacrificed, and to bolster his public image, Kennedy sent Vice President Johnson and General Lucius D. Clay, hero of the Airlift, to Berlin. Then he himself followed them. He climbed onto a wooden viewing platform to look across the grim divide. Behind him thousands of Western residents cheered his visit. In front of him, on the far side of no man's land, a dozen East Berliners saluted him in silence. Their courage stirred – perhaps even transformed – Kennedy. As his motorcade wove towards Schöneberg, he amended his prepared speech. He asked his translator to remind him how to say in German 'I am a Berliner' and scribbled the response phonetically on his script.

Freedom has many difficulties and democracy is not perfect, Kennedy declared from the podium outside the City Hall. 'But we have never had to put a wall up to keep our people in.'

In the broad square, on the surrounding rooftops and balconies, half a million Berliners roared in response. His audience was roused and Kennedy caught their mood.

'There are many people in the world who really don't understand, or say they don't, what is the great issue between the free world and the Communist world. Let them come to Berlin,' he said with feeling, now hardly glancing at his speech cards, departing from the carefully prepared script.

'There are some who say that Communism is the wave of the future,' he went on, his voice rising, the warm June breeze stirring his hair as well as the flags of city, nation and superpower guardian. 'Let them come to Berlin.'

'And there are some who say in Europe and elsewhere we can work with the Communists. Let them come to Berlin,' he insisted, his voice filled with a new cadence.

'And there are even a few who say that it is true that Communism is an evil system, but it permits us to make economic progress,' he called, banging home his point and fist. 'Lasst sie nach Berlin kommen. Let them come to Berlin.'

Then Kennedy cried out, 'All free men, wherever they may live, are citizens of Berlin, and therefore, as a free man, I take pride in the words "Ich bin ein Berliner".'

In response the crowd howled, applauded and wept. Adrift on their 'defended island of freedom', surrounded by twenty Soviet divisions, Berlin began to define itself anew. Its identity, destroyed by the Nazis, was restored by the Airlift and the Wall, by its transformation from villain to victim. Kennedy told Berliners that one day their city would be rejoined, in a peaceful and hopeful globe, and that the people of West Berlin could then take sober satisfaction in the fact that they had been on the front line for so many decades.

His speech was more than one of the defining moments of the Cold War. It marked the end of centuries of Prussian warrior culture, now irrelevant in a Western Europe protected and pacified by the strategic might of the United States.

Five months later Kennedy was assassinated. But before the fateful trip to Dallas, the president had met Bill Harvey at the White House. The shapeless patriot had become the CIA's heaviest hitter. Champion of the tunnel, nemesis of the KGB, recruiter of false defectors to the Soviet Union (he knew of Lee Harvey Oswald) and recipient of the secret Distinguished Intelligence Medal, he was destined for a role at the top of the Agency.

As Harvey was ushered towards the Oval Office, Edward

Lansdale, an Air Force Brigadier General and Kennedy's 'Cuba Commander', asked him, 'You're not carrying a gun, are you?'

'Sure I am,' replied Harvey, pulling a revolver from his pocket.

'Keep the damn thing in your pants,' whispered Lansdale, looking around for a guard to whom Harvey could turn over the weapon.

A Secret Service agent was found. The gun was surrendered. With a shake of his head, Lansdale again reached for the door handle. Harvey then cleared his throat.

'Sorry,' he said, as if apologising for an oversight. He reached behind his gabardine jacket and unsnapped a .38 Detective Special from its hidden holster. He handed the second gun to the startled agent. 'It slipped my mind.'

As the two men entered the Oval Office, Kennedy rose from his desk.

'Mr President sir, I'd like to introduce you to America's James Bond,' said Lansdale.

Around the same time in London, George Blake was exposed, arrested and sentenced at the Old Bailey to forty-two years' imprisonment, then the longest sentence ever to have been handed down by a British court. His confession led to accusations that the Soviets had used the tunnel to purvey disinformation. In truth such deception would have been impossible given the massive number of different voices monitored, recorded and cross-referenced. Yet the KGB – including Yevgeny Pitovranov – had known about the tunnel throughout its operation. On the night of its 'discovery' two of his officers were recorded saying, 'We know what the matter is, so we must speak carefully.'

So why didn't the Soviets act?

First, the KGB needed to protect Blake. If the tunnel had been exposed earlier, the British and Americans would have suspected a traitor.

Second, Operation Gold had tapped military lines. The Red Army's internal intelligence service, the GRU, was responsible for military security. The KGB and GRU were rivals, not unlike the CIA and FBI. By keeping knowledge of the intrusion to itself, and shifting some of its own traffic to other channels, the KGB ensured maximum embarrassment for the GRU.

Third, and above all, the Soviets did not act so as to give themselves time. In the 1950s America had far greater weapon superiority. The Soviets could not afford to attack – yet. With the Americans lulled into complacency, Russia had the chance to build up its nuclear arsenal.

Soon after the closure of the tunnel 'Big Bill' left Berlin, never to return. By the time of his death from complications arising from alcoholism, technological advances – such as the U-2 spy plane and satellite reconnaissance – had ended the need for physical telephone taps. Other tunnels would be dug in Berlin's sandy soil; some seventy-one subterranean passages enabled more than 200 East Berliners to escape under the Wall to freedom between 1962 and 1982. But Harvey's Hole, in helping to hold the world back from Armageddon, remains the most important and imaginative Allied intelligence operation of the Cold War.

Or does it?

Years later John le Carré – whose real name was David Cornwell – recalled his first visit to Berlin in 1961, while working as Second Secretary in the British Embassy at Bonn. The sight of the Wall had filled him with disgust and outrage, and inspired him to write his seminal book in five intense weeks. Berlin had seeped into his soul: its black winter canals, its deep dark shadows, the 'weasel faces of the brainwashed little thugs who guarded the Kremlin's latest battlement'. In turn *The Spy Who Came in from the Cold*, published two years later, would also transform the city, weaving further intricacy into its mythology, conjuring up a place both perilous and clandestine, drawing shades of grey out of the old black and white townscape.

'But the Berlin tunnel was blown before the first top-secret spade went into the ground,' le Carré told me, dismissing the remarkable, multi-million-dollar SIS-CIA project. 'It wasn't a triumph, it was a cock-up.'

CHAPTER 19

*John F. Kennedy, and
Politics as Theatre*

John F. Kennedy making his 'Ich bin ein Berliner' speech at West Berlin (Schöneberg) city hall, 26 June 1963. (*akg-images*)

Rathaus Schöneberg, 1963

Wednesday, 26 June

ACT ONE
Scene 1 At Tegel Airport, West Berlin (1963)

Enter JOHN F. KENNEDY, a President, and LUCIUS D. CLAY, a General. KENNEDY is forty-six years old, with brown hair and eyes that seem to look into the future. CLAY is sixty-six, the retired hero of the Airlift and a man with muscle enough to wrestle order out of chaos. He is nicknamed 'the Kaiser'.

Off stage the engines of Air Force One are heard winding down.

KENNEDY and CLAY descend the Boeing 707 gangway. In front of them waits a reception committee: German politicians stand on stage right, Allied commanders on stage left. A military band plays 'Hail to the Chief'.

KENNEDY shakes hands and mounts the podium at the beginning of his eight-hour visit to West Berlin.

KENNEDY: The legendary morale and spirit of the people of West Berlin has lit a fire throughout the world. But it is not so surprising for through history those who live in the most danger, those who live nearest the adversary, those who keep the watch at the gate, are always prouder, more courageous, more alive, than those who live far to the rear.

Flourish. KENNEDY inspects the assembled American, British and French honour guard as well as a detachment of the West Berlin police. Sounds off stage of starting motorcade engines.

Exeunt KENNEDY, CLAY and Attendants.

Scene 2 On a rubble mountain (1947)

It is fifteen years earlier. Hundreds of ragged, hungry Children cluster on a mountain of broken bricks to watch a US 'candy bomber' deliver food to the besieged city. Stalin has blockaded West Berlin in an attempt to drive the Americans out of Europe but the Allies are retaliating by launching the Berlin Airlift to sustain it.

Enter a younger CLAY and FRANK HOWLEY, a Colonel.

CLAY: Why are we in Europe? We have lost Czechoslovakia. We've lost Finland. Norway is threatened . . . If we mean that we are to hold Europe against Communism, we must not budge. If America does not know this, does not believe the issue is cast now, then it never will and Communism will run rampant.

CLAY and HOWLEY gaze up stage at a backdrop sky illuminated with rows of pearl-like landing lights. Over eleven months in the largest airlift in history, British and US aircraft make over 270,000 flights to West Berlin, delivering 2,325,000 tons of food, fuel, medicine and tools. The Soviets buzz the unarmed Douglas C-47s, DC-3s and Avro Yorks, swooping down on them in snub-nosed Yak fighters, blinding pilots with searchlights and jamming

Allied radio frequencies. Over one hundred Allied crewmen die during the operation. In the end the humiliated Russians are forced to back down, and Stalin accepts that Germany will not be united under Communism. In an historical turning point the former enemies – West Germans and Americans – become friends.

HOWLEY: We are not getting out of Berlin. The American people will not stand by and let the German people starve.

Hershey chocolate bars and Reese's Peanut Butter Cups drift down onto the stage beneath handkerchief-size parachutes, dropped by American pilots for the excited, shouting Children.

Exeunt CLAY and HOWLEY.

Scene 3 Presidential Motorcade in West Berlin (1963)

Enter KENNEDY and CLAY. KENNEDY steps into a blue Lincoln convertible with KONRAD ADENAUER, German Chancellor (aged eighty-seven) and WILLY BRANDT (forty-nine), Mayor of West Berlin. CLAY travels in the second car. The motorcade comprises thirty-eight vehicles, including a dozen buses filled with Journalists.

The motorcade drives away from the airport and onto Scharnweberstraße. Immediately it is mobbed by jubilant, enthusiastic, cheering Berliners. Confetti, balloons and streams of coloured paper rain down on the cars. Kennedy's driver uses windscreen wipers to clear his view and see the road ahead. Over a million people line the fifty-kilometre route, reaching out their hands, offering bouquets of flowers, chanting.

CROWD: Ken-Ne-Dy! Ken-Ne-Dy!

KENNEDY, ADENAUER, BRANDT and CLAY are standing, waving, overwhelmed by the outpouring of public emotion. No foreign visitor has ever had, or ever will receive a larger, more spontaneous welcome in Germany.

Scene 4 On the Kurfürstendamm

Fifty Police motorcyclists in bright white dress uniforms and helmets lead the motorcade past Café Kranzler and into the heart of West Berlin, swinging by ruined Kaiser Wilhelm Memorial Church. No mention is made of the Second World War during the trip. Focus is on the Cold War and the Wall. No attention is to be drawn to Kennedy's two previous visits to Berlin: in August 1939 when he (aged twenty-two) collected a secret message for his father about the imminence of the German attack on Poland, and in 1945 when he returned to the devastated city as a special correspondent for Hearst Newspapers.

CROWD: Ken-Ne-Dy! Ken-Ne-Dy!

Motorcade drives through Tiergarten and loops around the Siegessäule, with its gilded Victoria. No reference is made to the French flying the tricolour from the Victory Column in 1945, or their proposal to tear it down in an act of revenge.

Scene 5 In the Congress Hall

Enter KENNEDY, GEORG LEBER, a Trade Unionist, and Attendants.

Berlin is a political stage on which links are to be made between Germany and the United States. The Congress Hall on John Foster Dulles Allee is America's gift to Berlin. The conference and cultural centre is built on an artificial mound close to the border so it can be seen from the Communist East. Nearby are other bold, new buildings by Alvar Aalto, Corbusier, Walter Gropius and others.

LEBER presents KENNEDY with flowers picked that morning in East Berlin.

KENNEDY (quoting Benjamin Franklin): 'God grant that not only the love of liberty but a thorough knowledge of the rights of man may pervade all the nations of the earth so that a philosopher may set his foot anywhere on its surface and say "This is my country".'

KENNEDY is the first Western head of state to address a German labour congress.

KENNEDY: West Berlin is my country.

Applause. KENNEDY waves and exits. Duration of Congress Hall visit: twenty-five minutes.

ACT TWO
Scene 1 At the Brandenburg Gate

Silence. Enter KENNEDY. He mounts the wooden observation platform. The Berlin Wall is before him, and beyond it the Brandenburg Gate. The space between its columns is filled with huge, blood-red banners, hung by the East Germans expressly to block his view of Unter den Linden.

Television cameras focus on KENNEDY. The assembled Press Corps lift their microphones, cock their ears, but he says not a word. The script prohibits a speech. His silence is to speak volumes. The only sound is the click of shutters and the whirr of Arriflexes.

On his visit KENNEDY is to see and be seen. Every stop, every prop, every moment is chosen for its impact. He stares at the concrete divide, in front of 1,500 accredited Journalists. He looks at the Wall, and the world watches him look. The visit is jointly broadcast by Germany's two main networks, ARD and ZDF.

KENNEDY descends from the platform and exits.

Scene 2 To Checkpoint Charlie

KENNEDY rides in the open Lincoln with ADENAUER and BRANDT. Yet theirs is not the first vehicle in the motorcade. In front of them drives a

*khaki-coloured Ford truck, its flatbed stacked with rear-facing, tiered benches.
Dozens of Cameramen ride in it, their lenses trained on KENNEDY, snatching every gesture, every look. Like the President, they too are caught up in the
excitement, waving at the crowds, being photographed themselves, becoming
both viewer and viewed.*

*At Checkpoint Charlie, the main Allied crossing point, Soviet and American
tanks faced each other only eighteen months earlier. A single shot could have
escalated into nuclear war.*

*Enter KENNEDY. JAMES POLK, a US Commander, guides him and At-
tendants onto another viewing stand. Low voices are heard, but again – with
no microphone allowed on the platform – nothing can be recorded. Again
silence and the absence of dialogue are used to heighten the impact of the speech
to come. KENNEDY looks into the East as per script. A change comes over
him. His movements suggest a depth of feeling. He keeps staring even as his
Attendants turn away, looking back over his shoulder as he descends the steps.
A smile no longer lingers on his lips.*

*Across the divide on Lindenstraße a small clutch of East Berliners shout out
their greeting.*

The time is twelve o'clock noon.

Scene 3 In the Presidential Lincoln

*Enter KENNEDY, ADENAUER and BRANDT in the Lincoln. The Chan-
cellor and Mayor are talking to the President (BRANDT acting as translator).
But KENNEDY is distracted, even as the limousine passes the Airlift Memorial at Tempelhof. He keeps touching the carefully prepared speech cards in
his breast pocket. In the distance 450,000 Berliners await his arrival at West
Berlin's City Hall.*

ACT THREE
Scene 1 In front of City Hall

Enter KENNEDY. A thunderous roar rises up from the crowd. In Brandt's office, Kennedy had sat with his speechwriter TED SORENSEN and interpreters, annotating by hand the small index cards on which his speech had been typed. Now he stands stage left with his hands clasped behind his back as ADENAUER introduces him.

ADENAUER: Dear friends, you have come here today to hear President Kennedy . . .

Flourish. KENNEDY crosses the narrow platform to the podium. He draws the cards from his pocket, smiles, sways from right to left as he waits for almost a minute for the ecstatic cheers to die away.

KENNEDY: I am proud to come here in the company of my fellow American General Clay, who has been in this city during its great moments of crisis and will come again if ever needed.

Enter CLAY from stage right, where he stands with the West German politicians. CLAY acknowledges the applause and America's commitment to West Berlin. He shakes Kennedy's hand then steps away.

KENNEDY: Two thousand years ago the proudest boast was *civis Romanus sum.* Today, in the world of freedom, the proudest boast is 'Ich bin ein Berliner'.

Kennedy's speech has been crafted over months so as not to provoke Soviets or disappoint Germans. In it he is to recall key post-war events: the Airlift, the 1953 East Berlin uprising, Khrushchev's threats and the erection of the Wall. He is to advocate a new, conciliatory policy of East-West coexistence.

KENNEDY: I know of no town, no city, that has been besieged for eighteen years, that still lives with the vitality, and the force, and the hope, and the determination of the city of West Berlin.

*Now at the podium Kennedy appears to abandon much of the prepared text
and speaks off the cuff, from the heart, responding to the crowd's emotions
with his own.*

KENNEDY: Freedom has many difficulties, and democracy is not
perfect but we have never had to put a wall up to keep our people
in, to prevent them from leaving us.

*His voice rings through loudspeakers, echoing across the square and globe. He
calls the Wall an offence against history and humanity, separating families,
dividing husbands and wives and brothers and sisters, dividing a people who
wish to be joined together.*

KENNEDY: Let me ask you as I close to lift your eyes beyond
the dangers of today to the hopes of tomorrow, beyond the freedom merely of this city of Berlin, or your country of Germany,
to the advance of freedom everywhere, beyond the Wall to the
day of peace with justice, beyond yourselves and ourselves to all
mankind.

*The crowd roars in relief, with liberation, as the President distances them
from both their Nazi past and Communism, from nationalism and old
destructive habits. Then KENNEDY links West Berlin's identity with America's national myth.*

KENNEDY: Freedom is indivisible, and when one man is enslaved, all are not free. When all are free, then we can look forward
to that day when this city will be joined as one and this country
and this great continent of Europe in a peaceful and hopeful globe.
When that day finally comes, as it will, the people of West Berlin
can take sober satisfaction in the fact that they were in the front
lines for almost two decades.

He pauses as his interpreter finishes each translation.

KENNEDY: All free men, wherever they may live, are citizens of

Berlin, and therefore, as a free man, I take pride in the words 'Ich bin ein Berliner'.

As he finishes, the play's lead actor slips his cards into his jacket pocket. The phrase 'Ich bin ein Berliner' is not typed on them. Instead he had scribbled phonetically, 'Ish bin ein Bearleener' on the blank back of one card.

As the Freedom Bell (financed by public subscription in the United States and given to West Berlin along with the signatures of 16,000,000 Americans) begins to chime, citizens bow their heads in the hope that the President's symbolic, eight-hour visit will secure the liberty of their city. Kennedy has personified a new political future, and Berliners' enthusiasm has helped to reshape international politics. He turns away from the podium to whisper to speechwriter TED SORENSEN.

KENNEDY: We'll never have another day like this one as long as we live.

Exeunt.

CHAPTER 20

*David Bowie,
and 'Heroes'*

David Bowie on the set of *Just a Gigolo* in the Alte St-Matthäus cemetery near to the graves of *Victory* sculptor Friedrich Drake and the Brothers Grimm, 1978. (*Alain Dejean/Sygma/Corbis*)

Köthenerstraße, 1977

A dozen doves wheeled overhead, their bellies flashing white in the clear spring sunshine. The cyclist ducked through their weaving circle and swung off Hauptstraße onto the deep, tree-lined streets. His bicycle tyres thrummed on the cobbles. The warm air ruffled his hair. He pedalled past the buildings where Isherwood and Riefenstahl had lived. At a co-op café pale-faced students in PLO scarves looked up from their copy of Kierkegaard and ordered another espresso. Above them 'US Army Go Home' was graffitied on the walls of a squat. Beyond them a Bolivian busker played the panpipes. A geriatric bicyclist rode by in the opposite direction, her cheeks caked in rouge, a black silk flower stitched onto her mauve stalker hat, smoking a cheroot as she pedalled, with a Chihuahua balanced in her basket.

At Brecht's blitzed apartment block on Spichernstraße he veered north, retracing the old playwright's daily stroll to the Romanisches Café. Over coffee and chess – the cyclist had read – Brecht and Grosz had called for a new kind of art, and gifted it to the world.

Some mornings the cyclist turned left rather than right and rode

south to where Ernst Kirchner – one of the fathers of Expressionism – had had his studio. As he coasted along Körnerstraße, he
thought of Kirchner's struggle to free himself from older, established forces. Kirchner had built a bridge – *Die Brücke* – between
the past and the present, until the Nazis tore it down and destroyed
600 of his paintings, driving him to suicide.

The three-gear Raleigh carried the cyclist past places forever
haunted by absence: the vacated bunkers, the demolished Sportpalast where Goebbels had declared Total War, the People's Court
where Hitler's would-be assassins had been sentenced to death.
Tempelhof's vast arrivals hall and cold stone eagles rose behind
him. Ahead of him on Potsdamerstraße, where he paused to catch
his breath, Dieter Werner's Children's Crusade had dispersed years
before, leaving no trace.

Each ride through the divided city made the cyclist feel more
whole, each pedal push carrying him through space, through time,
both back to his core and towards his future. In those days Berlin
seemed to stand at the centre of everything that had happened,
and would happen, in Europe. His bicycle exhilarated him, lifting his heart, at once grounding and freeing him in his adopted,
pulsing new home.

'I have really now got the will. I will be and I will work,' he had
written in his diary.

At Mies van der Rohe's New National Gallery, built on the abandoned foundations of Speer's Germania, he turned right to follow
the canal. Along the bank a stagger of arguing drunks fell into a fist
fight. The cyclist swept past them into Köthenerstraße, avoiding
the tracks of the trams which no longer ran, and glided towards the
Wall. At the edge of no man's land he coasted to a stop, and rolled
his bike into the Hansa Sound Studio.

David Bowie was nine years old when he decided to give himself to music. His father had bought a brand new gramophone and
a stack of 45s: The Platters, The Moonglows, Fats Domino and
Little Richard. When the young Bowie first heard 'Tutti Frutti', his
heart nearly burst with joy.

He had been born David Jones in blitzed south London, growing up in a small terraced house in Bromley, scheming of a means to escape cosy suburbia. The wide, wild world came to him through music, in his father's records, in his mother singing along with the wireless, her voice soaring with Ernest Lough's 'O for the Wings of a Dove'.

He first performed on the Isle of Wight with the Bromley Cubs, playing skiffle music. His elder step-brother Terry then thrust him beyond Lonnie Donegan by introducing him to The Beats, thrilling the young teen with tales of Kerouac and Soho jazz cellars. Bowie picked up a guitar, learnt the piano and joined a school band called George and the Dragon. His father helped him to buy an alto sax and, in his bedroom, he set up a simple recording studio with a reel-to-reel tape recorder and cellotape. He formed The Kon-Rads and then The King Bees, morphing from mod to rocker, envisaging himself as an English Little Richard. He had thousands of ideas, recalled early bandmate David Hadfield, 'a new one for every day – that we should change the spelling of our name, or our image, or our clothes ... he also came up with lots of sketches of potential advertising campaigns for the band'. Bowie painted both his image and music with chameleon-bright colours.

At seventeen while still at school he began touring in an old ambulance. In his search for a stage persona he studied Mick Jagger at the Marquee and Bo Diddley at the Lewisham Odeon. To find a look he collected cast-off clothes from Carnaby Street dustbins. He renamed himself Bowie after the singer Davy Jones joined the TV band The Monkees. He cut his first important single, 'Can't Help Thinking about Me', and hand-delivered it to Paul McCartney's recording studio. When the Beatle didn't respond Bowie climbed onto the roof of his house and, in disappointment, threw away his complete record collection.

As he played Bognor and Bournemouth, building up a loyal local following, Bowie feared not breaking into the mainstream. His frustration honed his desire to understand the public, as well as pushing him to the fringes of the art world and into books. He devoured Brecht, Burroughs, Camus and Kafka. *Metamorphosis*

spooked him, its tale of transformation penned by another quest-
ing, imaginative soul who fabricated alter egos and lived for a time
in Berlin.

Bowie toured the UK with the mime artist Lindsay Kemp. Kemp
encouraged him to play with identity. On stage, Bowie tested the
theories of French theatre director Antonin Artaud. Artaud wanted
the audience to be at the heart of a 'spectacle' – his term for the
play – so as to be engulfed by it. Through his work, Bowie came to
see the theatre as a place where the spectator was exposed rather
than protected, and art as a vehicle for risk. He saw how performance could both embody and intensify life, recreating the thrill
of experience. He tried his hand at musicals and in an arts lab.
He toyed with movies. He jumbled together narrative, mime and
vaudeville, drawing new ideas into his music and conjuring up an
exuberant personal mythology.

At the age of twenty-one he wrote 'Space Oddity' but couldn't
interest a record company in the song. The Beatles' George Martin
turned it down. Brooklyn-born Tony Visconti – who in time would
produce a dozen Bowie albums – considered it a gimmick track.
When the spacey, naive tale of Major Tom – an heroic astronaut
and vulnerable, alienated everyman marooned in orbit – was finally
released in the year of the moon landing, it became Bowie's breakthrough single.

Over the next five years, in London, New York and then Los
Angeles, Bowie rose to become the first, great post-modern pop
star. He dyed his hair red and dressed in flamboyant costumes to
create androgynous Ziggy Stardust, subsuming his own life into
that of his glittering conception.

'Off stage I'm a robot. On stage I achieve emotion,' he declared
as he lost himself in the character. 'It's probably why I prefer dressing up as Ziggy to being David.'

Then he discarded the alien rocker for *Aladdin Sane*, traded
glam, post-apocalypse *Diamond Dogs* (its tour stage inspired by
Fritz Lang's *Metropolis*) for plastic-souled *Young Americans* and
masked himself behind the Thin White Duke. Self-risk motivated
both the changes and his career. Time and again he channelled the

avant-garde into the populist mainstream without compromising its subversive, liberating power. Yet with every transformation he became less and less able to separate himself from his creations, as Isherwood and Dietrich had discovered before him. 'That was when it all started to go sour,' he said, describing his professional life as an act. 'My whole personality was affected. It became very dangerous. I really did have doubts about my sanity.'

Bowie was driven by a relentless urge to create, as well as a great deal of cocaine. He had little personal self-worth. He thought his work was the only thing of value. He lived in a kind of prolific mania, especially when on tour: reading, talking, listening to the revolutionary electronic band Kraftwerk, writing songs, checking out new acts after his own show. He stayed up late. He hardly ate. His body weight dropped to eighty pounds. He believed his manager had cheated him of millions. He became haunted by the occult, denying himself sleep for seven or eight days at a time, slipping into a bizarre, nihilistic fantasy world of imminent doom and Egyptian mysticism. Some mornings at his rented Doheny Drive house, his assistant Coco Schwab would find him lying like a dead man beside the drained pool, at the bottom of which he had burnt an image of the devil. She held a mirror under his nose to see if he was still alive.

Off stage he was deeply unhappy. He looked – as he himself admitted – as if he'd just stepped out of the grave. He needed to escape both LA celebrity culture and his own theatrical personas. 'I realised that what I had to do was experiment. To discover new forms of writing. To evolve, in fact, a new musical language,' he said, as if responding to the call of Brecht and Grosz. 'That's what I set out to do. That's why I returned to Europe.'

In 1976 rock 'n' roll's blazing star fell to earth in Berlin. Bowie had met Isherwood in California, the smooth old queen and impudent new king talking for an hour after his concert at the Englewood Forum. 'Berlin is a skeleton which aches in the cold; it is my own skeleton aching,' Isherwood had written in *Goodbye to Berlin*. Bowie had read his books, seen *Cabaret* and wanted Isherwood to clothe the skeleton for him. He asked him to tell him – as one storyteller to another – about its mythical, creative underworld. Six months later, on the edge of physical and mental collapse, he moved to the capital of reinvention.

In the dozen years since Kennedy's visit, Berlin had both changed and remained unchanged. Outside the Wall a quarter of a million Red Army soldiers still surrounded the city. Within it 12,500 American, British and French troops still guarded the island's freedom. But West Berliners had grown used to the barrier, planting clematis and rose bushes alongside it, using it as a 155-kilometre-long canvas for graffiti: Change Your Life, Learn Peace, Death to Mediocrity.

To rebuild their own devastated lives, most German war veterans had overlooked the acquiescence of the Nazi years. A story went the rounds of an Austrian Jew, Jitzhak Ben-Ari, who in 1938 had travelled by train to Dachau where his father was imprisoned. At the station he had asked for directions to the camp and the locals had 'gladly told him where the Jews were being taken'. But after the war when Ben-Ari returned to Germany as Israeli ambassador, and went back to Dachau, the camp had somehow been expunged from people's memories. No one had seemed able to direct him to it.

This vile omission was confronted in the sixties. To the new generation, West Germany's economic miracle – or *Wirtschaftswunder* – had been built not on initiative and hard labour but on a lie. In their minds their parents' unquestioning obedience to Hitler had led to the Holocaust. Slavish Prussian devotion to uniformed authority had almost annihilated the country. As a result young Germans – and especially young Berliners – rejected their elders' leadership for the first time in centuries. They chose to look at history from the perspective of its victims, not its perpetrators.

Since 1946 West Berlin had been kept alive by huge cash subsidies. West Germans who moved to the city had their taxes slashed and removal costs reimbursed. Male residents were exempt from military service. Hence tens of thousands of young people were drawn to the island, and then promptly rebelled against its authorities. The Nazi legacy – combined with the perceived diminution of the Communist threat and outrage over America's Vietnam War – convinced them that Western capitalism was a reincarnation of the Third Reich. To assuage their inherited guilt, they joined co-ops and sit-ins, protested against the Allied 'occupation', burnt the Stars and Stripes and marched in support of the Vietcong. 'Ho-Ho-Ho-Chi-Minh' not 'Ken-Ne-Dy' was chanted outside Amerika Haus.

In 1967 a visit by the Shah of Iran – who many believed was backed by the CIA – led to violent street battles and the killing of a protester. The death radicalised the Berlin student movement. Demonstrators stormed onto the streets, calling for the overthrow of the government. 'This fascist state is organised to kill us all,' declared a youth leader. 'We must organise resistance. Violence can only be answered with violence. They are the generation of Auschwitz.'

Riots spread from Berlin to Paris and Prague. In France students and workers manned the barricades. Idealists proclaimed, 'We will invent a new original world.' But their optimism was perverted by political extremists and the dogma of Sartre and Foucault. When Warsaw Pact armies invaded Czechoslovakia in August 1968, Berlin twisted itself in discord and dread. Czech refugees who had escaped the bloody crackdown, who had struggled to pull down the red flag, stared in disbelief as Western radicals tried to raise it. Hundreds knelt and prayed in the soft, soothing blue light of the Kaiser Wilhelm Memorial Church, waiting in fear for the roar of Soviet tanks on the Kurfürstendamm.

Yet Maoist and Marxist-Leninist groups like Baader-Meinhof, entangled by disgust for their parents' generation, remained blind to the reality of the Soviet threat. In their confusion they raged for random violence against the 'Nazi Federal Republic'. In Moabit Ulrike Meinhof, wearing a wig and carrying a gun in her briefcase, freed her imprisoned conspirator Andreas Baader, killing a bystander in the process. Their Red Army Faction – a deliberate allusion to both the Soviet Army and the Royal Air Force – bombed department stores, seized hostages and murdered almost three dozen people during the 1970s. The group aimed to goad the state into introducing illiberal measures that would stir public anger and spark civil war. A quarter of young West Germans expressed some sympathy for the movement. After Meinhof had been captured, and hanged herself in prison, 4,000 mourners attended her funeral at Berlin's Mariendorf cemetery.

At this pivotal point, after the horror, belligerence and firestorms, the '68ers – paradoxically with their safety assured by America – broke with the predatory past, freeing themselves from centuries of historical fear, and transformed Germany.

The bicycles sliced through the woods on a sword-straight path, wheels wobbling in the sandy soil. Orderly ranks of trees fanned away in every direction, catching the light beneath their canopy, blocking out the sky. The trail dipped and crested but it didn't deviate from its linear course, stretching away to the west and a verdant vanishing point. Iggy Pop rode a leopard-spotted yellow bike inherited from a departing neighbour. Bowie pulled ahead of him, lost his balance then regained it, stood up on his pedals and whooped. The sense of freedom thrilled him. He felt as if they could ride right off the island, through the Wall, as far as the English Channel.

When he and his friend Pop had first moved to West Berlin in late 1976, they'd fallen back on bad habits. In an open-topped Mercedes which had once belonged to the President of Sierra Leone, they'd cruised around the island city, drinking *KöPi* at Joe's Beer House, stumbling into gutters and transvestite bars, clubbing at the Dschungel and The Unlimited. In their rooms at the Hotel Gehrus they'd snorted coke while watching *Starsky and Hutch* and *Triumph of the Will*, read *Siddhartha* and *The Spy Who Came in from the Cold*.

'There's seven days in the week: two for bingeing, two for recovery, and three for any other activity,' Pop had said. Pop, the former Stooges frontman and future godfather of punk rock, had been derailed by drug abuse. He too wanted to haul himself back from the brink, yet at the same time he seemed ready to throw himself off it.

One night – whether in Berlin or LA, neither of them could remember – Pop had sat in the passenger seat as Bowie rammed their dealer's car again and again, for five crazed minutes. Bowie then drove around the hotel's underground car park, pushing 100 kilometres per hour, screaming above the screech of the tyres that he wanted to end it all by driving into a concrete wall. Until the car ran out of fuel and the friends collapsed in hysterics.

To defeat his demons Bowie needed space and stability. His estranged wife Angie no longer provided it – for much of the time she kept their son Zowie (later Joey then Duncan Jones) away from him in London or Switzerland – so his assistant Coco found him a modest, first-floor apartment in an Art Nouveau building in Schöneberg, a gold-album-throw away from Langenscheidtbrücke where Dietrich had once opened her skirt above puffing steam locomotives. Coco had its walls painted white as a private gallery for Bowie's dark images. She ordered in blank canvases and tubes of oil paint. She picked up his discarded clothes and scattered drawings. She read Nietzsche beside him beneath his fluorescent portrait of the Japanese author Yukio Mishima. Above all she went with him to the Brücke Museum, to gaze at the works of Kirchner, Kollwitz and Erich Heckel whose *Roquairol*, with its stark depiction of lunacy, would become the model for Pop's tortured pose on the cover of *The Idiot*. The Expressionists' rough, bold strokes, and melancholic mood, captured a sense of the ephemeral as well as Bowie's imagination. He was riveted by the strength and recklessness of Grosz's drawings. Egon Schiele's distorted, skeletal portraits entranced him. He stared for almost an hour at Otto Mueller's *Lovers between Garden Walls*, a portrait of a First World War parting, and began to reimagine it for a later, colder war and Wall.

At the Hansa Sound Studio, Bowie mixed 'Always Crashing in the Same Car'. In its bleak verse he despaired of his failure to change, of taking chances yet remaining trapped. He was always crashing in the same car.

In truth he was edging away from cocaine psychosis, finding his way out of his life of excess, remaking himself as an ordinary man – and one of the twentieth century's greatest artists. He dressed in baggy trousers and dowdy shirts and enjoyed the Berliners' disinterest in him. No one bothered him on the street. One night on a whim he climbed onto a cabaret stage to perform a few Sinatra songs. The local audience shrugged and asked him to step down. They had come to see a different act. Away from the limelight he composed, painted and for the first time in years 'felt a joy of life and a great feeling of release and healing'. Berlin was for him 'a city that's so easy to "get lost" in – and to "find" oneself, too'.

Bowie realised that his goal was not simply to find a new way of making music, but rather to reinvent – or to come back to – himself. He no longer needed to adopt characters to sing his songs. He found the courage to throw away the props, costumes and stage sets.

The first Berlin album *Low*, which he had started to record at Château d'Hérouville near Paris, both portrayed the darkness and purged him of it. Bowie linked his scarred emotions with Eastern Europe's uncertainty, depicting a life and location on the edge. 'Art Decade' was West Berlin, cut off from the world, its art and culture dying without hope of retribution. 'Subterraneans' evoked the spirit of the trapped East Berliners, its faint jazz saxophones stirring memories of the past. 'Warszawa' conjured up the capital of Communist Poland, its alien bleakness underlined by his singing in an imaginary Slavic language.

Low was a cathartic work, a collaboration between Bowie, producer Tony Visconti, guitarist Carlos Alomar and English renaissance musician Brian Eno, 'the Einstein of Pop', who once spoke about the need to create music 'that felt like it had a place in the world . . . that felt rooted and properly positioned'.

'All my songs are very personal and I combine this with an exaggeration so the meaning is clearly brought home to the listener,' an artless, younger Bowie had told *Melody Maker* in 1970.

Over the intervening years he had refined his working method. In the recording studio music was laid down first, with three or four musicians racing through the rhythm tracks, working with as much spontaneity as possible. Bowie has always been inspired in his choice of collaborators, selecting artists with a voice and tone that matched his own, or who had a spirit that he required in his work. He gave them creative freedom, willing them – as guitarist Adrian Belew said – 'to add a lot of colours and sounds, to play solos and to be involved in the shape and form of the music itself'.

After the rhythm tracks were finished, Bowie slowed down, replaying them, reflecting on them and building the overdubs. Cocaine sugared these 'sweetening sessions' when a shift of perspective was needed, teasing out a new guitar line, adding saxophone or piano, keeping minds bright and awake until dawn and beyond. The secret was not to stop but to keep working when on a roll. Finally when the music was finished he began to write the lyrics.

'He writes them in the studio now,' John Lennon marvelled in an interview. 'He goes in with about four words and a few guys, and starts laying down all this stuff and he has virtually nothing – he's making it up in the studio.'

Bowie had been inspired by Pop's risky working style. He'd watched Pop come up with the words for 'China Girl' while standing at the microphone. He began to emulate the method, combining it with William S. Burroughs's fragmentation technique, jotting down a line or two and then improvising as the tape rolled. Words never came before music, hence sound never simply echoed their meaning.

Hansa had a darkness about it, said Carlos Alomar, 'not foreboding, just that the air was thick with a darker vibe ... Germans, Nazis, the Wall, oppression'. In the war the converted concert hall had been used as a ballroom by the Gestapo. Goebbels and Speer had danced in its shadows. Now armed *Grenzpolizei* patrolled no man's land at the end of the street.

In the summer of 1977 Bowie, Eno and Visconti were on a creative high. Visconti arrived in Studio 2 with his new Eventide

Harmonizer, an effects processor which 'fucks with the fabric of time'. Eno brought from the UK his turquoise-keyed, toggle-sticked synthesizer-in-a-briefcase. With four key musicians – Alomar, George Murray, King Crimson guitarist Robert Fripp and drummer Dennis Davis – they began to make a new album.

Visconti recorded the rehearsals, which were often strong enough to use as rhythm tracks. Eno tweaked and twisted their sound, then startled the musicians into new thinking by flipping through his *Oblique Strategies* cards: Distort Time, Discover Your Formulas then Abandon Them, What is the Simplest Solution? He and Bowie worked in a kind of cyclone of febrile energy, and then like a pair of eccentric professors, addressing each other in the manner of comedians Peter Cook and Dudley Moore, breaking into fits of giggles. Bowie ate almost nothing, sailing home to Hauptstraße with Eno at dawn, breaking a raw egg into his mouth and sleeping a few hours before returning to the studio. Visconti edited down the spontaneous jam sessions, splicing the tape and songs into shape.

Once the music was recorded, cut and sweetened, Bowie turned his attention to the words. One of the first songs recorded that summer remained an instrumental track until the very end of production. Alone at the piano Bowie began to sketch out its lyrics, making it the title track, calling it 'Heroes'.

Visconti rigged up three microphones with electronic 'gates'. The first mike was twenty centimetres from Bowie, the second six metres away, the third fifteen metres away across the vast, dark hall. The gates were set to open when Bowie sang above a certain volume, forcing him to lift his voice from whisper to shout, using the room's natural echo. As Visconti adjusted the levels, Bowie wrote the lyrics. His bursts of inspiration were followed by periods of contemplation. Halfway through the song he asked to be left alone with his thoughts and piano. Visconti slipped out of the building, walked along Köthenerstraße and met backing vocalist Antonia Maaß. Maaß was Visconti's lover. From the studio control room Bowie saw them kiss, by the Wall.

Two hours later the final lyric was recorded. Bowie and Visconti added the backing vocals. 'Heroes' – with its reference to border guards shooting above the heads of a young couple – became Berlin's rock anthem, a droning, courageous wall of sound, fired with deep emotion, hammered by a clanging, metallic rhythm – produced in part by Visconti hitting a studio ashtray. Bowie called 'Heroes' – and his three Berlin albums – his DNA. Time and again it would be named as one of pop music's greatest and most original singles. The song may even have helped to bring down the Wall.

Many come to Berlin on a search, often for themselves. Bowie found himself in Berlin. He pulled away from addiction and shed his false personas, unlike many of his predecessors who remained trapped in their self-generated myths.

'I was David Jones from Brixton who wanted to do something artistically worthwhile,' he said at the end of his Berlin days, his voice rich and warm, his weight back at 130 pounds. 'But I hadn't the courage to face the audience as myself. It takes tremendous courage to face up to the adulation, the pressure, without cracking.'

The city changed him. Instead of an outlandish, alien superstar, he appeared to be himself: a defiant and gifted mortal searching for a saner future.

Berlin had also taught him to write about important things. He had grown up in the shadow of the Second World War, in blitzed Brixton and Bromley. His father had fought against Rommel in North Africa. His mother had survived the Luftwaffe's bombs. Like most of his generation he was fascinated by the Nazis. Their ideology hadn't moved him, in spite of a few ill-considered comments, but rather their theatricality. He had watched Riefenstahl's films and studied Goebbels' manufactured mythology. He had sketched out a musical based on the Propaganda Minister's life and lit the stage for the Thin White Duke tour with columns of light reminiscent of Speer's Cathedral of Light. At first there was a naivety in his fascination. Yet in time, surrounded by both victims and perpetrators of Nazi evil, he evolved a coherent vision for himself and a new age. He captured and defined its quintessence, speaking for a confused generation which had lost hope in ideals and dreams.

One Sunday afternoon in 1977, five months after he'd recorded 'Heroes', I watched Bowie create a new song at Hansa. In the 'Great Hall by the Wall' he sat down at the piano with only the inkling of an idea and – in less than an hour – had enchanted a tune out of the air as if by magic.

I'd heard the gossip about him before we met of course, the stories of a paranoid, egotistical thin white duke who flirted with fascism and the occult. But over the months that we worked together I saw only a gentle, articulate, warm and affable man, filled with self-effacing good humour, and on the cusp of finding his own true self. In his Hauptstraße home he played records for me and others, explaining how musicians and groups come together then break up in the pursuit of creative goals, likening the process to *Die Brücke* artists earlier in the century: the Beatles and Lennon, Roxy Music and Brian Eno, *Der Blaue Reiter* and Kandinsky. Early one morning, after film director David Hemmings and I had spent a night reworking some of *Just a Gigolo*'s dialogue, I knocked on his trailer door and delivered new lines for him to memorise. Bowie scanned the pink pages, smiled weakly and said, 'Now melody I can handle . . .'

We spent Christmas together: Bowie, Hemmings, partners and children plus add-ons like me. At a secluded restaurant in the Grunewald, we ate and drank too much and Bowie gave me a copy of Fritz Lang's biography. At the end of the happy evening I followed him downstairs to the huge, ceramic-tiled bathroom where – as we peed – we sang Buddy Holly songs together (or, at least, a line and a half from 'Good Golly Miss Molly').

For me, music is wonder-work. The charming of a tune, the hatching of rhythm, the whimsical concoction of lyrics are akin to a miracle. More than any other art, music is mysterious and unfixed, hanging in the air for a heartbeat, its every performance changed by mood, instruments, even weather. I understand how Schinkel reshaped his Italian studies into the Altes Museum, how Kollwitz transformed her husband's weeping patients into haunting engravings. I can imagine Wim Wenders devising his cinematic angels, willing them to speak from another world, and see Hermann Hesse shaping the words to propel Goldmund on a quest to embrace all that perishes in this life. But how could Beethoven have heard the 'Ode to Joy' or Little Richard written 'Tutti Frutti'?

'The Revolutionary Song' which Bowie recorded at Hansa that Sunday in November was neither finished nor officially released. Yet its creation remained so special that I played it again and again, with shivers running up and down my spine, as the cassette tape stretched and that clear, beautiful voice grew as muffled as a lost dream.

I last saw Bowie in New York. He was on Broadway, playing the lead in a stage adaptation of *The Elephant Man*, and I had arranged to meet him after the show. I was staying on West 72nd Street with friends. The evening before I was reading in their basement apartment, and heard what sounded like a car backfiring, three, four, maybe five times. I kept on reading until I sensed something was wrong. I went outside. Across the road a crowd had already gathered at The Dakota. The police had started to put up barriers. John Lennon had been shot dead.

But the music didn't die that night, as Don McLean might have had it, for artists live on in their work if not the flesh, in their songs, on their canvases. The next evening, as the cold December air crackled with emotion, Bowie went on stage wearing a loincloth and no mask, and gifted the audience with one of the most intense performances of his career. He took a single, swift curtain call. Afterwards I knew he wouldn't want to see me, or anyone except Coco. I asked for her at the backstage door. She looked as if she hadn't slept. I gave her a white rose for Bowie, and asked her to send him my love. As I turned to go I paused and said, 'And please say thank you. Tell him, thank you for the gift.'

*

Ten years after his departure from Berlin, seven years after *The Elephant Man*, Bowie returned to the divided city. In June 1987 his driver drove him past the old Hauptstraße apartment, by the Brücke Museum and Hansa, to a stage in front of the Reichstag. As night fell he performed to a crowd of 70,000 fans, their sparklers and candles glittering around the Platz der Republik. Towards the end of the show he read aloud a message in German. 'We send our best wishes to all our friends who are on the other side of the Wall.' Then he sang 'Heroes'.

On the other side of the hateful divide, hundreds of young East Berliners strained to hear echoes of the concert. They caught sight of stage lights flashing off blank, bullet-marked walls. They heard Bowie greet them. They listened to his song. Their song. Berlin's song.

'We can be heroes, just for one day,' he sang in a daring, ironic elegy to both the divided world and his past life. Everyone can be a hero, be their own hero, and love can prevail, if only for one day, if only in a myth.

As 'Heroes' reached its climax some of the East German crowd pushed towards the Brandenburg Gate, whistling and chanting, 'Down with the Wall'. They threw insults and bottles at the *Volkspolizei*, rising together against the Party's thugs in a rare moment of protest. On stage Bowie heard the cheers from the other side. He was in tears.

'It was one of the most emotional performances I've ever done,' he said later. 'It was breaking my heart. I'd never done anything like that in my life, and I guess I never will again . . . That's the town where it was written, and that's the particular situation that it was written about. It was just extraordinary.'

So it is that the creative spirit transforms the world, flowing forth from the mouths and pens of poets, painters and songwriters. A gift of talent is bestowed on an artist and he or she labours in its service. The fruit of their toil is then offered to us all, and it in turn can awaken our individual gift or dream. Through wonder-works like 'Five Years', 'Ashes to Ashes' and 'Sag mir, wo die Blumen sind', artists give themselves to us in the same way that we are given all that is truly precious in life: hoar frost, the taste of apples, a lover's laughter, favourite melodies.

In Berlin, Schinkel fought to realise his vision, Kollwitz struggled to shape her fears, Isherwood – living on a tutor's stipend – reworked reality, and Bowie made his journey from addiction to independence, from celebrity paranoia to radical, unmasked messenger who told us, all the fat-skinny people, all the nobody people who had dreamt of a new world of equals, that we were beautiful, that we could be ourselves.

Vietnamese mother and child, Vinh Phuc c.1971. (*Archive of Modern Conflict*)

Schönefeld, 1986

How much time went by, Ha did not know.

He'd gazed for hours in the rear-view mirror at the shadows moving around the apartment. He'd seen the blue television light flicker against the sheer curtains. He'd watched and waited. Visitors had come and gone. Residents had turned off their bedside lamps. Tom-cats had stalked each other behind the bins and later a fox padded across the icy lot. At one point a young *tay lai* couple had lingered at the front door, bidding each other goodnight, their warm breath rising in the frozen air like the mingling of spirits. When they finally parted, Ha's heart had stirred in sadness.

Then a figure appeared at the second-floor window and Ha was filled again with rage. A crystal glass glinted in the man's hand, no doubt filled with Red Label. He was smoking a cigarette. He tilted his head as he spoke on the telephone. Ha almost did it then, seized the moment and closed the circle, yet the silhouette had a familiarity about it which brought him a strange feeling of confusion.

Ha's car was parked at the back of the low, terraced building, out of the light, beneath the tall, dark trees of Zehlendorf, near to the

Grunewald, far from his corner of Berlin. Snow dusted the wind-screen and muffled sound. The smell of pines crept through the crack in the open window. The night was so still and quiet that he didn't dare to start the engine, to run the heat for even for a minute. He'd never get used to the cold. Nor would he ever understand why the gun always felt warm in his hand, no matter what the weather. He tightened his leather jacket around himself, and shivered.

The man's silhouette reminded him of home, which was even further – so much further – away. In the village of his birth, his mother had spread a bamboo mat on the ground and he – aged three or four – had laid his head on her lap, listening to the chir-ruping cicadas or cooing pigeons. She'd always placed the mat near to the river under the *thien ly* flowers. His mother had loved the *thien ly*, planting them in groups, training them up a bamboo trellis, and Ha's first job had been to water the plants, freshening their roots. The heavy fragrance of the golden-yellow blossoms filled his memory. He remembered their taste in rice field crab soup.

When South Vietnam fell to the People's Army, Ha's father had moved the family away from the Mekong delta, north to Vinh Phuc. He thought they would be safer there, and he could work on a plantation. The move saved them from the re-education camps but cost them dearly. The coffee trees withered and the enter-prise failed. The poor mountain soil also didn't suit the *thien ly* and years went by before his mother managed to coax new vines up a trellis. In the hills there were no field crabs and the flowers could only be cooked with minced boar meat, which Ha's parents could never afford. His father earned a mean existence by cutting fire-wood which his mother bartered for rice in the market place. They often argued about returning to the South, to her lowland home of Tay Thon. His father's voice would explode out in the bare room, roaring abuse. Whenever he struck them, Ha would run and hide beneath the house, his hands over his ears or smarting head, shak-ing with anger.

One cloudy June day during the rains his father walked away to town, never to return. Later uniformed men came demanding to know where he had gone. When his mother could not tell them, they ordered her to pull up the *thien ly* and to plant sweet potatoes. When she refused she was beaten. Away from her own family, with no man to protect her, she too began to wither away.

She died one afternoon in the month that the kapok flowers fell crimson on the stony highland ground.

Ha was seventeen years old when he stepped off the four-prop Interflug Ilyushin at Berlin-Schönefeld. Never in his life had he felt such cold; not in the mountains, not in the orphanage, not even when training in the far north on the Chinese border. In the bus it was no warmer, neither in temperature nor welcome. No one spoke Vietnamese apart from the other boys and girls from Hanoi, and they had not one word of German between them. Ahead, the unlit cobblestone road stretched away into the forest. At the crest of every hill Ha sat up in his seat, gazing forward to try to catch sight of Europe, but all was darkness.

At home Ha had volunteered to join a fraternal socialist co-operative abroad. His contract was for five years, as it was for most of the 60,000 Vietnamese 'specialist guest workers' in East Germany. They laboured at the Trabant motor works in Zwickau, as optical engineers at Zeiss or in cement factories in Erfurt and Magdeburg. Twelve per cent of their salary was paid to the government of Vietnam, another portion was given to them in consumer goods: sugar, soap, sewing machines and bicycles. They had to join the FDGB trade union confederation. They were required to make social insurance contributions yet could not use the social services network. They received little of their 400 Ostmark salary in cash.

Ha's Neubrandenburg dormitory was like a barracks. The language trainers slept on the top bunks, Vietnamese on the bottom. Tuition lasted eight hours a day, followed by homework. Only German was to be spoken. Fraternising with locals outside the compound was discouraged. Any Vietnamese woman who became pregnant was forced to have an abortion. Meals were eaten at a mess-like canteen, and no rice was served in the entire three months. At night the security lights cast a sulphurous glow across the ceiling. Ha looked around the regimental classrooms, across the parade ground courtyard, at the barbed-wire fences and asked him-self, 'Am I in prison?'

But he studied hard, unlike the sons of Party functionaries who dozed through their lessons. He knew that he had to succeed in his cold, new home. In Vietnam there was nothing for him, apart from bad memories.

On graduation Ha was assigned to a clothing collective in Berlin-Lichtenberg. On a misty morning he queued at a factory gate, looked up at the grey buildings and wondered if East Berlin looked like Moscow. A froth of pungent white smoke rose from a chimney capped by crossed hammers. Beneath it dispirited souls shuffled through the grimy light, descending a filthy glass-sided gangway to the assembly hall. To him the German workers looked tired, their skin sallow, with only alcohol bringing colour to their cheeks. But between the racks of polyester trousers, at the long line of sewing machines, sat bright, young Vietnamese seamstresses in white blouses and blue smocks. Ha worked among them, manhandling away the finished garments, delivering pre-cut panels, even – due to his 'clever fingers' – taking turns at the machines himself. Under a portrait of Party Chairman Erich Honecker, Ha helped to stitch parkas, uniforms and red flags in the run-up to May Day.

The deputy manager – an enterprising Hmong major who had fought in the Sino-Vietnamese War – noted Ha's industry, and con-vinced him of the advantages of serving a master other than the collective. 'A clever man must have money in his pocket, to buy himself a watch or a girl, and to gamble with on Saturday night,' he said over a bloodshot *Blutwurst* served in the canteen. His voice had the precise, resonant pitch of a man used to issuing orders.

The major considered his job to be demeaning and unworthy of his lineage. To make amends he'd instructed his seamstresses to make tailored jeans on the side, thereby turning over a tidy Ost-mark profit. To earn hard currency, he next hit upon the idea of buying original designer jeans from the West at Karstadt, and rep-licating them in standard sizes and large numbers. Every finished pair of jeans could be sold for ten times its cost price in East Berlin, or twenty times on 'the other side'.

As Vietnamese passport holders were allowed to visit West Berlin, Ha – with his chirpy manner and now-fluent German – became the major's right-hand man, negotiating with and delivering to the traders. The major also noted that – if the illegal business went wrong and a scapegoat was needed – Ha had no living relatives.

For the first time in his life Ha had money, and a sense of freedom, and he liked it. A new light shone in his eyes. Outside bleak, black Friedrichstraße railway station a housewife sold bunches of snapdragons for one Ostmark apiece. Ha took ten of them for the seamstresses, paying with a new five-Deutschmark coin, not knowing it was illegal. The old woman ran after him, brimming with happiness and gave Ha all the remaining flowers.

As their illegal business grew, the major ensured that Ha needn't clock into the collective, although he remained on the payroll. As the saying went, he pretended to work for them and they pretended to pay him.

Then the major instructed Ha to buy a computer. To maintain the illusion of Communist technical superiority, Western machines could not be brought into East Germany. But many individuals in the ministries and at Karl-Marx-University were willing to pay good money for their import. Together with Ha and Vietnamese friends, the major pooled 30,000 Ostmarks, which a Lebanese socialist brother-cum-money changer converted into 3,000 Deutschmarks. On Kantstraße in West Berlin Ha bought an IBM PC Convertible (running the new MS-DOS 3.0) and smuggled it over the border in a box of stinking durians. The major then sold it under the counter for 120,000 Ostmark, quadrupling their money.

Ha now put aside the rag trade work entirely to concentrate on computers, fulfilling specific orders for Dell Turbo PCs, Hewlett Packard thermal printers and ARM processors. The frequency of the orders made him brazen at the border, and his suspicions weren't alerted as the guards let his borrowed car pass with only a perfunctory inspection. He was young and cocksure so thought himself to be invulnerable, calling himself 'bullet-proof', all but ignoring the major's fall-back plans.

Ha concentrated on opening and emptying his real leather

wallet with heady abandon, buying himself a gold ring at KaDeWe, gambling in endless games of *bai ba la*, paying *tay lai* women to open the door to manhood. At West Berlin clubs he laughed while tucking the notes into dancers' g-strings. Over eighteen months he delivered more than eighty computers from the West, until the major vanished and the Stasi knocked down his dormitory door.

'Where is the money from your 7 October 1988 sale of an IBM 3090?' asked the interrogating officer. 'What happened to the profit from the illegal importation of Apple MacPlus serial number C6330ROM0001AP on 12 January 1989?'

In the interrogation room Ha learnt that the Stasi had records of every trade. They seized his savings, the income from all his efforts, and kept the computers, some of which – still stinking of durian – may well have graced desks at their own headquarters. In a cell pending extradition, Ha understood how he and the major had been used by the authorities. At Schönefeld before the departure of his Hanoi flight he asked to go to the toilet. Inside he met the major as arranged in secret. He switched coats with him and walked out past his guard – who like most Germans couldn't tell Asians apart – to catch the S-Bahn back to East Berlin.

Three months later the Wall fell. Ha came out of hiding and walked through the open border. At Café Kranzler – on the corner where Kennedy's motorcade had turned towards the Brandenburg Gate – he bought himself a glass of beer, and fell in with a group of celebrating Vietnamese drinkers, from the former South.

In the decade after the Vietnam War, as Party loyalists began to fly to East Germany in fraternal socialist brotherhood, some one and a half million Vietnamese who had opposed the Communist regime fled as boat people. Adrift aboard crowded, leaky boats as many as 200,000 of them perished at sea. Of those who reached international waters, and the West, 38,000 refugees were taken in by West Germany. Many of them settled in West Berlin and so, in November 1989, found themselves face to face with their former enemies.

In the euphoria at Café Kranzler there was no mention of the

tragic decades, at first. Ha laughed with the other men, sharing
memories of field crabs and *thien ly* flowers, his crisp Northern
accent at odds with the relaxed, melodic burr of the South. Other
differences soon emerged between them. Ha – who'd embraced
risk-taking to survive in the East – seemed to them to be wildly
ambitious. In contrast, the South Vietnamese – scarred by the hor-
rific trial of their escape – wanted a quieter life, with a stable job,
state support and an open bottle of Johnnie Walker Red Label. It
was a paradox that those who had risked so much to escape Communism now embraced socialism. In a world so full of suffering
they were content in their peaceful corner of it. By the end of the
evening, their conversation lapsed into silence, especially after Ha
had mentioned the name of his mother's village.

Within weeks of the collapse of East Germany, Ha had lost both
his job and right of abode, as had every other fraternal guest worker.
The Mozambican, Cuban and Angolan *Gastarbeiter* took up the
government's cash offer of 3,000 Deutschmarks to return home.
But Ha decided to stay, even though knock-off jeans and smuggled
electronics no longer brought any profit. For a time he dabbled in
pirate CDs but the returns were poor. Next he bulk-bought ETZ
motorbikes through a friend at the Zschopau factory, bypassing
the long waiting list, until people began to chose Suzukis instead.
Then the major – who had also emerged from hiding – asked him
to help deal with a Russian officer at the Karlshorst barracks.

At the time Soviet soldiers still stationed in the vanished coun-
try could buy unlimited numbers of cigarettes at huge discount.
To turn a quick profit, the major had ordered 200 cartons, but the
Karlshorst officer had understood him to want 2,000. On the spot
Ha agreed to buy the extra 1,800 cartons on credit, selling them
on at half the usual, taxed price. Within a week he was back at
Karlshorst to order 4,000 more cartons of Marlboro and Golden
American. Ten days later he took another 5,000. After the second
weekend he bought a second-hand Mercedes. Within a month his
profit was enough to make the down-payment on a small Kreuzberg
apartment in which he installed three of the seamstresses, and himself. The girls, rescued from their stark Marzahn billets, shrieked

and giggled and chattered, collapsing onto the floor to compare the new clothes – now of lilac, fawn and russet brown – which he had bought them. He loved how it showed off their umber skin and gleaming, long hair.

Ha liked the taste of money, and the pleasures which it could buy. Money made him feel safe, and powerful when it was fleeced from Germans. He kept it in blue garbage bags in the freezer and, every time he withdrew a cold bundle of notes, it seemed to melt away between his fingers.

Ha's Vietnamese street dealers stood outside supermarkets, lined Karl-Marx-Allee, gathered in Alexanderplatz. As the trade snowballed, propelled by the acumen and ambition of himself and others, KGB officers became involved. Vast new shipments were organised, delivered by military trucks and aircraft to Berlin. Whole Soviet battalions facilitated the trade. At its peak – according to unreleased official statistics – every one of the 350,000 Russian soldiers stationed in East Germany appeared to smoke three cartons (that is, 600 cigarettes) every day. The German government tolerated the trade, and the huge loss of excise duty, for it distracted those frustrated soldiers, most of whom were confined to barracks.

The withdrawal of the Red Army from Germany in 1994 ended the easy supply of cigarettes. The big dealers changed their tactics, ordering through false Belarus companies full shipping containers for delivery from Rotterdam to Minsk. As the trucks crossed Germany they were stopped, robbed and – if the driver was complicit – refilled with bricks of the same weight, resealed and driven on to the border weighing station and out of the country. Later smugglers welded false bottoms into agricultural tankers to bring in hundreds of thousands of tax-free smokes from Poland, Lithuania and Slovenia.

Ha no longer enjoyed the exchanges, deep in the night and in the seemingly endless pine forests which surround Berlin. Once a month he and a dozen drivers would meet a seven-and-a-half-ton truck, transferring its boxes to their cars in minutes, unloading the garbage-bagged bank notes in return. No one counted money as fast as the Vietnamese. His men – testosterone-pumped and serious

– aimed to offload the cigarettes to street distributors within two hours, and be on their backs at the King's Club by dawn.

Every forest meeting point needed two escape routes, as the major had ordered. Only once did Ha fail to organise them. At the height of summer, as the moon thinned away and darkness lingered in the sky, he met his usual Polish supplier. The deal was big, his biggest ever, and the unloading of 48,000 cartons took less than twenty minutes. Ha raised the proffered glass of vodka and toasted the strength of their 'fraternal' relationship. But 100 metres away the exit road was blocked. Armed Russians surrounded the convoy, ordering the Vietnamese out of the cars and into the deep, dark forest, shooting into the air to scatter them. Above Ha's head a tree exploded, showering him in sap and bark fragments. The Russians then stole the cars, the money, all the cigarettes and even the Polish truck.

Greed and the scale of profit changed the business. Until the involvement of Russian gangs, violence had been contained within the Vietnamese community – a punishment beating in a tenement, a murder outside a karaoke bar – and the German police took little interest in it. But as bigger players from Kiev and Moscow moved into town, disseminating brutality and heroin, adding cigarettes to their already profitable line in human trafficking, the authorities could no longer look away. In the Berlin turf wars opposing gangs bribed local politicians, sold Ukrainians into sexual slavery, buried a Serbian competitor up to his neck in the earth then scythed off his head. The city became a transit point for drugs, girls and, again, barbarity.

Ha's men – and their wives – began to worry about risk and rein-carnation. Those who already had lost friends made offerings and prayed at the cemeteries, pouring out rice wine for the ghosts. By 1998 most of the men had gone legitimate, cashing in their shares, opening Asian food wholesalers or sushi restaurants. Ha didn't. He bought a gun. The bullet-proof boy went from strength to weakness for the third time in his life, much like twentieth-century Berlin. The Russians had taken all his money and his eyes were stained with the dust of living. He cursed and bemoaned the loss of his old life and his childhood in Vietnam. There seemed to be only two races of men, he mused, echoing thoughts of Colin Albany in the Thirty Years' War, of chemist Fritz Haber's wife and Dieter Werner's father in 1945: the wild and the tame, the soldier and the civilian, who pursue each other with cruelty.

Ha needed to start anew. He settled on computers, although not the hardware which he'd once lugged across the former border. He saw a future in software design and the new internet. Berlin was the ideal location for such a startup company, he believed, with its low rents and under-employed young people. Capital outlay would be small. English was widely spoken. American websites for online gambling and property sales could be cloned. His aim was to disrupt the German incumbents and drive them out of business within a handful of years.

To raise money Ha turned to the cautious Vietnamese in the old West. Over the years the animosity between the two sides had softened, not least because of intermarriage. The majority of former boat people were men. The Vietnamese women in the East – like some of the seamstresses from the Lichtenberg clothing collective who had shared his bed – needed to acquire citizenship to stay in Germany. An agreeable accommodation was reached between the former enemies and, through his former blue-smocked colleagues, Ha found his way into the moneyed living rooms of Zehlendorf.

One evening – after outlining his startup plans to a group of elders – one of the wives took Ha aside to ask if his mother's old village had been Tay Thon. 'Because our next-door neighbour says he was born there,' she said.

Ha asked his name.

'He's called Lieu Van Khung. But he never seems to be free to meet you.'

Lieu was not a common surname in Vietnam, especially when linked with Khung, a given name which translates as 'Crazy'. It had been Ha's father's name. But Ha's father had always claimed to be ill at ease in the old South.

'Our neighbour is a bachelor and I thought you might have known him when you were a child, especially as he talks about growing *thien ly* flowers along the Mekong.' The woman paused, then added, 'The thing is that his accent isn't right. He sounds like a Northerner.'

Ha gazed on at the shadows moving across the apartment windows. The heinous border between East and West, North and South, along that 'great half-circle' which Kennedy had said stretched from Berlin to Saigon, had torn apart families, turned brother against brother, broken innumerable hearts. The Cold War, the Wall, North and South Vietnam often felt like ancient history to Ha. Yet he knew that it was his history, that he could never move on, never step into the modern world, until he had avenged the betrayals of the past. He felt the warm gun in his hand, as he waited and watched through the long, dark night.

How much time went by, Ha did not know.

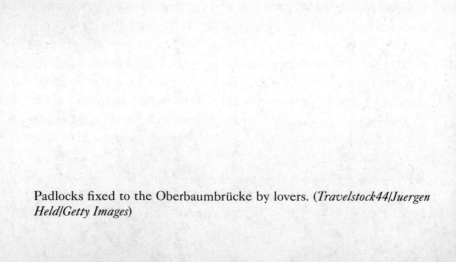

Padlocks fixed to the Oberbaumbrücke by lovers. (*Travelstock44/Juergen Held/Getty Images*)

Zoologischer Garten, 2011

She had no name, or at least when the boy woke he no longer knew it. Her father was Russian, he remembered that, a Jew who had come to Berlin within days of the fall of the Wall. Her old man had learnt to say hello in Vietnamese before German, traded cars and lived off couscous for months, billeted at a home for aliens in Marzahn. On the night he was granted refugee status, he drank a bottle and a half of Stolichnaya and collapsed into her mother's arms on the dance floor of a punk club on Kollwitz Platz.

Her mother was an American who had arrived a couple of years earlier. She'd worked as a runner in New York, landed a job on *Wings of Desire*, tumbled into love, fell pregnant, got dumped. Her plan had been to stay on in Berlin. But on her daughter's sixth birthday she'd moved back to the States alone for a dream job at DreamWorks. She remarried and her daughter hadn't seen her for three and three-quarter years.

The girl, she was a Berliner. *Eine echte Berlinerin.* She'd been raised by her father in Alt-Moabit (where Frederick the Great had planted royal potatoes and factory chimneys first smoked), danced the *Ziganochka* for his lunatic friends, cleaned up their bottles and butts before school. She taught herself to read music, raided her father's old CDs, listened to Lou Reed, Juan Atkins, Nina Hagen and Ellen Allien. At sixteen she mixed her first tracks. At eighteen she landed a job behind the bar at Knaack, working the DJs who came to the club after their shows. In the capital of global dreamers she had a dream. She wanted to dance to her own tunes. The mix was everything for her, the 'braincandy' as Allien called it, pushed to the limit, sweating, shaking, until the room buzzed, until the world belonged to the dance.

He also thought himself to be a Berliner, but by way of Stuttgart and London. Like her he was twenty-one years old. He'd been born at the Charité hospital but soon afterwards his parents had moved west. He'd built Lego cities in his sandbox and trained as an architect at the Architectural Association. He landed his first job with Milla & Partner, the firm due to build the new Schlossplatz monument *Citizens in Motion*, the slender, sculpted barque that would be set in motion by visitors, tilting on its plinth, reminding people that together they can change the world.

Last night – his first back in town since he was a child – he'd met the girl on a dance floor, spinning on life's great turntable. He hadn't been able to stop staring at her eyes. He remembered her green eyes now. Green as jade, he had told her.

'Sorry, ich steh auf Mädchen' – 'I prefer girls' – she'd replied, but with a smile.

The girl's mother hadn't voted for Reagan; not as governor, not as president, not for street sweeper, as she told her daughter. In 1987 her mother had marched at the front of a crowd of 24,000, protesting against his Berlin visit, against American power, against Star Wars, even against Disney. She'd believed in something in those days, about the way the world should be, or at least how it shouldn't be. She could have joined America's birthday party for Berlin – at Tempelhof, replete with cake and balloons to mark the city's 750th anniversary – but she chose instead to march with the Greens, anarchists and gangs like Anonymous. They stormed along

Ku'damm between solid rows of policemen in full riot gear, throwing bottles at the shop windows and setting cars alight. Reagan was a has-been actor waddling towards retirement yet at the Brandenburg Gate – where Harvey, Kennedy and Bowie had once stood – he'd called out with a rhetorical flourish, 'Mr Gorbachev, tear down this Wall! . . . Es gibt nur ein Berlin.' 'There is only one Berlin.' She hated to admit it but the tears that had pricked her eyes weren't from the tear gas.

Soon afterwards East Germans found a new way to escape their utopian prison, streaming to the West through liberal Hungary. In 1989 Soviet President Mikhail Gorbachev refused to use the Red Army to staunch the flow, and the East German regime collapsed in confusion and shame. With eyes gleaming, Berliners flooded across no man's land, crying 'Wir sind das Volk,' and then 'Wir sind *ein* Volk.' 'We are one people.' Bouquets of flowers covered the windscreens of police vans. On Potsdamer Platz British squaddies served cups of scalding tea to the rippling crowd, among them the boy's parents. Again and again they glanced back at the concrete barrier, fingers crossed just in case, hardly believing they were finally free. At Schinkel's Neue Wache the goose-stepping NVA guards were replaced by a single policeman. Lenin's bust was covered with a melamine box then removed from outside the Soviet Embassy. The two halves of the country were reunited and Germans called the change *die Wende*. The turning point.

Over that remarkable winter the girl's mother had strode between abandoned watchtowers, down flights of hidden steps, past the bricked-up entrances of an underground station into the steel-reinforced concrete chamber of a forgotten bank vault. Tresor – meaning safe or vault – was the first, great post-*Wende* dance club. In the reunited city, clubbers came together beneath the death strip which had once separated them.

A decade earlier Lou Reed had walked on the wild side, his rock tragedy *Berlin* washing a new, Mohican-crested wave over Kreuzberg and Schöneberg. Bowie and Pop had opened the SO36 music club. Nick Cave had then moved onto Oranienstraße, hanging out at Risiko where Blixa Bargeld tended the bar. Together they sowed the Bad Seeds onto Berlin's dark, feverish dance floors. Grex became the city's first House club. Riehmer's was *the* pick-up spot. Club rats scuttled between it and Dschungel, to Turbine Rosenheim and Loop di Loop. At Trash, a Berlin Electric Ballroom run by Hell's Angels, party people had gazed out of the second-floor windows at the annual May Day ferment as Nirvana's 'Smells like Teen Spirit' boomed from the speakers.

The dancers never stopped.

When the border cracked, a third of all buildings in the east of the city were vacant. Techno activists stormed across the Spree to Ostkreuz and Friedrichshain, improvising new clubs in abandoned basements, warehouses and fuel depots. Their music – born in motor city Detroit, revved up in Berlin – swept through the gaps in the Wall, beating out a new pulse towards the future.

Clubbers never knew how long any night might last, a venue stay open, or where to go next. Transience imbued Berlin's nightlife with a sense of mystery. Yet the subterranean Tresor remained, its steel vault doors at once entrapping and freeing the dancers as the Wall had done. Its BOSE tube speakers blasted and smashed all the glasses in the bar every couple of weeks. Along the line of the late great division of the world, between a Communist East and a capitalist West, totalitarianism was replaced by total entertainment, and the girl's mother danced the nights away, until the city sold the land to developers and she heard the call of DreamWorks.

Thick smoke filled the pungent air. Coloured spots swept across the throng of semi-naked bodies. Strobe lights flickered and froze their movement. Metal staircases loomed out of the mist, rising towards a surreal labyrinth of hidden bars, disconnected balconies and dim, crowded alcoves.

A fierce, feral punk-bouncer, pierced and tattooed on every inch of exposed skin, had stood at the club's entrance like a sentinel from hell. He'd blocked the young architect's path for a moment, then stood aside to usher him into the darkness. In a concrete chamber – beneath painter Piotr Nathan's mural *Rituals of Disappearance* – he'd been frisked, stamped and relieved of his jacket.

Now a rhythmic, thunderous sound rose around him. The bass beat gripped his chest and pounded his body in waves so powerful that – in the second when they stopped – he felt like a dust mote floating up into the yawning cavern of the building, towards the eighteen-metre-high ceiling.

Berghain was no secret. The converted power station held 1,500 dancers. Its scene was both gay and straight, as well as accommodating every intermediate deviation. In time he would venture up to the packed Panoramabar, with chill-out House music and wraparound black leather counter. He'd perch on stained sofas, beside butcher's block tables, around immense, down-lit steel and concrete pillars.

But before that he just danced.

Around him moved buffed shirtless boys, slender gleaming girls, a camp crew-cut dancer with chunky boots and diminutive Hello Kitty backpack. A man in lens-less Elvis Costello spectacles circled a laughing, bare-chested invalid in a wheelchair. For the most part the dress code was minimal, black or proletarian, apart from a dancing queen in white bridal dress and tiara who stood on a plinth above the throng, stirring the smoke with her wand. In front of him against a Funktion-One speaker stack a couple made love without removing – or even unzipping – their clothes. A tall, smiling beauty in a long frock stroked his arm, and turned out not to be a woman at all.

He saw her then, dancing alone amidst the groping, grappling bodies. He slipped between them and into her orbit. She made no objection and soon they were dancing together, mirroring each other's movements. At times she moved with such lightness that she hardly seemed to touch the floor.

After a hands-up moment, he offered her a drink. She led him up the stairs to a bar. She wore a long, loose top and tight black leggings. She drank Bionade. He missed her name in the din. They talked about clubs, a thrill racing through him as she pressed her mouth against his ear. She told him that she loved Richie Hawtin, calling him a pioneer, and admired Ellen Allien, the club DJ who merged music and fashion: jersey shirts printed with iconic silhouettes of raised hands, the image of a dancer seen through a curtain of smoke. 'If a DJ doesn't have a feeling for what people want, they won't get into the set and it clears the floor,' she shouted to be heard. 'You have to be an emotion reader, a people reader.' She told him that she too wanted to start a label, to brand herself. Like Allien, she saw herself as a *Stadtkind* – a child of the city.

Later they fell back onto the dance floor, its atmosphere – at once crowded and intimate – charged by the raw lust throbbing from one corner: muscular torsos, braces, blindfolds, bondage. The sweating concrete walls seemed to amplify the hedonism and carnality. She brushed his arm. He held her waist. As dawn leaked through the slatted windows of the Panoramabar he told her again that he couldn't stop looking at her eyes. She laughed and, taking both his hands, said, 'Let's see what happens.'

They led each other away from techno central. In the cool sunlight near the Ostbahnhof he bought her a coffee. At a corner table another young man, with thin arms and legs crossed as if he were a puzzle of blood and bone, coughed and coughed.

On the way to his hotel the taxi passed through Schlossplatz, where Schinkel had stood and the *Citizens in Motion* memorial was to take shape, if the designer, architects and planners could get their act together, if the city archaeologists would stop unearthing medieval graves and bones. In front of Frederick's renascent palace, through the open window, in his buzzing ears, he imagined hearing the air of a flute.

A minute later the girl was stretching across him, pressing against him, pointing to the place where *Wings of Desire* had been filmed.

Wings of Desire, that was a film, a Berlin film as much as *Metropolis*, *The Blue Angel* and Fassbinder's *Berlin Alexanderplatz*. The girl effused about director Wim Wenders, dug up her mother's stories of writer Peter Handke, recalled one shot after another. There at Gleisdreieck the art department had mocked up sections of the Wall, she said, even though the real one had still been standing fifteen metres away. Here in this alley Wenders' angels had listened to the innermost fears and desires of Berlin's lonely, traumatised

population. Over at the Havel Film Studio her mother had helped
to paint a plaster replica of Friedrich Drake's Victory, the statue
atop the Siegessäule, which Berliners had nicknamed *Goldelse* –
golden Else – for reasons that no one could remember. In the movie
the angels' role was to 'testify and preserve reality', not to live it,
not to feel it, until winged Damiel – played by actor Bruno Ganz –
decided to give up eternity and become mortal.

The boy knew the film well. He could even picture the girl's
mother, then a young American at the back of a crowd scene where
the real crew played pinball with actors in Nazi uniforms. He remembered the movie's skies, its clouds, the ribbon of motorways
and its million solitary voices in the divided city. But most of all
he thought the film revealed Berlin's true emptiness: the flattened
houses and war-blitzed streets, the bombed wastes behind Anhalter Bahnhof, the determined, disorientated old man – played by
Curt Bois – picking his way through the long grass field behind
Hansa's 'Great Hall by the Wall', wondering what had become of
the capital's crowds, its horse-drawn omnibuses and Café Josty
where he'd drunk coffee in his youth. 'I can't find Potsdamer Platz.
Here – this can't be it,' the actor cried.

After the wrap, with *die Wende*, conflicting visions of a new city
had taken shape in Berlin's empty heart. Cranes had upended the
Wall's concrete slabs to be sold to Los Angeles, Chicago and Singa-
pore. Sections went to both the Kennedy and Reagan presidential
libraries. Tumbleweed balls of barbed wire were rolled away to
other borders. Orange-tipped survey stakes began to dot the bull-
dozed earth. Lines of plastic tape marked out the location of new
shopping malls, office blocks, five-star hotels and a casino. The
artist Hans Haacke set a neon Mercedes-Benz star atop the last
watchtower for an exhibition entitled *Die Endlichkeit der Freiheit*,
warning *Ossis* that freedom was finite under capitalism as it was
determined by personal wealth.

Corporate Germany transformed Potsdamer Platz's barren
square into the largest building site in Europe, aiming to tame
Berlin with flashy, glass-clad new builds and plush Belle Époque
renovations. The counter-culture banded together to try to block

the slide towards gentrification. A new battle for Berlin was fought
in cold-water squats and overheated court rooms. Displaced anarchists slid disposable barbecue sets under the Porsches of
wealthy incomers in the hope of driving them back to California
and Cologne.

Some Berliners even came to see Berlin itself as a dynamic work
of art. In their urban landscape Libeskind conjured up the Jewish
Museum. Chipperfield reinvented the Neues Museum. Derelict
buildings reopened as 'living projects', like the vibrant, radical
Tacheles artists' co-op with studios, urban beach bar and the filthi-
est stairwell in the city.

But the city fathers rejected the boldest chances for experimenta-
tion. Cautious planners buried almost all traces of the Wall beneath
oddly-shaped parks and safe American paradigms. They mutated
Checkpoint Charlie into a tourist ghetto and set about resurrecting
Frederick's hulking Schloss, which had been ripped down by the
Communists in 1950 as a loathed emblem of Prussian imperialism.
Tacheles' last squatting artists were evicted by its bank owner. The
debate – between homogeneity and diversity, community and cor-
poration, courage or poverty of aspiration – had drawn the young
architect to the profession. It was easy to design a dream city, he
recalled from the writings of the urban thinker Jane Jacobs, but it
took imagination to rebuild a living one.

In the hotel near to the Zoologischer Garten the girl couldn't sleep,
didn't sleep she said. He pulled a bottle of *Sekt* from the mini-bar
and they drank it looking out over the waking city. He kissed her
neck, tasting the dry salt sweat of dance on her skin. The dark
branches of the chestnut trees swayed in the breeze.

'I'm not tired,' she said again. She leant back against the window,
talking about music and clubs in both her mother's time and
now, about Ostgut, Bang Bang and Kaminer's Russian Disco as a
crowded, sweaty *Resteficken* pick-up joint for leftover meat.

Her phone rang and she slid it open. 'Mischa?' said the voice. 'I
have to talk to Mischa.'

'You have the wrong number,' she answered, her English tinged with both an American and Russian accent. 'Don't call this number again.'

She clicked off, waited a moment and – when the mobile rang again – switched on voicemail. She shook out her hair and said, 'I'd like a shower. Can I take a shower?'

He started the water for her, pointed out the white hotel bath-robe, closed the door as steam drifted out into the room. He pulled the curtains and turned on the bedside lamp. He lay on top of the duvet and listened. She was singing to herself, although so softly that he couldn't catch the words. Sparrows squabbled under the eaves. The morning light slid through the gap in the curtains, moving across the ceiling as if over a sundial.

When she turned off the mixer tap, he imagined water droplets dripping off the shower head, running down her skin. He liked the last, silent moments when a woman was alone in a bathroom, fixing her hair, looking in the mirror, bending forward to touch a new line at the corner of an eye.

She slipped into the robe and onto the brass bed, leaning back against the headboard, hugging her knees. 'Do you have a cigar-ette?' she asked.

He didn't.

'I envy my mother,' she said. 'She had an idea of what was right, and what was wrong.'

'The ancient age of certainties,' he said. 'As angels walked along the Wall.'

'But she – and my father – had something to believe in: Commun-ism, capitalism, whatever,' she went on. 'What do we have now?' she asked, starting to rock herself like child. 'Ecology? Ourselves? The new iPhone?'

He reached for the bubbly and offered to refill her glass. 'Music?' he said, probing. 'One another?'

She turned to face him then, stretching out on the bed, rumpling the covers.

'When I'm on the dance floor, I'm full of emotion, I'm loving the moment, I'm me, but are my small inner desires such a big deal? Haven't we lost sight of something . . . larger?'

He reached out to stroke her hair.

'Will you hold me?' she asked him. 'I'm cold. I'm not tired but I'm cold.'

He took her in his arms and kissed her. She touched the back of his hand to delay its advance.

'Just hold me first.'

He took a pillow and settled it under their heads. He pulled the duvet around her. He lay back and looked at the ceiling. The red diode on the smoke detector pulsed in the half-light. He hadn't slept since his flight. He was tired.

'Do you know that David Bowie song? "Never Get Old"?' she asked. He shook his head. 'Something about capturing the moment yet losing it, breathing deep when the movie gets real. My mother was so into him.'

She talked about her music then, happy again. She'd have her own label, she said, it was important for a woman to set up a record label to showcase her tastes and promote her name. He passed the glass to her. She drank and the bubbles caught in her nose. She laughed, her legs bumping against his under the duvet.

'When I was little my parents told stories to try to make sense of the world,' she said. 'Wonderful dreamlike stories in which, once I'd achieved my desires, my dreams, I would be fulfilled, I would become my own true self. That's what they told me.'

'It's an idea, one way of feeling and thinking,' he said, and started to talk about the firm's planned Schlossplatz project, returning to her question. 'We can believe in the things we can make. The sculpture is not simply an object to be looked at. It's about people making it into something, by stepping onto it and making it move.' He added, not unknowingly, easing himself closer to her, 'Imagine what an architect and a dancer can make together.' The *Citizens in Motion* monument had been designed by his boss at Milla & Partner and the choreographer Sasha Waltz.

With a peel of laughter the girl moved away, jumbling the covers as she slipped down to the foot of the bed. She stole three of the pillows, plumped them up to support her back then settled down alongside him, head to toe, laying her hand on his knee.

'Did you hear that Knut the bear is going to be put on display by Dr Death?' she asked suddenly, teasing his earnestness, breaking the current for a moment.

'It's a joke,' he said.

'No, really. I saw it on the news.'

Rumour had it that Gunther von Hagens, the controversial *Body Worlds* anatomist, was to skin the Zoo's favourite polar bear, which had just died, coating its body parts with resin, laying bare its muscles, nerves and tendons.

'It'd be too weird,' he said, shaking his head.

'He's going to have himself preserved too,' she went on.

'Who? Dr Death?'

'He says he's got a disease, Parkinson's I think. When he dies his wife will plastinate his body.' She shivered and pulled the duvet tighter around her. 'His last show in Berlin he had a couple, the skinless corpses of a real man and a real woman, locked together in, you know, fucking.'

Now he laughed.

The girl looked around the room, taking in its white walls, the sketchbooks on the desk, his unopened backpack in the corner. The sliver of sunlight fell across her hair which gleamed as she tucked it behind an ear. He noticed that she wore no jewellery, apart from petite conical earrings encircled with bands of colour. He began to massage her feet, softly, slowly. She closed her eyes.

He moved forward then to kiss her. He eased open the white robe, breathing deep, electrified by her warmth. Together the boy and girl tilted on the slender balanced barque of the bed, setting each other in motion, coming so close that the walls between them seemed to melt away.

Later, much later, he listened to the sound of her breath on the pillow and said, 'I heard you singing in the shower.'

She opened her eyes, looking as if her privacy been violated. Then she softened and quietly began to sing. 'Lunapark und Wellenbad, kleiner Bär im Zoo.'

'Stop thinking about the bear,' he said.

'Ich hab' noch einen Koffer in Berlin,' she sang. 'Deswegen muss ich nächstens wieder hin.' 'I still have a suitcase in Berlin.'

Dietrich had recorded the song, then Hildegard Knef and Udo Lindenberg. Reagan had used its title in his 1987 speech at the Wall. Now the girl sang the sad, dated lyrics – about the beauty of Paris, and the wonder of Rome, about the strange attraction of Berlin – as if it were a lullaby. 'Die Seligkeiten vergang'ner Zeiten, sind alle noch in meinem kleinen Koffer drin.' 'The bliss of bygone days is all still in my little suitcase.'

'It's an old person's song,' whispered the boy.

The girl shook her head, sang on and the young architect tightened his arms around her. When she finished, they fell back into silence, letting the words and music hang in the air of their little room. After all, the moment – *that* moment – was what it was about, all those pages, stanzas and touches of colour. One reached a place of beauty, of intimacy, a brief tender moment of love yet as soon as it was in one's hands, it was gone.

In the distance church bells rang and a plane passed high overhead.

'When my mother fell ill she started recording videos of television programmes,' the girl said into the shadows. 'Dozens and dozens of them, more than she could ever watch in the time she had left. It was her way of trying to extend her life, or at least the *idea* of her life.'

'I didn't know . . .'

'Three and three-quarter years ago,' she said. She paused and then added, 'There's so much I want to do.'

Sleep is not something that many people admit to doing in Berlin but in the blue half-light the young couple closed their eyes. Their breathing slowed and their limbs relaxed. Side by side they began to dream. They were sitting together in a sunny square full of people, all of whom were having the same dream as they. They were holding hands.

Suddenly on the hotel bed the girl lashed out, her fists windmilling in her sleep. She called out a name as the bedclothes tumbled off them. The boy jerked awake, half scared to death. He curved forward to take her back into his arms, to stroke her brow. At the same moment her phone rang. She groped for it, flipped it on, said without thinking, 'Don't call me. Lass mich allein.' She threw the mobile across the room then fell against him, head to head, their limbs and breath tangled and linked. Her heart was racing. Her skin was warm. She said, 'I don't want to die.'

When he woke again he was alone. Her DMs weren't under the desk. Her top was no longer slung across the chair. The white robe was draped over the TV. He threw back the covers in the hope of finding some sign of her, of them, but found nothing, no evidence of her touching his life. Their history had lasted a single night yet he sensed already that he must lock it in his memory, and somehow give it form.

He sat on the edge of the bed. He breathed in the air. He imagined a whiff of her perfume. He rose to his feet and pulled open the curtains. Beyond the window the grey city now appeared to be made up of an infinity of colours. Everyone who came to Berlin, he realised, came to make or find themselves in some way or other, their own creation changing the place itself, making them a part of it, and it a part of them, becoming Berliners. 'Ich bin ein Berliner. Wir sind Berliner.' It was a city of the imagination, its people making and embracing its myths, forging – in their minds at least – a sense of cohesion, of unity, of purpose.

The young architect stepped into the bathroom and flicked on the shower. As the clouds of mist filled the room he turned to face the mirror. Across its glass, written in lipstick, were words that had once been graffitied on the Berlin Wall, '*Alles hat ein Ende, nur die Wurst hat zwei.*'

Everything has an end. Only a sausage has two.

CHAPTER 23

*Ilse Philips,
in Another Berlin*

Stolpersteine 'stumble stones' on Gieselerstraße, Berlin-Wilmersdorf, 2013 (*Rory MacLean*)

Gieselerstraße, 2013

A crescent of tall windows opens onto the Linden trees. Late afternoon sunlight spills across the parquet floor. I've set my desk at the back of this light, elegant ballroom with its soaring ceilings and high double doors, and I'm excited enough to dance.

I live in Berlin now. I returned here to write this book, swapping a rambling quarter-acre of rural England for this polished oak field in the centre of the city. Now that it's finished I have decided to stay on for a time, or at least for as long as I am able. On summer evenings I like to sit at the window and look out at the street, at the cellar wine bar where the lamps burn all day, at the top-heavy balconied façades, at the creative tourists with their guitar cases and joints, at the woman opposite in a kimono washing her dreadlocks.

About a year after my arrival I heard the tap-tap of hammers beneath my window. Workmen were re-laying cobblestones, levelling them by hand in sand. I went down to investigate and a glint of brass caught my eye. I stopped, as had a dozen other passers-by, and read:

HERE LIVED FLORA PHILIPS
BORN 1896
DEPORTED 2.3.1943
MURDERED AUSCHWITZ

Next to it were more brass-capped stones, recording the names of seven other Jewish residents who had been pulled from their homes in this leafy and peaceful neighbourhood, and murdered in the camps. Hugo Philips, Flora's husband. Their neighbour Regina Edel. Selma Schnee. Doris Warwar. Dr Kurt Jacobsohn, his wife Liesbeth and little Hans Adolf who was six years old when he was gassed to death.

In 1939 Hugo and Flora Philips's sixteen-year-old daughter, Ilse, had walked away from her home and boarded a *Kindertransport* train bound for London. Her rescue from Nazi Germany had been arranged by Wilfrid Israel, friend of Einstein and Rathenau, whom Isherwood had portrayed in *Goodbye to Berlin*. Hugo and Flora had waved her off at the station. After the war, when she learnt of the execution of her parents and neighbours, Ilse vowed never to return to Berlin. But six months after I'd seen the white roses and brass *Stolperstein* cobbles, she came back.

On a sunny spring morning she stood at the doorway which she had last walked through seventy-two years earlier. With tears in their eyes, the building's gathered residents welcomed her, along with four generations of her English family. The Berliners spoke – in English, in German and with humility – of being overwhelmed by her family's 'open friendship' towards them. They expressed the need to 'commemorate the unbearable fate of our fellow citizens'. They said that as one stumbles upon the brass stones, and stops to read them, one has to bow – in respect for those who were so cruelly and needlessly killed. One by one today's residents – none of whom had lived in the building during the war – read aloud the names of their Jewish predecessors, and the dates and places of their murder. Their voices, wracked with emotion, echoed down the street where the deceased had once walked, talked, laughed . . . and wept.

Then it was time for Ilse's family to speak. Her daughter Miriam told the gathering that her grandparents had been ordinary German citizens who happened to be Jewish. Hugo had served the Reich in the trenches during the First World War. Their forefathers had lived in Germany for centuries. She said that saving their children – Ilse's late brother had also been sent away – 'had been the only light in the last years of Hugo and Flora's lives'. As Miriam held her mother's hand, the men donned their *kippah* prayer caps, and the family recited the *Kaddish*. Finally Ilse – white-haired, stooped and silent – laid two white pebbles onto the *Stolpersteine*.

Later that day in the apartment which had once been Ilse's family home, Miriam told me that her mother had decided to return to Berlin on reading a blog which I had written about the *Stolpersteine*. As a last witness to an older, colder Berlin she'd wanted to be a part of the act of remembrance. Miriam said, 'We have a huge sense of a circle completed.'

As we spoke a stranger joined us, introducing himself as a fellow neighbour. He told me that he was an artist, a painter. He listened to our conversation about the ceremony, about Berlin's history and then about my reasons for choosing to live in this haunted, vibrant city of absences. We talked about the past of course, for in Berlin one can never escape it, and the noble and necessary act of remembering.

'I do not want to say that they – the SS officers, the camp guards, even the soldiers by the Wall – are like us,' the painter said, looking across the room at Ilse. 'It is different, worse I guess. They *are* us – and we would have been them, in our respective times. It does not mean that I think we – the Germans – are likely to ever become Nazis or Communists again. Germany is a profoundly different land now, its identity reshaped for ever by cataclysmic events. But it is the potential of us, them, me, to have been part of such events that is the horror today.'

In a courageous, humane and moving manner, modern Germany is subjecting itself to national psychoanalysis. This painful process is evident in Berlin's Holocaust Memorial, in the Jewish Museum, in the black husk of the Kaiser Wilhelm Memorial Church, destroyed by Allied bombs in 1943 and in the Stasi's former Hohenschön-hausen prison. Above all it is evident in the *Stolpersteine*. Across Germany, in perhaps the largest artwork of all time, some 40,000 brass 'stumble stones' have been planted among the cobbles of 500 towns and cities, engraved with the names of individuals who were murdered during the Nazi years. Each plaque begins with the same words: *Hier wohnte* – here lived – followed by the name, date of birth, year of deportation and identity of the death camp or place of execution. In almost every case the *Stolpersteine* have been paid for by the residents of the deceased's former home.

At the heart of this process is a Freudian idea that the repressed (or at least unspoken) will fester like a canker unless it is brought to light. The insistence on memory is anciently Jewish, and now Western: the conviction that for the psychic health of a society – as well as an individual – past atrocities must be unearthed and con-fessed, as a condition of healing.

'So what is it that makes one person a collaborator and another a dissident?' I asked the young German painter.

He paused before he replied. 'All I can say is that even now, even after so many years, we still do not trust ourselves. Every German leader since 1945 has been wary of his own countrymen, because of their individual experience of the war. Perhaps this has prevented us from committing suicide again, and taking the rest of Europe with us.'

'But almost all of today's politicians were born after the war,' I said.

'So they have no personal experience of it. So they now listen to the *Stammtisch*, to popular opinion,' answered the painter, shak-ing his head. 'Goethe once wrote, "Germany is nothing, but every individual German is much, and yet the Germans imagine the re-verse to be true". Too often in our history we have surrendered ourselves to the group. So what makes one of us a collaborator and another a dissident? I wish we knew.'

As we spoke I remembered my first visit to West Berlin forty years earlier. I had popped out on a Saturday morning to buy a loaf of bread. The pavements were busy and I'd waited with other pedestrians to cross a main street. After a moment I looked to the left. Then I looked to the right. The road was free of traffic. I tried to catch a fellow pedestrian's eye in the hope of gleaning an explanation but no one looked back at me. So I asked the man at my side, 'Why are you waiting?'

'The light is red.'

'But no cars are coming.'

'The light is red.'

Get a life I thought, and strode across the deserted street.

Now came the shock.

On the opposite pavement, another small crowd of pedestrians were also waiting. As I approached them they closed ranks and blocked my path. No words were spoken between them. It was an instinctual, communal response. I stood stock still before them, stunned by their behaviour, wanting to laugh out loud. Not only did they obey a light bulb like well-trained sheep, they also rejected my independence. They were leaving me stranded on the road, which was now a concern as cars were rapidly approaching the intersection.

I stepped left, and the pedestrians shifted with me. I stepped right, they mirrored my movement. I no longer had time either for a philosophical discussion or to retreat back to the other side. Simply put, I was within seconds of being run over for my non-conformity.

In his autobiography *The World of Yesterday*, the novelist Stefan Zweig remarked of the Germans that they could bear anything, wartime defeats, poverty and deprivation, but not disorder. By crossing against the red I had mocked the other pedestrians' need for order. In response they seemed to have had no qualms about watching me be squashed like an audacious bug.

In those early days I had wondered if there was a fundamental absence in Berlin, one that had shaped the city and its people for over five centuries. It was an absence which helped me to explain the obsession with rules, the hunger for conformity, even the Holocaust. It was a lack of empathy.

Empathy lies at the heart of our humanity. Without it – or a substitute – a society will destroy itself. To compensate for this lack,

I told my teenage self, Germans developed strict laws to enshrine respect for fellow citizens. They waited at lights. They fell into ranks. They obeyed orders.

But the world is not as simple as it appears to a naive nineteen-year-old. Only thirty years had passed since the Red Army had butchered its way along those streets, less than two decades since the last German POW had returned from a Siberian gulag to his corner café, tears rolling down his hollow cheeks as he sipped his first coffee. As I came to know the city, I began to understand that, rather than lacking in empathy, Berlin was in trauma. Its collective memory was so wracked by historical suffering, so injured by emotional history, that Berliners – like Germans as a whole – had developed rules as defences.

Rules help to overcome a sense of instability, providing a means of dealing with shared memories of pain and deprivation, helping to forge a collective identity. As I learnt about the Thirty Years' War and the Hohenzollerns' wrestle against chaos, I began to appreciate the virtues of collectivity. I realised that the flipside of trauma is resilience, that the obsession with order and efficiency had produced an economic miracle. I became aware that collective introspection had created – in time – some of humanity's most moving public expressions of the past, in the monuments and symbols across the city which testify to the Germans' capacity for deep, empathetic feeling.

It's natural that a conformist society should produce radicals. Rebellion grows out of convention, it's the correlate. So on Berlin's sandy foundations, built by the steady labour and hidden fears of the dutiful, hard-working burghers, the free thinker, the reformist, the anarchist and the artist lashed out at the status quo, goading the conformists to question, to rethink, to be independent.

Throughout Berlin's brutal history these contrary forces have been bred into the volatile and moody virago. They have nurtured a complex society tangled with contradictions, uneasy with itself yet marked by pride, at once stoic and hedonistic, resilient and fragile, obedient and rebellious, where pierced and tattooed punks still wait for the light to change at deserted intersections, and the children of murderers bow their heads before their parents' victims.

Back on my street, as I took leave of Miriam, her mother and the painter, I searched for the right words of farewell. I was in no position to thank Ilse for coming to Berlin, to talk of the bitter pain of the family's loss, or to mention the courage of new generations of Berliners who are confronting the darkness in their past. I did not need to ask who will lay stones on the *Stolpersteine* of the other lost, former residents. We all knew that the search for their surviving relatives at Yad Vashem, Israel's memorial to the Jewish victims of the Holocaust, had been in vain. It would be up to other chroniclers to speak their names out loud, to ensure that they lived on in memory, in the imagination. All I could say to Ilse's family – my own voice croaking with emotion – was, 'It is good to have met you, here in Berlin.'

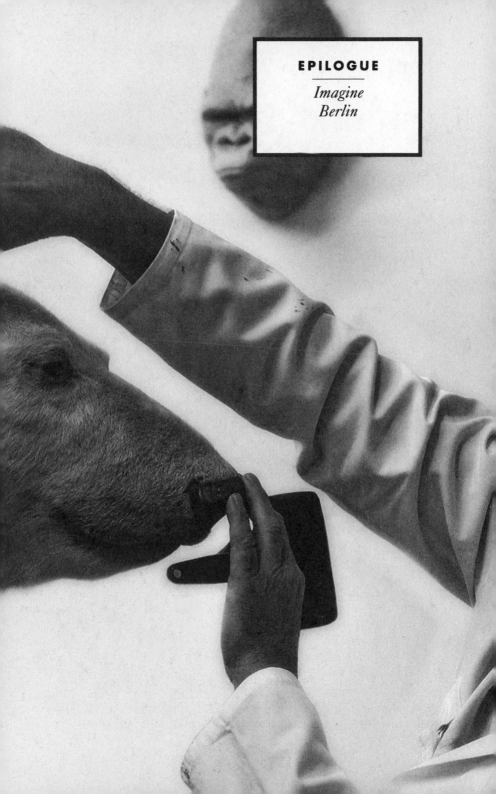

EPILOGUE

*Imagine
Berlin*

Knut the polar bear retouched by a taxidermist at the Natural History Museum, 2013. (*Museum für Naturkunde, Berlin/Carola Radke*)

Imagine Berlin. Imagine a city of fragments and ghosts. Imagine a metropolis which inspired countless artists and witnessed uncountable murders. Imagine a laboratory of ideas, the fount of both the brightest and darkest designs of history's most bloody century. Imagine the most arrogant capital of Europe devastated by Allied bombs then divided. Imagine it reunited and reborn as one of the creative centres of the world.

In my lifetime I have known three Berlins: West Berlin where I made movies with David Bowie, East Berlin where I researched my first book, and now the unified capital. Over the years I have visited so often that today, if the notion took me, I could find my younger self in almost any corner of the city.

If I waited long enough at Bahnhof Zoo, I would see myself aged nineteen fall from the Hoek van Holland train and into waiting arms. At night on Savignyplatz I would catch sight of myself, four years older, cycling home in the summer rain, soaked to the skin, my companion and I throwing off our clothes as we rode: shirts in the Tiergarten, skirt in the Spree. Along Friedrichstraße I'd watch myself – over thirty by 1989 and losing my hair – run between East German ministries, applying for travel permits for a country that might no longer exist (none of the bureaucrats knew for sure).

Later in the Grunewald, the dense urban forest which hugs the city's western fringe, I'd linger until I spotted myself – with notebook in hand – bow my head in the forest cemetery. In the black earth at my feet the stones were engraved *Unbekannter, Unbekannte, Unbekannt*. Unknown man, unknown woman, unknown. Some victims of the Allied bombing were so disfigured that their sex could not be determined.

Finally today I see myself lost in the memorial to the Jews murdered in the Second World War. The vast, undulating labyrinth of concrete plinths rises and falls away into the darkness of Gertrud-Kolmar-Straße. I stumble between its hard-edged, disorientating stelae, built on top of sealed Nazi bunkers, spooked by dusky sounds and shadows, moved by the echo of children's voices and footsteps.

Like so many others I inhabit Berlin, and it inhabits me.

Our memories are not fixed and lifeless fragments to be retrieved like dusty books from a library shelf. Instead they impel an evolving dialogue between our past and present selves. All our histories – personal, collective – become imaginative reconstructions, the ever-changing stories into which we look to understand the chaotic tumble of new events.

Similarly Berlin's identity is not set in stone, or brick. Its story is also ongoing. Again and again the city reinvents itself, reconciling a mythic idea of itself with its bitter, bloody, buoyant past. The Berliner Schloss rises again as Germany becomes paymaster of Europe. Mel Brooks's *The Producers* runs at the Admiralspalast, 'Springtime for Hitler' ringing out in the theatre where the Führer once kept a private box. After every performance of the Cold War musical *Hinterm Horizont*, the audience spills across the former death strip whistling 'Mädchen aus Ost-Berlin'. Knut the bear hasn't been laid bare by Dr Death, with exposed muscles, nerves and tendons coated in resin, but his fur is on display at the Natural History Museum. In the shadow of the Brandenburg Gate out-of-work actors don Chinese-made East German uniforms to sell fake East Zone passes. Fat Tire Bicycles offers Nazi and Red Berlin tours every hour on the hour. Not so long ago one visitor even asked their tour guide, 'Can you direct me please to the Third Reich?'

'Just walk down this street and turn right at 1933,' the guide replied.

With *die Wende*, Berliners at last can come to terms with their history, and so are able to believe in something again. At the Potsdam Institute for Climate Impact Research, once the Albert Einstein Science Park, the environmental pioneer John Schellnhuber talks about accepting responsibility for tomorrow, drawing a direct line from the darkest memories. 'We never again want to look the other way when we face wrong developments. It is a century-long exercise in responsibility.'

In Berlin-Mitte the internet crusader Burckhardt Bonello champions the city as Europe's startup capital, building virtual worlds from his elegant Wilhelmine workshops. One of a new generation of entrepreneurs, he is – like SoundCloud's Alexander Ljung – creating wealth for the twenty-first century as industrialists Borsig and Rathenau did 100 years ago. 'Today the startup scene is like the early days of electricity,' Bonello says. 'Everything seems possible.'

At the Chancellery, the boss of Deutsche Bank celebrates his sixtieth birthday in the company of the country's political and corporate leaders, among them heads of telecom, insurance and automobile groups, the 'rapacious West German business elites' so feared by Dieter Werner. Yet outside the gates, beyond the rank of bullet-proof Mercedes, activists work to break up the party, to change the old ways, harnessing 'big data' to expose abuses of power and privilege (for example, revealing plagiarism by Defence Minister Karl-Theodor zu Guttenberg – since nicknamed Baron von Googleberg – and cut-and-paste politicians who slip lobby groups' requests into German and European legislation).

Meanwhile at their own parties, the speeding tattooed tourists step onto the stage, the canvas, the film set that is modern Berlin, to play their role like movie extras, refashioning themselves – or being refashioned – as has happened here time and again, embracing the myth.

In this fractured capital, every citizen – whether perfectionist or revolutionary, collaborator or dissident, resident or visitor – can dare to imagine a place which no one else has ever seen. Some, like the writer and cultural observer Michael Schindhelm, even ascribe its astonishing ascent to its reinvention as a virtual city. Brick-and-mortar Berlin – being equalitarian, eccentric and communicative like the internet – has itself become a network, across which the e-generation surf as if on a comfortable global platform. Both on and offline its poets, scientists, performers, politicians and digital natives conjure up visions as potent as its actuality. Ideas rather than evil now spiral out from the centre, from all its neighbourhoods, filling the absences, creating a city that, in its constant state of becoming, is as much a conceit as a reality.

Berlin is a living city, for all its ghosts. It is fresh and green because of its woods and lakes but especially because it is always reinventing itself. 'Berlin ist eine Stadt, verdammt dazu, ewig zu werden, niemals zu sein,' wrote author Karl Scheffler over a century ago. 'It is a place doomed to forever become, never to be.' In its streets, on its avenues, atop the Victory Column, the living walk alongside the dead, remembering, forgetting and, together, imagining the world anew.

AFTERWORD AND BIBLIOGRAPHY

Berlin is a city of the imagination. A portrait which hopes to capture this aspect of its nature needs to let invention co-habit with reality, to juxtapose fiction with fact, as on its streets and amongst its inhabitants. To tell Berlin's story, to reflect its creativity and reveal both its seen and unseen sides, I have used some of the techniques of the novel. I have developed characters from historical sources, selected and tailored personal experience, arranged the action so as to give the narrative shape and momentum. My aim is to make the place and its history more engaging and accessible, to mirror the city's essence of perpetual reinvention.

History, which used to be written about princes and potentates, has become more personal. Now it's told from the bottom up. This change – which can be explained by the decline of collective loyalties and the rise of individualism – has made history more subjective. In our less deferential age, and in biographies which use narrative to propel the facts, both writers and readers are challenging the old assertions of objectivity, to the point of suggesting that the notion of non-fiction may itself be a myth.

'All art is unstable,' David Bowie once said. 'Its meaning is not necessarily that implied by the author. There is no authoritive voice. There are only multiple readings.' Each individual's experience colours their interpretation, in literature and the other arts, even hesitantly in science, adding secondary and tertiary layers of subjectivity, in a process of interaction which enriches our understanding. After all, it was in Berlin that Einstein set about refining his theory that reality isn't fixed, that all is relative.

The following selected bibliography is provided to enable

interested readers to know the sources and – to an extent – unpick the parts which have been combined to create the whole.

No records exist of Konrad von Cölln. His story, and that of the *Berliner Unwille* or citizens' defiance, was assembled from the fourteenth-century Codex Manesse, the *Berliner Stadtbuch* and the *Dialogverse zum Totentanz in der Berliner St Marienkirche* (translation from Niederdeutsch by Renate Hermann-Winter). Modern texts which enabled me to portray medieval times include Alwin Schulz's *Das höfische Leben zur Zeit der Minnesinger* (1889), H.F.M. Prescott's *Jerusalem Journey: Pilgrimage to the Holy Land in the fifteenth century* (1954), Margaret Aston's *The Fifteenth Century: The Prospect of Europe* (1979), *The Medieval German Lyric: The development of its themes and forms in their European context* (1982) by Olive Sayce, Bronislaw Geremek's *The Margins of Society in Late Medieval Paris* (1987), *Voices and Instruments of the Middle Ages* (1987) by Christopher Page, Ronald Taylor's *Berlin and its Culture: An Historical Portrait* (1997), Alexandra Richie's superb *Faust's Metropolis: A History of Berlin* (1998), *The Oral Epic: Performance and music* (2000) edited by Karl Reichl and Leoni Hellmayr's *Berlin im Mittelalter – auf den Spuren einer Doppelstadt* (2012, in *Archäologie in Deutschland*).

Colin Albany's wartime story is based on *Simplicius Simplicissimus*, the great epic of the Thirty Years' War, from which I borrowed freely both incident and language in an attempt to give the narrative – as Brian Eno said almost 400 years later – 'a place in the world . . . that felt rooted and properly positioned'. I first read of John Spencer and his peripatetic *Englische Comödianten* in Taylor's *Berlin and its Culture*. Also consulted were Gothard Arthusius's *Comet Orientalis* (1619), Daniel Defoe's *A Journal of the Plague Year* (1722), Schiller's *History of the Thirty Years' War* (1789) and Ricarda Huch's *Der grosse Krieg in Deutschland* (1914).

By the 18th century there was no paucity of written records. In addition I could visit the places which Frederick the Great had known. I could stand in the rooms where he had argued with Voltaire, follow the paths along which he had walked his greyhounds, feel the geography of his world. Frederick's story springs from his own writings as well as Nathaniel William Wraxall's *Memoirs of the Courts of Berlin, Warsaw and Vienna 1777–79* (1806), Thomas Carlyle's *History of Friedrich II of Prussia* (1899), *The Scottish Friend of Frederick the Great* (1915) by Edith Cuthell and Nancy Mitford's *Frederick the Great* (1970). General Hasso Freiherr von Uslar-Gleichen, who in 1990 oversaw the incorporation of the East German Volksarmee into the Bundeswehr, gave me an understanding of Prussian military tradition. I am grateful to him and to the Projektgruppe Friederisiko of the Stiftung Preußische Schlösser und Gärten Berlin-Brandenburg.

Schinkel's biography and the story of his restless imagination were distilled from the vast body of available literature. In English an accessible work about him is *Karl Friedrich Schinkel: A Universal Man* (1991) edited by Michael Snodin. Also read was Alfred von Wolzogen's *Aus Schinkels Nachlaß: Reisetagebücher, Briefe und Aphorismen* (1862, 1863) and Stephen Spender's 1992 essay *The Significance of Schinkel*. Both Prof. Dr Helmut Börsch-Supan and British architect David Chipperfield, who recreated Friedrich August Stüler's Neues Museum, helped me to understand the practical, political and aesthetic pressures that weighed on Schinkel's mind and influenced his work.

As with Konrad von Cölln, no records exist of Lilli Neuss. She was one of the hundreds of thousands of migrants whose lives have been totally forgotten and can now only be imagined. Her story was related to me by a friend in Alt-Moabit (during our discussions about her uncle who had worked with Albert Speer). Else Hirsch's history could not have been told without Jill Suzanne Smith, Bowdoin Professor of German, who shared with me her *Reading the Red Light: Literary, Cultural, and Social Discourses on Prostitution in Berlin 1880–1933* (2004) and the then unpublished manuscript of her provocative *Berlin Coquette: Prostitution and the New German Woman, 1890–1933* (2014). I fleshed out the material by reading between the lines of Margarete Böhme's *Diary of a Lost Girl* (1905), for which additional thanks are due to Andrea Claussen and Angelika Zöllmer-Daniel.

Central to my understanding of Emil and Walther Rathenau

were Harry Kessler's *Walther Rathenau: Sein Leben und sein Werk* (1928), David Felix's *Walther Rathenau and the Weimar Republic* (1971), D.G. Williamson's *Walther Rathenau* (1971), Zara Steiner's *The Lights That Failed: European International History 1919–1933* (2005) as well as Walther's own books and official AEG histories. Fritz Fischer's *Griff nach der Weltmacht: Die Kriegszielpolitik des kaiserlichen Deutschland 1914/18* (1961) and *World Power or Decline: Controversy Over Germany's Aims in the First World War* (1974) were my main sources on the economic motivation for war. Details of Otto von Bismarck's life are from A.J.P. Taylor's *Bismarck: The Man and the Statesman* (1955).

The two other First World War biographies are of Fritz Haber and Käthe Kollwitz. For my research on Haber I consulted Charlotte Haber's *Mein Leben mit Fritz Haber* (1970), Dietrich Stoltzenberg's *Fritz Haber* (1998), Daniel Charles's *Between Genius and Genocide: The Tragedy of Fritz Haber, Father of Chemical Warfare* (2005) and G.W. Fraser's BBC Radio 4 play *Bread from the Air, Gold from the Sea* (2001) as well as Bretislav Friedrich's *Fritz Haber* (2005, in *Angewandte Chemie*). The Kollwitz narrative was distilled from her diaries and letters (excluding those from her lover Hugo Heller, all of which were burnt before her death) as well as from *Käthe Kollwitz: Woman and Artist* (1976) by Martha Kearns, Elizabeth Prelinger's *Kollwitz Reconsidered* (1992) and *Kollwitz in Context* (1992) by Alessandra Comini. Also vital for creating a picture of those years was Erich Maria Remarque's *All Quiet on the Western Front* (1929) and Hans Gatzke's *Germany's Drive to the West* (1950).

In the 1920s Christopher Isherwood conjured up his own Berlin and parts which went into its creation – along with my portrait of it – were drawn from his *Goodbye to Berlin* (1937) and related stories, *Kathleen and Frank* (1971) and *Christopher and His Kind* (1976). Also read were Cyril Connolly's *Enemies of Promise* (1937), Jonathan Fryer's *Isherwood* (1977), Edward Upward's *Christopher Isherwood: Notes in Remembrance of a Friendship* (1996), Norman Page's *Auden and Isherwood: The Berlin Years* (1998) and Peter Parker's *Isherwood: A Life* (2004). I am grateful to the Kinsey Institute for the succinct history of Magnus Hirschfeld's Institut für Sexualwissenschaft.

To many, the 1928 premiere of Bertolt Brecht's *The Threepenny Opera* was the greatest night in the greatest decade of twentieth-century theatre. The musical ran for two years at the Theater am Schiffbauerdamm and – over the coming decades – was translated into eighteen languages and performed over 10,000 times around the world. Both Berlin's image (as an anarchic, amoral, free-thinking capital) and Brecht's fame were further enhanced by his death, after which East Germans elevated him from troublemaker to theatrical genius, and West German intellectuals laid the foundations of the 'Brecht industry'. As a result almost nothing original can be gleaned from the exhausted facts. To try to imagine him anew I created an earnest, everyman narrator from my readings in *Brecht Directs* by an anonymous colleague (1952, in *Theaterarbeit*), Walter Benjamin's *Understanding Brecht* (1983) and Ronald Hayman's *Brecht: A Biography* (1983). For better or worse, Brecht remains one of the most dominant influences on – or obstacles to – the development of German theatre.

Marlene Dietrich's portrait emerged from my own diaries from the time of *Just a Gigolo* (1977/8), Alexander Walker's *Dietrich* (1984), Steven Bach's *Marlene Dietrich: Life and Legend* (1992) and her daughter Maria Riva's biography of the same year. Other sources include Heinrich Mann's *Professor Unrat* (1905), Josef von Sternberg's script of *The Blue Angel* (1929) and his 'Acting in Film and Theatre' from *Film Culture* (1955), Lotte Eisner's *Fritz Lang* (1976) as well as Kenneth Tynan's *Curtains* (1961) and *Profiles* (1989).

Of the some hundred books read and films screened on the National Socialist years, the main titles include:

– for Leni Riefenstahl, Susan Sontag's *Fascinating Fascism* (1975), Ray Muller's documentary *The Wonderful, Horrible Life of Leni Riefenstahl* (1994), Clive James's *Splurge of the Swastika* (2007), Susan Tegel's *Nazis and the Cinema* (2007), Steven Bach's *Leni: The Life and Work of Leni Riefenstahl* (2007) as well as Riefenstahl's autobiography *Memoiren* (1987) and films *Ways to Strength and Beauty* (1925), *The Holy Mountain* (1926), *The White Hell of Pitz Palü* (1929), *The Blue Light* (1932), *Victory of Faith* (1933), *Triumph of the Will* (1935) and *Olympia* (1938).

– for Albert Speer, his memoirs *Inside the Third Reich* (1970) and *Spandau: The Secret Diaries* (1976), the biographies of Joachim Fest (1999) and Gitta Sereny (1995) as well as Robert R. Taylor's *The Word in Stone: The Role of Architecture in the National Socialist Ideology* (1974), Léon Krier's *Albert Speer: Architecture, 1932–1942* (1985), *Hitler's Berlin: The Speer Plans for Reshaping the Central City* (1985) by Stephen D. Helmer and the recollections of the niece of Stefan Schönecker.

– for Joseph Goebbels, extracts from his diaries (1923/45), Andrea Morgenthaler's NFP/Das Erste documentary *Joseph Goebbels* (2008), *Dietrich's Ghosts: The Sublime and the Beautiful in Third Reich Film* by Erica Carter (2008), Toby Thacker's *Joseph Goebbels: Life and Death* (2009) and Georg Bönisch's *Das böse Genie* (*Der Spiegel* 2010).

Other general books on the Third Reich read include Klaus Mann's *Mephisto* (1936), *The Rise and Fall of the Third Reich* (1960) by William Shirer, A.J.P. Taylor's *The Origins of the Second World War* (1961), Renata Stih and Frieder Schnock's *Orte des Erinnerns: Denkmal im Bayerischen Viertel* (1993), Ian Kershaw's biography of Hitler (1999, 2000), Michael Burleigh's *The Third Reich: A New History* (2001), Sebastian Haffner's *Defying Hitler* (2002), *A Woman in Berlin* (1954, 2002) by Marta Hillers, Saul Friedlander's *The Years of Extermination* (2007) and Antony Beevor's *Berlin: The Downfall* (2007).

The portrait of East Germany, and of Dieter Werner, is based on many journeys to and meetings in that vanished country during the 1970s and 1980s. The uncounted books read since those grey days include Hans Reichhardt's *Raus aus den Trümmern: Vom Beginn des Wiederaufbaus 1945 in Berlin* (1987), Anna Funder's *Stasiland: Stories from Behind the Berlin Wall* (2003) as well as works by Timothy Garton Ash, Thomas Brussig, Robert Cooper, John Lewis Gaddis, Josef Joffe, Robert Kagan, Don Oberdorfer, Gabriel Partos, Joseph Rothschild, Angus Roxburgh, Bernhard Schlink, Ingo Schulze and Christa Wolf. Dieter Werner is a pseudonym.

In 1984 when I first wrote about Bill Harvey and the tunnel many of the participants were still alive. John Wyke, leader of the British tunnelling team, became a friend and provided introductions in London and Washington. Through them and at the Library of Congress I was given access to declassified documents including NSA reports, CIA Special Evaluations and Clandestine Services Histories (*Berlin Tunnel Operation 1952/56*). Subsequently I consulted David C. Martin's *Wilderness of Mirrors: Intrigue, Deception and the Secrets that Destroyed Two of the Cold War's Most Important Agents* (1980), David Stafford's *Spies Beneath Berlin* (2002), Niko Rollmann and Eberhard Elfert's *Die Stadt unter der Stadt* (2006) and *Flawed Patriot: The Rise and Fall of CIA Legend Bill Harvey* (2006) by Bayard Stockton. Most recently John le Carré generously provided fresh insight into the operation.

JFK's script is based on research at the John F. Kennedy Presidential Library in Boston and at the Allied Museum in Berlin as well as on Andreas W. Daum's *Kennedy in Berlin* (2003, 2008) in which I learnt the origin of 'Ich bin ein Berliner'. The template for his crucial, Cold War performance was a short speech given a year earlier in New Orleans. In it Kennedy expressed pride for that city and his country, quoting Cicero, saying, 'Two thousand years ago the proudest boast was to say, "I am a citizen of Rome". Today, I believe, in 1962, the proudest boast is to say, "I am a citizen of the United States".'

My diaries (1977/80) provided the heart of the David Bowie chapter, as did the memories of some of the friends he left behind in Berlin. These were put into context by Kevin Cann's *David Bowie: A Chronology* (1983), David Buckley's *Strange Fascination: David Bowie – The Definitive Story* (1999), *Gimme Danger: The Story of Iggy Pop* (2002) by Joe Ambrose, *Helden: David Bowie und Berlin* (2008) by Tobias Rüther, Thomas Jerome Seabrook's *Bowie in Berlin: A New Career in a New Town* (2008) and Peter Doggett's *The Man Who Sold the World: David Bowie and the 1970s* (2011). Notable among the many articles consulted were William S. Burroughs's *Rolling Stone* interview (1974), Steve Turner's 'The Great Escape of the Thin White Duke' (1991) and 'The Forgotten Hero' by Torsten Hampel (2009, in *Der Tagesspiegel Berlin*). Victoria Broackes of the V&A Museum kindly let me read an early draft of her *Designing David Bowie* and shared a few pages of Bowie's 1976 diary.

Finally, Lieu Van Ha's history came to me through members of Berlin's two Vietnamese communities under the guidance of Kristóf Gosztonyi. The truth of the story – although not its facts – was checked by author and translator Nguyen Ngoc Bich. The portrait of twenty-first-century Berlin is the result of long conversations and nights with Berghain/Ostgut Ton's Ben Klock, the Balkan Beat *Wunderkind* Shantel and Dr Oliver Scholz. Thanks to them as well as to Ellen Allien, Bas Böttcher, Martin Dammann, Marianne Faithfull, Heidi Lüdi, Mark Thomson for *Die Endlichkeit der Freiheit: Art in the Two-Hearted City* (1990), Sasha Waltz & Guests and Milla & Partner Architects. I am grateful also to Ilse Newton (née Philips), Miriam and Tony Book for letting their story be told.

Libraries used – and not yet mentioned – include the Staatsbibliothek zu Berlin, the Staatliche Museen zu Berlin, the Gedenkstätte Berliner Mauer, the Bundesarchiv and the British Library.

As essential as historical research and recce trips may be, as ever my real travelling is done at my desk, in the intense distillation of the journey. It is on the page that I am best able to understand the lives of my subjects. And then, by enabling readers to empathise with those lives, I hope we will better know them and ourselves, and to sense the real meaning of things.

ACKNOWLEDGEMENTS

Many hundreds of people made this book possible, giving their time and knowledge with forbearance and goodwill.

In Berlin I am grateful for the insight, expertise and friendship of Burckhardt Bonello, Corinna Brocher, Molly, Mark, Henry and Oscar Brown, Thomas and Kathrin Brussig, Jan and Steffi Bullerdieck, Jens Casper, David Chipperfield, Suparna Choudhury, Katy Derbyshire, Kristina van Eyck, Kristóf Gosztonyi, Matthias and My-Linh Kunst, Sharmaine Lovegrove, His Honour Judge Percy MacLean, Axel Monath, Dana Monzer, Alina and Maren Niemeyer, Dr Maria Nooke of the Gedenkstätte Berliner Mauer, Nadine Rennert, Niko Rollmann, Clemens Schaeffer and Anne-Marie Weist. I thank them as well as painter Martin Dammann for his gift of clarity and Wilfried Rogasch who encouraged me to look anew at Wilhelm II.

Prune Antonie, Greg Baxter and Rachel Hill – as well as the formerly mentioned Ben Klock and Dr Oliver Schloz – guided me towards Berlin's hedonistic side, while Andreas Uthoff explained the 1980s club scene. I am grateful to Lady Plaxy and Sir Michael Arthur, former British ambassador in Berlin, for looking after me (i.e. feeding me up) during the lean, early writing days, as well as Richard Wyldes for his care after their departure.

In the UK I am grateful to Frank Barrett, Martyn Bond, David Chater, David and Jane Cornwell, Peter Doggett, Drs Marlie and Michael Ferenczi, Christine Gettins, Mwape Will Goble, Rosie Goldsmith, Toby Latta, Jacqueline Pritchard, the Airlift pilot Paul Nathan Sapirstein, Sarah Spankie, Christopher Thornhill, Colin Thubron and Lord Weidenfeld, as well as David Thomson and the remarkable Archive of Modern Conflict, especially Timothy Prus and Ed Jones. In Paris Dimitri de Clercq and Sophie Schoukens brought me understanding of more than Leni Riefenstahl. I thank Nguyen Ngoc Bich and Penelope and Alex Privitera of Washington DC. Justin Jampol of the Wende Museum in Los Angeles shared with me many unforgettable photographs and thoughts.

Great thanks are due to the Goethe Institut, especially to Elisabeth Pyroth, Claudia Amthor-Croft and Sabine Hentzsch who supported me throughout this five-year journey. I am grateful to them, as well as for the generous support of the Authors' Foundation and the Royal Literary Fund.

Bea Hemming has been a dream editor, caring, principled and intuitive, and Peter Straus wasted no words in his steadfast support. I value their candidness, enthusiasm, energy and determination for excellence, as I do the professionalism and passion of my US editor Daniela Rapp. My wife Katrin remains my most enduring guide. For ten books and double that number of years she has supported, encouraged, cheered and tolerated my need to put pen to paper. Without them this book would not have been written.

INDEX